MW01224047

Psychology and Indigenous Australians: Effective Teaching and Practice

Edited by

Rob Ranzijn, Keith McConnochie and Wendy Nolan

Cambridge Scholars Publishing

Psychology and Indigenous Australians: Effective Teaching and Practice,
Edited by Rob Ranzijn, Keith McConnochie and Wendy Nolan

This book first published 2008

Cambridge Scholars Publishing

12 Back Chapman Street, Newcastle upon Tyne, NE6 2XX, UK

British Library Cataloguing in Publication Data
A catalogue record for this book is available from the British Library

ISBN (10): 1-84718-920-2, ISBN (13): 9781847189202

Psychology and Indigenous Australians

TABLE OF CONTENTS

ACKNOWLEDGEMENTS

Support for the project 'Disseminating Strategies for Incorporating Australian Indigenous Content into Psychology Undergraduate Programs throughout Australia', which included the 2007 Conference, has been provided by the Australian Teaching and Learning Council in Higher Education Ltd, an initiative of the Australian Government Department of Education, Science and Training. The views expressed in this document do not necessarily reflect the views of the Australian Teaching and Learning Council. The editors would also like to acknowledge the support of the Australian Psychological Society, Charles Sturt University, and Victoria University, our partner institutions in the above-mentioned project.

Introduction and Overview

Rob Ranzijn, Keith McConnochie and Wendy Nolan

This volume contains the edited proceedings of the inaugural Psychology and Indigenous Australians annual conference, held in Adelaide, South Australia, on July 12-13 2007. In keeping with Indigenous protocol, the conference participants were welcomed to Kaurna country (where Adelaide is located) by Uncle Lewis Warritja Yerloburka O'Brien, an Elder of the Kaurna people, and most of the speakers commenced their presentations with an acknowledgment of country, of being on Kaurna land. Also in keeping with tradition, most of the speakers mentioned their own country, where their own people had come from.

The conference was held soon after the Australian Commonwealth Government initiated its controversial intervention into Northern Territory Aboriginal communities, sparking a lively media debate, with strong passions on all sides. Many of the informal conversations at the conference, as well as audience discussions in the formal sessions, were focused on the intervention and its implications, and many of the presenters referred to it in their presentations.

The *Bringing Them Home* Report, the report of the Royal Commission into the Removal of Aboriginal Children from their Parents (Human Rights and Equal Opportunity Commission, 1997) called for an apology to the Stolen Generations. While all of the State and Territory governments had apologised in the meantime, it took eleven years for an apology from the Commonwealth Government. On February 13th 2008, the first day of the first parliament of the incoming Labour Government which replaced the Liberal/National Party coalition which had governed Australia for those eleven years, the first piece of business was to endorse the public apology by the Parliament of Australia to the Stolen Generations, delivered by the Prime Minister Kevin Rudd. The apology has been widely welcomed as an essential step in the healing of Indigenous Australians and in improving relations between Indigenous and non-Indigenous Australians. However, a deeper understanding of Indigenous cultures, non-

Indigenous cultures, and cultural competence is required in order to keep moving forward as effective practitioners and responsible citizens. The papers presented at the conference addressed many of the important current issues in these areas: theory, effective teaching, and effective practice.

These proceedings are not in the chronological order in which they were presented at the conference, but have been arranged to provide a sequence beginning with racism, a central factor in all areas of Indigenous disadvantage, and ending with a discussion of cultural competence, which all practitioners require in order to work effectively with Indigenous people or anyone from a culture different from their own. The chapters have been edited where required to give non-Australian readers an understanding about places and concepts with which they may not be familiar. Reflecting the diversity of presentations, some of the chapters are theoretical and academic, with extensive referencing and footnotes, while others are more narrative or discursive, telling stories of engagement between Indigenous and non-Indigenous people. The atmosphere of the conference was one of generosity and sharing, so the academics and the practitioners all gained a lot from listening to each other.

The first chapter was written for this volume in order to explain the context of the conference. The story of relations between psychology and Indigenous Australians has not always been a happy one, but there seems to be a growing goodwill to repair historical injustices and work together to make psychology more effective in Indigenous affairs in the future. This chapter briefly relates some of the past history and tells the story of how the conference came to be held.

Next are two papers on racism. Racism has plagued Australia since the First Fleet sailed into Botany Bay on January 26th 1788, and continues to be one of the key factors in perpetuating Indigenous disadvantage (Paradies, Harris, & Anderson, 2008). There is growing recognition that racism will not be reduced unless it is understood and challenged from both sides: understanding the psychology of racism and its effect on those who are disadvantaged by it (Australian Psychological Society, 1997; McDermott, 2006), and reflecting on and challenging the many subtle ways in which the perpetrators perpetuate racism (see, for example, (Green, Sonn, & Matsebula, 2007; Kessaris, 2006; Liu & Mills, 2006). These papers illustrate both sides of the story and the nature of the challenges to overcoming racism.

The first is by Dennis McDermott, an Aboriginal psychologist and one of the three keynote speakers at the conference. In a very personal account, he outlines current thinking about racism, and in particular about how racism is experienced on a daily basis by Indigenous people as 'wounds that break their stitches every morning'. Dennis makes many powerful points in his paper, including a remark which may point to a new way forward in resolving some of the emotional turmoil and discomfort around racism: acknowledging that Australia is *both* a tolerant *and* a racist society. Damien Riggs and Martha Augoustinos then explore racism from the other side, by analysing 'everyday' conversations of non-Indigenous students and how they reinforce white privilege, thereby perpetuating racist discourse.

The section on teaching how to work with Indigenous Australians contains four papers. Educating for anti-racism and pedagogical strategies for teaching cultural competence are areas of great theoretical and applied interest at present (see for example American Association of Medical Colleges, 2005; Betancourt, 2004; Ranzijn, McConnochie, Day, Nolan, & Wharton, 2008; Wells, 2000). These papers go beyond the theory and rhetoric to illustrate how the pedagogy works in practice.

First, Michelle Dickson discusses the head/heart dichotomy that tends to characterise contemporary Western psychology. She makes a strong case that teaching in this area needs to involve the heart as well as the head, and indeed 'guts' as well, and shows how to integrate these three elements in teaching practice. Her approach is centred around Indigenous ways of teaching and learning, and both her Indigenous and non-Indigenous students respond extremely well to this form of pedagogy. Diane Gabb and Dennis McDermott, in their paper about training health professionals, make a distinction between cross-cultural and trans-cultural communication, trans-cultural interaction requiring the 'professional' to be self-disclosing and self-reflective in order to avoid the common trap of 'othering' the 'client'. They argue that the Indigenous concept of Dadirri ('deep listening') can be a powerful tool in creating a trans-cultural conversational space. Hence, both of these two papers are revolutionary in that they apply Indigenous pedagogical tools to what is normally a non-Indigenous context, and thereby contribute to the development of what may become a truly Australian form of psychology.

The third paper in this section is by Tracey Powis, who takes the theme of 'doing our own work' (as non-Indigenous people) to a deep personal level in a reflective presentation which makes pertinent points about contemporary psychology, reinforcing Michelle's points about psychology's tendency to disconnect 'the heart' from 'the head', in contrast to the Indigenous understanding in which the heart and the head are inseparable. Danielle Every then elaborates on the theme of self-reflection, emphasising that understanding racist discourse is important, but not enough – we need to challenge it in order to change the way people discuss Indigenous issues, and furthermore work to transform the discourse into action to overcome oppression.

Next comes the powerful second keynote address, by the Aboriginal academic and author Judy Atkinson, who outlines a model of healing which builds on traditional healing practices centred on stories of relatedness – relationships with 'people, land, animals, plants, skies, waterways and climate' – and indicates ways for psychologists and Indigenous healers to work together. This is followed by the third keynote presentation, by Aboriginal psychologist Tracy Westerman, whose wide-ranging paper discusses a host of practical guidelines for psychological practice, including her development of psychological assessment strategies and interventions appropriate for specific Indigenous cultural contexts. She emphasises the importance of 'starting from scratch' by getting to know the people and understanding culture. She provides many insights into Indigenous understandings of mental health and the primacy of cultural understandings of psychological phenomena. She also discusses the need to 'be growled' by Indigenous elders, to test whether the psychologist has the personal qualities required to work collaboratively. These two papers show that it is possible for non-Indigenous psychologists to work in Indigenous contexts, especially if they are able to utilise Indigenous methods to increase the effectiveness of their own practices.

The next four papers are case studies of working with Indigenous Australians in specific contexts, papers which illustrate many of the principles discussed in the earlier papers. There have been numerous publications with advice on how to work effectively (for instance, Australian Psychological Society, 2003; Bishop, Vicary, Andrews, & Pearson, 2006; Dudgeon, Garvey, & Pickett, 2000; National Health and Medical Research Council, 2003; Sheldon, 2001; Vicary & Bishop, 2005; Westerman, 2004) but, as with pedagogy, there is a dearth of practical worked examples of how to apply the principles in diverse contexts. These papers make a valuable contribution to the literature by providing specific examples of how to work effectively in particular, local, contexts.

The first in the series, by Sarah Sutton and Kathryn Stone, is about Aboriginal and non-Aboriginal workers collaborating in the treatment of Aboriginal male sexual offenders. Kathryn and Sarah show how effective it can be for Indigenous and non-Indigenous practitioners to work together in partnership, using Indigenous methods of developing trust and communication. They raise a number of issues which often concern non-Indigenous practitioners, including being afraid to ask questions so as not to offend: They maintain that "I don't think I could ever offend someone by asking a question: it's all about the way that the question is asked." Joylene Warren, Lisa White and Trish Hickey then describe their work of reuniting Aboriginal families with children who have been removed from their care. This is a particularly challenging task for them since they work for the same welfare system that removed the children in the first place. It takes great persistence and cultural sensitivity to enable the families and agencies to work together in a system governed by Western ways of delivering services.

In the third paper, Rachel Reilly, Joyce Doyle and colleagues describe a health promotion program in the Goulburn Valley in rural Victoria, the success of which is due to the fact that it was designed, controlled and directed by local Indigenous communities. The authors emphasise that non-Indigenous academics and organisations do have a useful role, but have to be prepared to be true partners and not 'leaders in the process' as has tended to be the case in interventions of non-Indigenous professionals into Indigenous affairs. The final paper in this series, by Harold Stewart, Kerry Dix and Jennene Greenhill, outlines a program of suicide prevention in rural South Australian communities. They refer to the potential barrier of 'cultural dyslexia', which takes time and patience to overcome. Kerry and Jennene, young white women, were able to work effectively with male Indigenous Elders and other members of Indigenous communities because of their respectful attitude and willingness to learn. The paper illustrates that it is the personal qualities of non-Indigenous people that are most important in interactions with Indigenous people. Taken as whole, and reflecting the thrust of the keynote addresses by Judy Atkinson and Tracy Westerman, the four papers reinforce the point that non-Indigenous service providers can be effective as long as they are willing to work in real partnership and to learn from Indigenous communities.

The final paper in the book summarises a panel discussion by three practitioners working in the area of cultural competence – Keith McConnochie, David Egege and Dennis McDermott. Cultural competence is a contested term, and many people are not convinced about how useful a concept it is. A number of important issues are raised in this panel conversation, including: ensuring that cultural competence training is not just a matter of 'ticking a box'; the need to involve all levels of an organisation in training; and the usefulness of including cultural safety and cultural ease in the concept of cultural competence.

As conference organisers and participants, we learnt a lot from the 2007 conference, and we look forward to future conferences. Another very exciting recent development is the inaugural meeting of the Australian Indigenous Psychologists Association which was held in April 2008. This is likely to give a great boost to the development of a critical mass of Indigenous psychologists, which may have a major effect on the evolution of Australian psychology into the future.

A note on terminology: While the most appropriate terms and labels are continually contested, the current consensus seems to be that 'Indigenous Australians' is the most appropriate term for the Indigenous inhabitants as a whole. However, many Indigenous Australians prefer to refer to themselves as 'Aboriginal Australians' or 'Torres Strait Islanders', Islanders having different cultures and ways of life to people on the mainland. There is huge diversity within Indigenous Australia, with over 270 distinct original language groups, most with a number of dialects such that there were over 500 distinct groups throughout Australia in 1788, each with its own defined geographical boundaries, and many of these groups have retained some or most of their unique cultures. Where possible and appropriate, Indigenous groups are referred to in this book by connections to country (traditional land), and footnotes and other explanatory terms are used to explain where country is located.

We hope that you find this book interesting and informative and that it helps you in understanding a little better the culture of Indigenous and non-Indigenous Australians. We hope that it will provide some useful indications about how to work effectively with people from diverse cultural groups

References

American Association of Medical Colleges. (2005). Cultural Competence Education for Medical Students. [Electronic Version] from http://www.aamc.org/meded/tacct/culturalcomped.pdf.

Australian Psychological Society. (1997). *Racism and prejudice: Psychological perspectives*. Melbourne, Australia: Australian Psychological Society.

—. (2003). *Guidelines for the provision of psychological services for, and the conduct of psychological research with, Aboriginal and Torres Strait Islander people of Australia*. Melbourne, Australia: Australian Psychological Society.

Betancourt, J. R. (2004). Becoming a physician: Cultural competence - Marginal or mainstream movement? *New England Journal of Medicine, 351*(10), 953-955.

Bishop, B. J., Vicary, D. A., Andrews, H., & Pearson, G. (2006). Towards a Culturally Appropriate Mental Health Research Process for

Indigenous Australians. *Australian Community Psychologist 18*(2), 31-41.

Dudgeon, P., Garvey, D., & Pickett, H. (2000). *Working with Indigenous Australians: A handbook for psychologists*. Perth, WA Australia: Gunada Press, Curtin Indigenous Research Centre.

Green, M. J., Sonn, C. C., & Matsebula, J. (2007). Reviewing Whiteness: Theory, Research and Possibilities. *South African Journal of Psychology, 37*(3), 389-419.

Human Rights and Equal Opportunity Commission. (1997). *Bringing them home: National inquiry into the separation of Aboriginal and Torres Strait Islander children from their families*. Sydney, Australia: Sterling.

Kessaris, T. N. (2006). About Being Munungay (Whitefulla): Making Covert Group Racism Visible. *Journal of Community & Applied Social Psychology, 16*, 347-362.

Liu, J. H., & Mills, D. (2006). Modern racism and neo-liberal globalization: The discourses of plausible deniability and their multiple functions. *Journal of Community and Applied Social Psychology, 16*, 83-99.

McDermott, D. (2006). Growing up brown in a white-shirted time. *Medical Journal of Australia, 185*(8), 464-466.

National Health and Medical Research Council. (2003). *Values and Ethics: Guidelines for Ethical Conduct in Aboriginal and Torres Strait Islander Health Research*. Canberra, ACT: National Health and Medical Research Council.

Paradies, Y., Harris, R., & Anderson, I. (2008). *The impact of racism on Indigenous health in Australia and Aotearoa: Towards a research agenda* (Discussion Paper Series: Number 4). Darwin, Northern Territory: Cooperative Research Centre for Aboriginal Health.

Ranzijn, R., McConnochie, K., Day, A., Nolan, W. & Wharton, M. (2008). Towards cultural competence: Australian Indigenous content in undergraduate psychology. *Australian Psychologist, 43*(2), 132-139.

Sheldon, M. (2001). Psychiatric assessment in remote Aboriginal communities. *Australian and New Zealand Journal of Psychiatry, 35*(4), 435-442.

Vicary, D. A., & Bishop, B. J. (2005). Western psychotherapeutic practice: Engaging Aboriginal people in culturally appropriate and respectful ways. *Australian Psychologist 40*(1), 8-19.

Wells, M. I. (2000). Beyond cultural competence: A model for individual and institutional cultural development. *Journal of Community Health Nursing, 17*(4), 189-199.

Westerman, T. (2004). Engagement of Indigenous clients in mental health services: What role do cultural differences play? *Australian e-Journal for the Advancement of Mental Health, 3*(3).

STEPS ALONG A JOURNEY – THE GROWTH OF INTEREST IN THE RELATIONS BETWEEN PSYCHOLOGY AND INDIGENOUS AUSTRALIANS

ROB RANZIJN, KEITH MCCONNOCHIE AND WENDY NOLAN

Abstract

The discipline and practice of psychology have historically had a fraught relationship with Indigenous Australians. The colonisers brought with them the prevailing Western worldview of their day, that the Indigenous people were inferior and, according to the principles of social Darwinism, would die out within a few generations. As psychology emerged as a profession in the 20th Century, psychological research was used to confirm the prevailing stereotypes of inferiority in multiple domains, and as agents of the state psychologists were instrumental in the removal of Aboriginal children from their families. Even today psychology is viewed with suspicion and mistrust by many if not most Indigenous Australians. However, the situation is slowly changing. Better relations between Indigenous Australians and psychology have been largely initiated by Indigenous Australians themselves, especially Indigenous psychologists, in collaboration with non-Indigenous psychologists. Since about 1990 there has been growing interest in improving these relations, and this movement has accelerated in recent years. This chapter briefly summarises the history of relationships between psychology and Indigenous Australians which has led to the conference whose proceedings form the content of this book. The conference and other events are encouraging signs that psychology may have a useful role to play in the future in overcoming Indigenous disadvantage and contributing to social and emotional well-being.

Until 1788 the inhabitants of Australia had lived for 60,000 years or more in peace and harmony with the environment of this beautiful land. The invasion (as Indigenous Australians call it – many non-Indigenous Australians prefer to call it settlement), which began in Sydney on January

26th 1788, was an unmitigated disaster for the Indigenous peoples. Within two generations around 95% of the original population had been wiped out, the majority from introduced diseases but many also from starvation, resulting from lack of access to the land which provided their essential resources, poisoning of waterholes and food, and outright slaughter and massacres of the few who tried to resist the white invaders. Since then, a constantly changing series of government policies have had disastrous effects on the lives of most Indigenous Australians – arbitrary relocation to missions and reserves, restrictive legislation which kept the Indigenous people away from white society except as virtual slaves, and the removal of Aboriginal children from their families, to name just a few. The Indigenous peoples have never had the opportunity to recover from the cultural trauma (Halloran, 2004) resulting from the actions of the colonisers, and the negative psychological and social effects have been cumulative, cascading and intergenerational. As a consequence, on any social or health indicator, the traditional owners of this land are the most disadvantaged of any group of people in the country.

The colonisation of Australia occurred at a time when many of the nations of Europe were establishing their empires around the globe, and the colonisers brought with them the worldview that Western ways were superior to all others and that people in other lands were inferior, generally regarding them as savages at a more primitive stage of evolution. There was an unquestioned assumption that the 'superior' Western powers had the right to take over other peoples' lands and 'claim' them in the name of their various kings and queens. The rest of the world was viewed as a vast resource to be mined for the benefit of the conquerors – including the people, who were commonly enslaved to serve the invaders. In Australia this attitude was taken to an extreme. The land was declared to be empty of human habitation (the principle of Terra Nullius) (Chamarette, 2000). The original inhabitants were regarded as animals, not people, and hence had no right to resist the spread of white settlement. Until after the referendum of 1967 Indigenous Australians were not included in the five-yearly population census, rather being counted, if at all, among the flora and fauna.

The early psychologists in Britain and Europe were fascinated by the 'native' peoples in the colonies, since they were thought to be relics or vestiges of earlier stages in human development and hence to give insights into the prehistory of Western people, who of course were at the pinnacle of evolution. This zeitgeist dominated research into Indigenous peoples, including Australians, throughout the 19th and well into the 20th Centuries. Psychology in Australia emerged as a separate discipline towards the end of the 19th Century and grew slowly in the first half of the 20th (O'Neill, 1987). As was the case with Western psychology generally, the First and particularly the Second World War accelerated the development of Australian psychology, sparked primarily by the growth in psychological testing to classify soldiers for different war duties and, towards the end of the Second World War, to rehabilitate the soldiers and fit them for civilian life. The testing movement dominated psychological research into Indigenous Australians until the 1970s. With few exceptions, the research 'showed' that the cognitive and other skills of Indigenous Australians were deficient to those of other Australians, and the few areas in which Indigenous Australians appeared to excel were those regarded as relatively unimportant by mainstream society, such as visuo-spatial orientation (Kearins, 2000).

Children were removed from their parents from the earliest days of white settlement. It is estimated that up to 100,000 children were removed between 1814 and 1975 (Human Rights and Equal Opportunity Commission, 1997), removal reaching its height in the Protective Legislation era (1920s – 1960s). All the Australian states passed legislation to establish 'Protectors' of 'Aborigines' who had unlimited power over all Aboriginal people. The extent of the forced removal of Indigenous children has been widely reported and discussed following the publication of the Bringing Them Home report in 1997 (Human Rights and Equal Opportunity Commission, 1997). As many as 1 in 5 Indigenous children were removed from their families, with the majority of these removals (about 80%) being girls. These statistics suggest that almost one third of all girls (16/50 or 32%) were removed from their families over this period.

If a young mother, say aged 25 at the time, whose five-year-old child was removed in 1975 is still alive today, she would now be about 58 years old, and her child would now be about 38 years old. If the young mother was herself taken from her family as a young child, as often happened, her mother would be about 78 if she is still alive. The Stolen Generations are not just a historical event for Indigenous Australians, they are still with us, and the grief and loss are still very real for all Indigenous Australians, since in the kinship system, which is still strong, every Indigenous Australian is closely related to all the members of their communities, not just their 'immediate' family members as in the Western system (Clark, 2000; Koolmatrie & Williams, 2000).

What was psychology doing during the time of the Stolen Generations? This removal was widespread during the two decades between 1950 and 1970 and psychologists were actively involved in aspects of this process, although the extent of this involvement remains poorly documented. Over the same two decades there was a major debate within psychology over the impact of maternal deprivation on children, initiated by the publication of Bowlby's *Maternal Care and Mental Health* in 1951 and culminating with Michael Rutter's *Maternal Deprivation Reassessed* in 1981.

While psychologists in Australia were actively involved in this debate they failed to link the evidence or the theoretical models relating to maternal deprivation to the removal of Indigenous children from their mothers. As Bretherton and Mellor (2006, pp. 92 - 93) comment:

> "Few white psychologists challenged the idea that taking Aboriginal children away from their families was in their best interests and, indeed, practising psychologists working for welfare agencies after 1950 probably had a complicit role in many such cases........ Given the prominence of the debates on maternal deprivation during the 1950s to the 1970s, and psychologists' awareness of the complexity of psychosocial sequelae that tend to follow the breaking of bonds with primary caregivers, it is salutary to note psychologists' lack of concern for Aboriginal mothers and their children. ......Psychology and psychologists could have used their disciplinary knowledge and social standing to act as advocates for Aboriginal children, but did not do so."

That is, psychological research, including Australian research, was demonstrating the importance of maternal attachment to subsequent child development, and yet, as far as we know, no psychologist spoke out on behalf of the Aboriginal children who were being taken away. Instead, many psychologists were actively working on behalf of the state, as part of the welfare system, to remove children from their families and place them in institutions where they were commonly neglected, not fed properly, denied access to their families, in many instance told lies such as that their mothers did not want to see them, punished for speaking their language or wanting to retain any element of their culture, and in many case physically and sexually abused, after which they were farmed out as servants and labourers to pastoralists and rich white people in the cities, and even the pittance to which they were entitled was held in trust by the white authorities and often never paid to them. The enormous fear and distrust of 'the Welfare', that took the children away (and is still taking Indigenous children away at far higher rates than non-Indigenous children) has become generalised to psychologists, who are regarded by many Indigenous Australians as part of 'The Welfare' (Ranzijn et al., 2008). Many Indigenous Australians are fearful of going to a psychologist because they may be labelled 'crazy', hence incompetent to look after their children, and liable be taken away themselves or have their children taken from them.

Psychology was silent about the Stolen Generations, yet at the same time it was growing fast as a profession. For instance, up to World War Two there were only two departments of psychology in Australia (the Universities of Sydney and Western Australia). By 1956 there were seven more, by 1977 there were ten more, and currently there are 38. The membership of the Australian Psychological Society (APS) has grown from 893 in its founding year of 1966, to about 1700 in 1974, to 4321 in 1985 (O'Neill, 1987), to close to 16,000 in 2008, an exponential increase from its founding. The influence of psychology has grown greatly over the past 50 years, and increasingly psychology is taking a leading role in the mental health arena. In 2006, after many years of lobbying, clients of registered psychologists received the right to claim Medicare benefits (the Commonwealth Government-funded universal health care system). Yet, in spite of its increasing prominence, the profession and discipline of psychology have been almost entirely silent on social justice in relation to Indigenous Australians until quite recently (Gridley, Davidson, Dudgeon, Pickett, & Sanson, 2000).

The impetus for change started at the International Conference of Applied Psychology held in Sydney in 1988 at which an Indigenous delegate stood up in the final plenary session and pointed out that, even though the conference was held in Australia, there were no Indigenous Australian presenters or delegates (Dudgeon, 2003). This shamed and spurred the Board of the College of [Australian] Community Psychologists to action, resulting in the first symposium on the Psychology of Indigenous People at the APS National Conference in Perth in 1990, at which for the first time Indigenous Australians spoke at an APS conference. In the late 1990s university courses containing Indigenous content and addressing issues such as racism were developed by Indigenous academics working in collaboration with non-Indigenous colleagues, most notably at Curtin University of Technology in Perth (Sonn, Garvey, Bishop, & Smith, 2000). Two important developments occurred in the year 2000. The first was the publication by *Australian Psychologist*, one of the two main academic journals of the APS, of a special edition on Psychology and Australia's Indigenous Peoples. The second was the publication by Pat Dudgeon, Darren Garvey and Harry Picket, all Indigenous academics, of *Working with Indigenous Australians: A Handbook for Psychologists* (Dudgeon, Garvey, & Pickett, 2000). There was also a flurry of academic publications in other journals on Indigenous-related matters, written by both Indigenous and non-Indigenous authors, often in collaboration.

The late 1990s also saw the commencement of university psychology courses[1] that taught some elements of what is now commonly referred to as cultural competence. However, this work was being undertaken by only a few individuals working in isolation from each other. Australia is a large continent, and it is often difficult and expensive for colleagues from different parts to meet together to develop new ideas and teaching practices, especially if they are as far away from each other as Perth and Melbourne, or Darwin and Adelaide. Also, they were also working in relative academic isolation, since teaching in this area was, and still largely is, regarded by most academics as interesting work but a fringe activity, of lesser importance than the 'core business' of psychology such as teaching about research methods, learning theory, or cognition and perception. Hence, when financial and other resources became scarce, it was the Indigenous-related courses that tended to be cut back or watered down by incorporating them into other courses or reducing the proportion of the courses that addressed Indigenous issues. Added to this were the emotional and intellectual demands on the teachers, especially Indigenous teachers, of delivering what is often very emotional content and dealing with student reactions which can range from grief and sorrow through to possible guilt and shame and even to aggressive racist resistance to what is being taught. Therefore, the few teachers active in this area started to become burnt out and the impetus was starting to falter.

In 2004 we started work at the University of South Australia (UniSA) to more comprehensively help our undergraduate psychology students to learn what we thought was important for them to know about Indigenous history and culture and psychology's role in redressing Indigenous disadvantage. We developed two new courses, a compulsory first-year course 'Indigenous Australians: Culture and Colonisation' and an elective third-year course 'Psychology and Indigenous Australians.' The first-year course has around 200 students each year and the third-year course around 30. Both courses are extremely well-received by the students (Ranzijn et al., 2008), and we believe we have developed effective teaching strategies to overcome student resistance and deal with some of the emotional issues that arise in the course of such teaching.

Soon after starting work on developing the courses we received two small internal grants from UniSA to generalise the curriculum work

---

[1] A course (may also be called a unit, subject or topic) is a 13-week sequence of instruction comprising a quarter of a full-time student's workload during that period

beyond the discipline of psychology and to extend the psychology work within UniSA more broadly throughout Australia. The grants enabled us to travel to meet some of the 'pioneers' referred to above, to develop curriculum guidelines to advise other academics, and to present two interactive workshops, in 2005 and 2006 (Ranzijn & Severino, 2006, 2007), aimed primarily at testing and refining the curriculum guidelines. However, while we aimed the first workshop primarily at psychology academics, the majority of participants were not in this category but included psychology practitioners, other mental health or welfare practitioners and academics, Indigenous community members and field workers, and students. We realised that there is a huge thirst for knowledge across the board about not only teaching in this area but also about how to practise and intervene effectively and appropriately with Indigenous peoples. While we thought that our commencing students would have a low knowledge base to start with, we soon realised that most practitioners are also quite ignorant about Indigenous history and culture and their role in either perpetuating or overcoming racism. Therefore, the 2006 workshop was a two-day event, with one day devoted to teaching issues and the other to practice. We also recognised early on the need to build a critical mass of academics and practitioners working in this area, for moral, practical, and informational support. Hence we initiated an email distribution list which continues to grow rapidly, with over 500 email addresses in 2008, including a growing number of interested persons outside Australia, from South Africa, Aotearoa (New Zealand), the United States, and Canada. The last three countries in particular have similar histories and issues with Indigenous peoples to Australia (with important differences of course).

  With our limited resources we were starting to progress this work quite well, but we felt that with extra support we would be able to do more work more quickly. Therefore, we applied for and received a grant from what was at that time called the Carrick Institute for Learning and Teaching in Higher Education Inc, a Commonwealth Government - funded organisation. This enabled us to do a number of things: to travel around Australia to deliver seminars on 'Indigenising the Curriculum' to schools of psychology, to undertake site visits by invitation to particular schools of psychology, to establish a website (www.unisanet.unisa.edu.au/pia) with a large range of teaching and other resources, and to present national conferences in 2007 and 2008. The edited proceedings of the 2007 conference make up the content of this book.

  What does the future hold for psychology in relation to Indigenous Australians? Increasingly, both Indigenous and non-Indigenous psychologists and other professionals are saying that psychology can have a major role in redressing Indigenous disadvantage and promoting social justice and well-being (Dudgeon, 2003; Ranzijn, McConnochie, Clarke, & Nolan, 2007). However, this will require some major changes in the way that psychology is practised. First, psychologists need to work in true partnership with Indigenous peoples and communities. Secondly, they need to have an expanded view of their role to go beyond the individualistic one-on-one therapeutic relationship and become advocates for social and political change, since it is not possible to separate the well-being of individual Indigenous Australians from the broader social and political contexts of their lives. Thirdly, they need to become culturally competent, since without this any work they do with Indigenous Australians is likely to be ineffective at best and destructive at worst. Much work has been done in recent years on developing detailed guidelines for working effectively with Indigenous Australians and people from diverse cultural groups, and increasingly the professional bodies and government regulators are encouraging and requiring professionals to become culturally competent (Australian Psychological Society, 2003; National Health and Medical Research Council, 2003). Psychology in Australia is well behind other countries in this regard (for instance, Aotearoa (New Zealand) and Canada), but is trying to catch up fast. Many of the papers in this volume address some of the complex issues in effective practice, with practical suggestions that show that the task is not impossible, but requires patience, humility and goodwill.

With regards to research, the discipline of psychology is in a good position to increase understanding of the dynamics of racism, cultural and trans-generational trauma, identity, social and emotional wellbeing, community wellbeing, self-determination and empowerment, healing practices, and other concepts particularly relevant to Indigenous lives. While there has been some good research conducted in recent years, much remains to be done. There is an increasing need to address issues of diversity within Indigenous Australia, since Indigenous Australians are not homogeneous but extremely diverse – at the time of the invasion there were somewhere between 500 and 600 distinct dialect groups within over 250 distinct language groups, each with its own unique culture. Add to this that there has been much intermarriage between the groups, largely as a result of forced relocation, that at present the majority of Indigenous relationships are with non-Indigenous partners, and that there are big differences in the lives and experiences of people living in the big cities, rural centres, and smaller non-urban communities, and it is clear that it is unrealistic and unhelpful to categorise Indigenous Australians as all having the same culture and the same needs.

It is an exciting time to be involved in this area. The formation of the Indigenous Australian Psychologists Association in April 2008 has the potential to bring about a major change in Australian psychology, which may finally become a truly 'Australian' psychology relevant to Australian needs rather than a product imported virtually unchanged from the United Kingdom and the United States. We look forward to the next few years with great interest.

References

Australian Psychological Society. (2003). *Guidelines for the provision of psychological services for, and the conduct of psychological research with, Aboriginal and Torres Strait Islander people of Australia.* Melbourne, Australia: Australian Psychological Society.

Chamarette, C. (2000). Terra nullius then and now: Mabo, native title, and reconciliation in 2000. *Australian Psychologist, 35*(2), 167-172.

Clark, Y. (2000). The construction of Aboriginal identity in people separated from their families, community,and culture: Pieces of a jigsaw. *Australian Psychologist, 35*(2), 150-157.

Dudgeon, P. (2003). Australian psychology and Indigenous people. *Network, 14*(1), 38-44.

Dudgeon, P., Garvey, D., & Pickett, H. (2000). *Working with Indigenous Australians: A handbook for psychologists.* Perth, WA Australia: Gunada Press, Curtin Indigenous Research Centre.

Gridley, H., Davidson, G., Dudgeon, P., Pickett, H., & Sanson, A. (2000). The Australian Psychological Society and Australia's Indigenous people: A decade of inaction. *Australian Psychologist, 35*(2), 82-87.

Halloran, M. (2004). Cultural maintenance and trauma in Indigenous Australia. *E Law, 11*(4), (e-journal).

Human Rights and Equal Opportunity Commission. (1997). *Bringing them home: National inquiry into the separation of Aboriginal and Torres Strait Islander children from their families.* Sydney, Australia: Sterling.

Kearins, J. (2000). Children and cultural differences. In P. Dudgeon, D. Garvey & H. Pickett (Eds.), *Working with Indigenous Australians: A handbook for psychologists* (pp. 167-175). Perth, WA Australia: Gunada Press, Curtin Indigenous Research Centre.

Koolmatrie, J., & Williams, R. (2000). Unresolved grief and the removal of indigenous Australian children. *Australian Psychologist, 35*(2), 158-166.

National Health and Medical Research Council. (2003). *Values and Ethics: Guidelines for Ethical Conduct in Aboriginal and Torres Strait Islander Health Research.* Canberra, ACT: National Health and Medical Research Council.

O'Neill, W. M. (1987). *A Century of Psychology in Australia.* Sydney: Sydney University Press.

Ranzijn, R., McConnochie, K., Clarke, C., & Nolan, W. (2007). 'Just another white-ology': psychology as a case study. *Counselling, Psychotherapy and Health, 3*(2, Indigenous Special Issue), 21-34.

Ranzijn, R., McConnochie, K., Day, A., Nolan, W., & Wharton, M. (2008). Towards cultural competence: Australian Indigenous content in undergraduate psychology. *Australian Psychologist, 43*(2), 132-139.

Ranzijn, R., & Severino, G. (Eds.). (2006). *Psychology and Indigenous Australians: Effective Teaching and Practice - Report on the proceedings of a workshop on developing curriculum guidelines.* Adelaide, SA: University of South Australia.

Ranzijn, R., & Severino, G. (Eds.). (2007). *Psychology and Indigenous Australians: Effective Teaching and Practice - Report on the proceedings of the second national workshop on developing curriculum guidelines.* Adelaide, SA: University of South Australia.

Sonn, C. C., Garvey, D. C., Bishop, B., & Smith, L. M. (2000). Incorporating Indigenous and cross-cultural issues into an undergraduate psychology course: Experience at Curtin University of Technology. *Australian Psychologist, 35*(2), 143-149.

KEYNOTE ADDRESS:
WHAT CURE FOR TAMWORTH SYNDROME?
THE ACCUMULATIVE EXPERIENCE OF RACISM,
BLACKFELLA WELL-BEING AND
PSYCHOLOGICAL PRACTICE

DENNIS MCDERMOTT

Abstract

It's difficult for an Indigenous Australian to write dispassionately on racism. There is an unavoidable tension between the demands of academic rigour and the demands of community for 'truth-telling' about past and present Indigenous/non-Indigenous relations in this country (McDermott et al., 2008). The lesson from professional development for mental health practitioners, that Indigenous perspectives are satisfactorily served only when affective learning is privileged as much as cognitive (Gabb & McDermott, 2008), may, fortunately, prove as valid in relation to scholarship. This paper combines a narrative of 'official' Australian racism in operation in my home town of Tamworth[1], NSW, with an examination of the consequences of continually attracting racialised projection - here characterised as Tamworth Syndrome – and what that means for psychology in relation to Aboriginal and Torres Strait Islander Australians: how differently it may need to be construed, practised and taught. In good blackfella fashion, I combine insights from both the peer-reviewed and Indigenous 'grey' literature with a story from my family's experience (Garvey 2007, p.3). From an Indigenous perspective, neither the personal nor the emotional need be shied away from, as long as they chime with, and enhance, the scholarly.

The last ten years have seen a surge of interest in the links between racism and ill health: of over 100 studies now in existence that attest to

---

[1] Tamworth is a regional centre in inland NSW, lying roughly half-way between Sydney and Brisbane. The district population is around 50,000 people.

the health consequences of racism, the majority have been published since 2000 (Drexler, 2007). A 2006 meta-analysis of 138 studies, each examining the impact of racism on health, found that the strongest and most consistent findings were for negative mental health outcomes and health-related behaviour (Paradies, 2006). Yet, in terms of informing praxis in relation to Indigenous mental health / well-being in both the Australian and New Zealand context, racism is an under-researched area - one described in a discussion paper arising from a recent trans-Tasman Indigenous forum as in need of a cohesive research agenda (Paradies, Harris & Anderson, 2008). In relation to how psychology might better engage with these concerns, this paper takes up that challenge. In particular, it addresses three areas deemed important by that discussion paper: Indigenous "experience" of racism, the "impact" of racism on Indigenous peoples, with particular reference to the life course, and the "best ways to address systemic racism in Indigenous peoples" (Paradies et al., 2008, p.16). As we shall see, not only are the ways racism operates in such a first-world, allegedly-postcolonial society as Australia neither straightforward nor monolithic, but also neither are the best means to address them. Indeed, amongst other things, this paper aims to complexify the relationships between Indigenous and settler Australia. Tamworth Syndrome, then, becomes a handy rubric under which to gather the consequences for Aboriginal and Torres Strait Islander Australians of living within a matrix of ease, ambivalence and hostility, where the last two are comprehensive enough for many blackfellas to feel besieged, and potent enough for serious psychological impact. Exploration of this complexity, at times confusing and paradoxical, and its import for current projects to Indigenise psychological praxis and training (Ranzijn & Severino, 2007) requires a nuanced approach, a consideration of 'grey' areas that are yet incompletely addressed by peer-reviewed research.

Indigenous and non-Indigenous Australians share a country that has changed markedly since the official abandonment of policies of assimilation (Haebich, 2008a), yet racism has not only persisted, but resists attempts at satisfactory public discourse. In fact, such is the force of racism's tenacity and mutability over the decades since then that Haebich argues that the current period is one of "retro-assimilation" (Haebich, 2008b). Contemporary manifestations of racism are not necessarily overt, operating through opaque modalities, such as 'structural' or 'systemic' racism/discrimination (Davis, 2008), and internalised racism (Paradies et al., 2008, p.16). Racism, however, may also operate through less-obvious derivatives; measures tagged as rational, beneficent responses to intractable crisis, such as the recent, bipartisan re-deployment of paternalism (ABC News Online, 2008; Gratton, 2006). This paper asks whether continual experiences of racism - 'Ground-Hog Day' experiences - accrete to critical mass, and how such a charged accumulation of racialised experience, in all its forms, intersects with blackfella well-being.

The need for specific work on the range of possible interaction effects is interrogated through an exploration of the likely connections between racism and colonisation-related impacts on well-being - including 'traumatic' grief (Paradies et al., 2008) and trans-generational trauma (Raphael, Swan & Martinek, 1998). Finally, this paper examines the potentially significant implications, thus raised, for psychological practice and training.

Racism and Blackfella Well-Being

Indigenous Australia contends that racism is central to Indigenous mental distress. Racism is perceived as more than the 'behavioural problem' to which it was reduced by former Prime Minister John Howard (Howard, 2006; Sydney Morning Herald, 2005), in the wake of the 2005 Cronulla Riots[2]. Not only are there cognitive implications - that repeated exposure to racist treatment may build to the debilitating belief that there is no escape, that this is one's lot - but racism also affects how one emotionally, and thus physiologically, responds to the wider world (Mays, Cochran & Barnes, 2007). When one repeatedly absorbs negativity – at various times, simple hatred - the zeitgeist itself appears to change. Many Indigenous Australians perceive themselves as moving through a corrosive affective world that many non-Indigenous Australians would find hard to recognise as the same country they live in. Coming to grips, then, with Indigenous trauma requires models that help us track the dynamic interplay of population level factors and unique individual experience. For conceptual ease, some existing models emphasise that factors with potential, negative impact on Indigenous well-being tend to fall into one of two groups (Cripps, 2007; Memmott, Stacy, Chambers & Keys, 2001). These groups can also be conceived of as layers, with individualised interactions between layers (Human Rights and Equal Opportunity Commission, 2007): to facilitate comprehension of the dynamic constitution of Indigenous mental distress, one schema proposes

---

[2] The Cronulla riots were an outbreak, over some weeks during the Southern hemisphere summer of 2005-6, of serious, racialised urban unrest - centred on beach-side incidents involving Australians of middle-eastern and Anglo-Celtic heritage - in the NSW capital city, Sydney

a core of colonisation-related factors, surrounded by a range of contemporary determinants, all mediated by a variable exposure to trans-generational trauma (McDermott et al., 2008). Racism, thus, may oxygenate 'historic' (Duran & Duran, 2005) or 'collective trauma' (Atkinson, 1997). The contemporary damage from colonial dispossession, violence, child removal and social exclusion plays out in the number and severity of stressful life events routinely carried by significant numbers of Indigenous Australian families (Western Australian Aboriginal Child Health Survey (WAACHS), 2007). A family might already be saddled, but coping, with a burden of premature deaths, or chronic illness, high levels of mental distress, or community discord or violence – some unwanted legacy of colonisation – when an additional scenario starts playing out: one child starts skipping school to avoid abusive playground interactions; or store security continually targets a parent, following them from display rack to display rack; or Ku Klux Klan-styled leaflets start circulating in their home town.

Yet, whilst the literature on racism-related health outcomes now reflects a deeper understanding of the visceral power of racism's effects (Drexler, 2007; Tull, Sheu, Butler & Cornelious, 2005), the complexity of the processes involved, the consequences of accumulative experience and the indirect, political/structural aspect of much Indigenous experience of racism are satisfactorily addressed in neither the scientific literature nor public discourse (Davis, 2008; Paradies et al., 2008). A key enabler here, then, would be improved recognition of the pervasiveness of sometimes 'invisible', sometimes disguised, racism. In the process of making recommendations on Indigenous social and emotional well-being, the national and New South Wales peak Aboriginal community-controlled health bodies stated, in effect, that as a nation Australia doesn't really comprehend how racism affects Aboriginal people – neither the repetitive nature of exposure, nor the depth of the effects engendered. In their terms, racism *"permeat[es]"* Indigenous Australian experience (NACCHO/AHMRC Aboriginal and Islander Social and Emotional Well-Being Forum, 2003). I've described this elsewhere as "wounds that break their stitches every morning" (McDermott, 2003).

The peak bodies further note that the discourse around Indigenous health and well-being needs to reflect what is actually happening, every day, on an individual and institutional level. This call reflects the manner in which the Indigenous holistic perspective of health and well-being is applied, not only to service delivery, but also to theoretical frameworks and disease/disorder aetiology. Aboriginal and Torres Strait Islander Australia perceives the commonplace, conceptual and service delivery cleavage between people with a psychiatric diagnosis and what some call 'the worried well', to be unsatisfactory, simplistic and pejorative. From an Indigenous perspective, not only are the clarity and aetiology of many specific diagnoses questionable – so much so that there are moves to develop tools to assess non-specific mental distress (McDermott, 2007) - but also the distress displayed is supra-individual and is tied, inescapably, to colonisation and its sequelae.   One, then, not only considers a presenting situation from the social, spiritual and emotional well-being perspective of the person *and* the community, but also of the person in the context *of* their community – and their community's history.

Racism a 'Public Secret'

Why, then, does the pervasiveness of racism in Australia not have a proportionately-invigorating effect on both bio-medical approaches to Indigenous mental health and public/policy discourse?   One answer is that, for Australia, as for the USA, racism is a "public secret": "There are secrets that are kept from the public and then there are public secrets – secrets that the public chooses to keep safe from itself ... The trick ... is in knowing what not to know" (Daniel, 2006).

Sharon Daniel's term, used in her work with over-represented African-American and Latina women in Californian prisons, has resonance for Australia in regard to the persistence of racism.   It succinctly captures the notion that there are realities that the public is uncomfortable being reminded of.   Just like the Emperor's new clothes[3], there are naked truths that are hard to call, if no one wants to know about them.

Daniel's "public secret", the wilful ignoring of a vast and contentious Californian prison-industrial complex - particularly exemplified by the landmark 30 square miles of prison close to a major Californian freeway running between San Francisco and Los Angeles – helps complexify the operation of contemporary racism.   Her work echoes Angela Davis' construction of the massive over-incarceration of 'people of colour' in the US – linked, by Davis, to mechanisms behind Indigenous Australian over-incarceration - as a consequence of: "... the persistence and further entrenchment of institutional and structural racism [under conditions of] neoliberalism ... [combined with failure to recognise] the material forces of racism that are responsible for offering up such large numbers ... to the carceral state" (Davis, 2008, p.8).

---

[3] In the Hans Christian Anderson story

It is difficult to assess racism's accumulative effects on mental health / well-being – and, thus, adequately plan to ameliorate or prevent them – if the existence of the phenomenon in question, beyond individual breakouts of 'bad behaviour', is disavowed. Davis draws our attention to the (supposed) 'death' of racism as akin to Fukuyama's (alleged) "end of history": "Why does the word "racist" have such an archaic ring to it – as if we were caught in a time warp? ... [R]acism is [inaccurately] viewed as an anachronistic vestige of the past ..." (Davis, 2008, pp.9, 11.)

Davis' contention assists our understanding, and thus the combating, of the difficulty that Australia as a nation has in owning its racist face. Perhaps we see the term, racist, as exclusionary. Yet such a view would be simplistic, denying our complex make-up: Australia is both a tolerant *and* a racist society. It isn't necessary to erase or elide the *in*tolerance within a nation to embrace the tolerance. It would be primarily important, then, in seeking to respond appropriately to the effects of racism on mental health / well-being, to 'out' this public secret: to acknowledge the existence of such hybridity and the sheer multiplicity of possible negative experiences. One of the reasons Australians may disavow our racism is because we actually don't get to see enough of it in action. Many commentators have pointed out the invisibility, or relative invisibility, of racism (Davis, 2008). Unless one is actually on the spot, there is little chance of being aware of what has just occurred (Garvey, 2007, pp.1-4; McDermott, 2006).

Systemic discrimination is often oblique (Reconciliation and Social Justice Library), yet may have significant mental health consequences (Harris et al., 2006). Across the health, welfare and judicial systems, the shortfall in service delivery (Cunningham, 2002), and the existence of barriers to service access exist alongside either a lack of recognition or lack of professional, or political, will to address them (Hall et al., 2004). Obliqueness can play out in the way diagnoses, of far-reaching treatment significance for a client, may arise from a flimsy evidentiary foundation (Hunter, 1988; Westerman, 2003). Similarly, breathtakingly-careless assumptions concerning a presenting Aboriginal or Torres Strait Islander person (Reconciliation and Social Justice Library, 2008), may have profound consequences for that person's health and well-being and yet only receive wider attention when the situation is so clear, and so dire, that it's newsworthy (ABC Radio On-Line, 2008). This paper contends that interventions attempting to effectively address racism and its consequences have an inescapable political dimension: their first task is to make the 'invisible', visible.

Tamworth Syndrome

A recent episode of 'official' racism in my home town of Tamworth – in this instance, against Sudanese refugees - presents just such an opportunity for making both the phenomenon and its workings more discernible. Reference to my earlier exploration of the experience, and consequences, of growing up immersed in racial hostility (McDermott, 2006), allows a linking of 'Tamworth Past' and 'Tamworth Present'. Such linkage provides a vehicle to examine Tamworth Syndrome with its complexity intact.

In December, 2006, Tamworth Regional Council voted not to take up an offer to resettle five Sudanese refugee families in the city. The Mayor, James Treloar, remarked that their acceptance: "... could lead to a Cronulla-riots-type situation. Ask the people at Cronulla if they want more refugees" (Sydney Morning Herald On- Line, 2006).

He also claimed that: "... of the 12 Sudanese people who live in Tamworth, eight have been before the courts for everything from dangerous driving to rape" (Sydney Morning Herald On-Line, 2006). "These people don't respect authority" ('Tamworth's Rejection of Sudanese families "Racist"', 2006).

The situation blew up into a national and international story of Australian racism. More than one observer noted that the mayor's contention that Tamworth couldn't adequately find resources to meet the needs of five families should be ranged against the fact that, within weeks, the city would host around 40,000 visitors for its famous annual Country Music Festival. By mid-January, 2007, a combination of local pressure and widespread condemnation forced the council to a vote on a rescission motion, which was carried. Additionally, the Australian Human Rights Commission announced a move to mount legal action over anti-refugee leaflets that had been circulated in the Tamworth area. One way to read the latter decision to take action is in terms of recognition of the potential for physical and psychological harm arising from the unpredictable manner in which racist acts can multiply and accumulate. Racism multiplies rhizomatically: unchecked racist practice breeds further racism. As occurred with the Cronulla riots, even swifter replication - via text and e-mail - is possible now than in the past. A perceived groundswell of 'legitimated' racist acts may refresh and embolden a racism previously expressed only privately.

The Power and the Paradox of 'Mainstream' Racism

This paper posits that the way in which the racism feeding Tamworth Syndrome manifests is separable from, but equal in potency to, that arising from neo-fascist-style fringe organisations – although both engender negative blackfella experience. It is both widespread and entrenched, an inescapable part of the contemporary Australian atmosphere (Paradies et al., 2008). Anecdotally, many Pakeha (non-Maori) New Zealanders visiting Australia report being appalled at the everyday-ness of racist treatment of Indigenous Australians, and the 'tolerance' of such behaviour. Paradies and his co-authors draw our attention to the pull of 'elite' racism (2008, p.4): the phenomenon may be similarly powerful when presenting as 'offical' – the 'in-everyone's-best-interests' conclusions of an elected mayor – or as otherwise acceptably 'mainstream'.

Such 'mainstream' Australian racism, however, is not only hedged with ambivalence - possibly to maintain the integrity of our 'tolerant' view of ourselves, or to maintain our ignorance of the 'public secret' - but can also exhibit puzzling contradictions. The story of the interactions, over some decades, of my family (the McDermott family) and the Treloar family helps complexify any assumed White/Other straightforwardness in Australian Indigenous/settler relations. Further, it exemplifies how racism can perpetuate itself – until sufficiently challenged.

Mayor James Treloar is a lucerne farmer, but his father, Bruce Treloar, was a mercantile man, the descendant and inheritor of the Treloar who founded Tamworth's own department store in the 1880s, a large and significant institution in Tamworth. Bruce Treloar had been particularly kind to my family. When my brother worked for him, Bruce couldn't speak highly enough about my brother and gave him all sorts of assistance. When I was applying, at the age of 17 or so, for a trans-Tasman Youth Exchange, Bruce was an encouraging and steadying influence. Some years later, during a second bout of university study, Bruce's daughter (James' sister) and I struck up a friendship and went out a few times. Racist parental responses were nothing new to me, yet although I'd been through the experience a few times before, I was flummoxed by an edict to cease the relationship: the sense, if not the polite phrasing actually relayed, was to 'bugger off'. Given (what I'd presumed was) the family 'relationship', I hadn't seen it coming.

It was a minor, but nasty, personal experience of racism - one far from unknown to blackfellas - yet a confused and confusing situation. What does one make of such contradiction? What do *I* make of it, still? Her family had been genuinely kind - then crunch time came: I was stepping out with their daughter. I'd reached an 'Abo-proof' fence, beyond which lay a 'no-go' zone that Indigenous Australians are familiar with from this nation's history of 'virtual' apartheid (McDermott, 2004): the point at which, in seeking education, employment, rental accommodation – or real relationship – you discovered (or were reminded) that you were Other. The pertinence of this inter-family narrative doesn't hinge on hurt pride so much as on the ambivalence, or paradox, discernible in many such settler/indigene relationships. In Daniel's terms, the settler/coloniser may need to keep themselves safe from the 'secret' of the racist nature of their own urge to action when intimacy crosses some specifically-threatening threshold. Unless the feared Other is somehow de-Othered, through some genuine, alchemically-transforming interaction, the scene recurs and the racism may become normative, inter-generationally. If such racism is never called, never named, it may simply persist. I regret my lack of guts and action, back then. Thirty five years on, here is the younger Treloar, now mayor, railing in his official capacity against the lack of respect for authority, the criminality and disease-carrying potential of "these people" (Gratton, 2006).

I have drawn a localised picture – with a fuller account of some of the psychological ramifications of continually butting up against one's Otherness available elsewhere (McDermott, 2007) - but the phenomenon is nation-wide. The corrosive effects of unchallenged racist events have multiple negative consequences for the nation as a whole. Racism has a long 'half-life': racist events explode in individual lives, then their effects hang around. These events – and the practices that gave rise to them – float just outside public awareness, subtly poisoning public discourse, lingering like background radiation. The question for psychological schema, curricula, practice and training becomes: how do we deal with such inter-generationally entrenched, almost 'normative' racism – and its eroding of mental health and well-being - as it plays out in such environments as Australia's?

Questions Raised by Tamworth Syndrome

What Are the Long-term Effects of Living Inside Hostility?

The complexity of Australian racism – its varying along dimensions of ambivalence/directness, interpersonal/systemic and internalisation /

externalised response[4] – whilst crucial to apprehension of the phenomenon in operation, diminishes public perceptions of its ubiquity and hobbles both clinical and policy responses.   Tamworth Syndrome is also Townsville Syndrome, Perth Syndrome and Launceston Syndrome: a phenomenon unique in local presentation, but nation-wide in occurrence. In 2003, Dunn reported that surveys of Australians in Queensland and NSW revealed that Indigenous people, overseas-born people and people speaking a language other than English at home (LOTE) were around twice as likely to report experiencing 'everyday racisms' as other Australians (Dunn, 2003).   Vasta, however, in the book *The Teeth Are Smiling: The Persistence of Racism in Multicultural Australia*, positions Indigenous Australian experience of racism as "a much more extreme" experience of racism (Vasta & Castles, 1996).

What has been unclear is to what extent, and in which precise ways, this 'extreme experience' translates into nasty outcomes.   There are pointers in other fields of research. The last decade has seen a re-thinking of the potency and route of action of psycho-social risk factors in the causation and prognosis of cardiovascular disease (CHD: which includes such outcomes as heart attacks and strokes) (National Heart Foundation of Australia Expert Working Group, 2003). Utilising methods for critically-appraising systematic reviews, a convincing case has been made that factors such as depression and social isolation have an effect on CHD in the order of such accepted risk factors as smoking and high blood pressure (National Heart Foundation of Australia Expert Working Group, 2003). The recent work of Harris and her colleagues in Aotearoa/New Zealand, drawing on responses to the New Zealand Health Survey, supports a similar re-positioning of racism's significance in relation to effects on health: "Racism is a major determinant of health and a driver of inequalities in health" (Harris et al., 2006, p. 200).

In the previously-mentioned meta-analysis, Paradies had quite a few criticisms to make about how such research could be refined and results sharpened and better validated - including both the need to better define racism and better articulate the pathways by which racism actually affects physical and mental health - whilst still solidly connecting racism and mental distress (Paradies et al., 2008). Work on the mode of operation of the pathways involved *is* emerging (Mays et al., 2007), with particular attention being paid to links between racism and dysregulation of cortisol

---

[4] Dunn (2003) reminds us that: "While racism is quite prevalent in Australian society its manifestation is everywhere different. Locally sensitive antiracism initiatives are required to engage the **racisms** within Australian society" [my emphasis]

(Tull et al., 2005). The neuroendocrine and immune systems are increasingly viewed as part of a potential mechanism of operation (McKenzie, 2003). Whilst work on mechanisms and pathways continues, there is now broad agreement that "consistent relationships" (Harris et al., 2006) have been demonstrated between perceived racism/discrimination and poorer health and mental health outcomes, that the contemporary literature suggests "a robust link" (Gee, 2006). The evidence is 'in'. As Drexler has succinctly noted: "Racism hurts – literally" (Drexler, 2007).

The substantial literature on the effects of violence, abuse and neglect on the developing child, though, suggests that some interaction of acuteness of event, personal factors and chronicity of exposure to racism, to 'accumulative experience', may prove central to the kinds of system dysregulation referred to above (Perry, 2001). Further, the early-trauma literature provides evidence of mechanisms that resonate with long-standing Indigenous perspectives on the indivisibility of mind, body and spirit. Three decades of psychoneurobiological research now attest that the hurt is whole-of-person (Schore, 2002; Van Der Kolk , 1994, 1996). Tamworth Syndrome, then, suggests that continual exposure to racism is a multi-level process of embodiment (Krieger, 2005), that: "… piles up in your head and heart" (McDermott, 2006, p. 520)

What are the Interaction Effects between 'Accumulative' Racism and Indigenous Australian Dispossession, Forcible Removal and Traumatic Grief?

Any exploration of the pathways to distress serves to remind us that, not only is there great resilience, great strength, in Aboriginal Australia – that has enabled many to cope with multiple, grinding challenges - but also great diversity. Each person's situation is distinct: where there is impact on well-being, it reflects an individual interaction between a core of 'historic trauma' and a singular experience of racism, amongst other determinants. Racism is but one of the variables in play: its interaction with others offers avenues of possible further consequence for Indigenous mental distress. The literature on post traumatic stress disorder provides an exemplar with its suggestion that healing from serious trauma is affected by the post-trauma environment (Silove, 1999). Racism may play a role in not letting the wounds of colonisation heal. In particular, the work of Murphy and colleagues in the US, with Vietnam veterans, points to a particular barrier to recovery from Post Traumatic Stress Disorder (alongside, of course, that of persisting neurological adaption) related to that person's trauma symptomatology feeling: "… **'right'**, i.e.,

adaptive and protective with regard to safety and interacting with others"
(Murphy, Cameron, Sharp & Ramirez, 1999, my emphasis).

The findings of Murphy and his colleagues resonate with the
testimony of members of the 'Stolen Generations' still struggling with
their removal-related grief and, frequently, institutionalisation-related
violence, abuse or neglect. To the latter, the continual experience of
racism shows that nothing's changed. In particular, not only is the world
still unsafe, but there has been little acknowledgement - and less
validation - of their fate and suffering. The possibility of a 'validatory
effect' may prove not so much to hinge on whether *some* validation has
taken place but whether the trauma survivor perceives the surrounding
environment to be sufficiently changed ... sufficiently welcoming,
sufficiently *safe*. The Australian Federal Government apology of early
2008 to those forcibly removed from their families as children is,
therefore, a significant, but partial turn-around from the constancy of the
minimisation, trivialisation, even denial, emanating from conservative
media and 'mainstream' racist commentators over the previous eleven
years. A current member of the board of the Australian Broadcasting
Corporation (at time of writing), had likened the testimony of 'Stolen
Generations' as akin to False Memory Syndrome:

> ... accumulating research point[s] to the role of suggestion in creating false
> memories of **events that never actually happened**. It would be quite
> understandable, for instance, if in later life some children whose parents
> really did neglect them—and the parents themselves— reinterpreted the
> circumstances under which authorities intervened in the family (Brunton,
> 1998 - my emphasis).

If a personal experience of trauma is neither honoured nor validated,
nor even *believed* and accepted, might it not add another layer of
difficulty in healing from that trauma? If colonisation is the wound, then
the continual experience of racism might, serially, 'bump' the wound.

Thus, Tamworth Syndrome raises questions pertinent to the
Indigenising psychology task at the heart of this edited collection.
Drawing on the models of layered Indigenous Australian traumatisation
noted earlier, the ways in which such 'every-day racism' - experienced
recurrently, and for some *continually* - might interact with the 'collective'
or 'historic' trauma posited to lie at the very centre of Indigenous mental
distress, becomes a question of particular importance. If such is the still-
bubbling core of Indigenous mental distress - into which a stream of
'traumatic' grief, from early, unjust or cumulative losses, or the
consequences of violence, abuse and neglect are, already, known to sink –

the question becomes how much more would the addition of a person's accumulative experience of racism crank up the heat?

One answer is that racism may contribute further to the not-immediately-discernible burden of stress in many Indigenous lives. Quasi-official condoning of racist practices – including media demonisation of 'men's business', along with income sequestration and other aspects of the Northern Territory intervention[5] – may lead to demoralisation amongst blackfellas, which, in turn, is tied to a loss of hope[6]. Moreover, a diminished expectation of safety – as has been reported in some country towns, such as Kyogle and Albury in NSW, following periods of Ku Klux Klan threats – might, in turn, diminish levels of hope for the future. The research awaits on potential interaction effects between such factors and other determinants of Indigenous mental distress.

The aforementioned unconscionable burden of life-event stress being carried by Aboriginal and Torres Strait Islander adults (Lachlan & Evans Health Services; New England Health, 1998), and children (WAACHS, 2007), may be the most fruitful place to start. The area of accumulative stress is under-addressed by dominant models of mental health centred on biological psychiatry and psychopharmacology. A substantive critique of this model has emerged in the past two decades (Breggin, 2000, 2003). Read and Morrison, amongst others, have emphasised the role of trauma, even in relation to psychosis (Morrison, Read, & Turkington, 2005). Boelen has argued for the existence and potency of 'complex' grief (Boelen & van der Bout, 2005, 2006), a notion that echoes a long-argued Indigenous perspective (Swan & Raphael, 1995). Future research could profitably target racism's likely interaction with the inter-generational consequences of Indigenous dispossession, the multiplier effects of forcible child-removal, and a roll-out over one's life course of multiple losses unrecognised by, or trivialised within, the dominant culture.

---

[5] The Northern Territory (NT) Intervention is a massive, controversial Australian Government response – initiated by the Howard Government in 2007; under review, but continued (as of September 2008, the time of writing) by the Rudd Government – to a report detailing concerning levels of abuse amongst NT Aboriginal children. Its much-debated measures include: the use of army personnel, compulsory Aboriginal child health checks, changes to Aboriginal control over access to land, and Aboriginal welfare benefit sequestration.

[6] The issue of demonisation is felt keenly by Indigenous Australian men. One of the stated reasons given by the Central Australian Aboriginal Congress for organising an Aboriginal Male Health Summit in Alice Springs in July, 2008 was to: "Address the stereo type casting (sic) "labels" (drunk, unemployed, paedophiles just to name a few) that have been placed on all Aboriginal men since the release of The Children Are Sacred report and the subsequent NT intervention".

Dispossession is a cluster bomb: the original act scatters multiple bomblets that go off down the years. The contemporary losses with the most obvious impact on well-being are multiple, premature deaths – there is no low season for Aboriginal funerals. Other less-obvious losses may provide sources of psychological and physiological stress capable of additive, or multiplier, interaction effects with the stress of accumulated racist experience. Indigenous Australians still mourn the loss of land - not just loss of title to land, profound as it is when considered as economic base – but, for many, the anguish of severance of spiritual connection to the specific country over which they should be practising stewardship. Equally mourned are the losses of, or constraints on, culture and language. Work in both North America (HeavyRunner & Marshall, 2003) and Australia (McKendrick, 1997) has sharpened our comprehension of how subtle, yet potent, the process may be, by providing evidence of a reverse phenomenon, cultural resilience. A number of studies have reported improved health (and educational) outcomes through restoration of connections to culture, language and country and the enhancement of a secure identity (Durie, 1997; Raphael & Swan, 1997; Strand & Peacock, 2002). Such work resonates with research on the crucial role of control in life situations, including control over one's 'destiny' and a sense of 'mastery' in one's everyday dealings (Marmot, Siegrist & Theorell, 2006; Syme, 2004). Other commentators have provided striking Indigenous exemplars (O'Dea, 2008; Trudgeon, 2000). Yet 'control' and 'mastery' are a difficult hurdle when you are not only dispossessed of the fit and familiarity of your home place, ways and language, but also - for generations - actively denied a place within productive Australia through the operations of a system of 'virtual' apartheid (McDermott, 2004). The last-mentioned suggests a profitable direction for research: it could be argued that racism, in all its forms, now performs the work that was previously the role of this de facto form of apartheid: the long-standing containment and institutionalised Othering of Indigenous Australia. In its pervasiveness and power, racism operates as an effective gate-keeper for the ability to be in work, in a decent house, in education, under health care and more. Future research needs a dual focus, both how colonisation-related factors interact with experiences of racism in contemporary Australia, and how to *de-Other* – what might effective modes of combating racist practices look like in a land where public-domain anti-racist approaches are eschewed, since 'we're not racist!' (Gabb & McDermott, 2008).

What are the Implications for the Practice of Psychology?

Erika Apfelbaum's dictum, that psychology simply doesn't have the tools (Apfelbaum, 2000) to deal successfully with catastrophic events, aids our understanding of what Tamworth Syndrome implies for an Indigenised psychology. Apfelbaum, who lost almost her entire extended family in the Holocaust, found resonances between the catastrophic impact of that event and events, past and present, in Australia (Apfelbaum, personal communication, 1999). The burgeoning literature on the impact of racism on mental health, allied to its potential for interaction with other factors, mean that a meaningful incorporation and addressing of such phenomena might necessitate a "re-invention" of psychology (Guerin, 2007).

The lessons drawn by Syme from some, self-described, 'failed' work (often sophisticated, well-thought-out, multi-million dollar interventions) are helpful here.   Drawing on an array of solidly-conceived and implemented studies that proved manifestly ineffective, he concluded that clinical, individual approaches, or interventions that directly attack specific variables or risk factors - such as smoking, or in the mental health context, possibly depression - offer much less hope of success than dealing with people in their lived context and with the fundamental issues affecting their everyday existence (Syme, 2008). Syme's conclusions are as pertinent to psychology and Indigenous well-being as they are to their original field of public health.   Unconsciously, though unsurprisingly from an Indigenous perspective, they echo the holistic Indigenous approach to health / mental health referred to earlier. The lessons from this and other public health intervention experience now provide support for the value of 'Indigenising' psychology as the best way to serve the needs of Indigenous mental distress. As Syme notes, with unintended but particular resonance for racism: "[W]e rarely identify and intervene on those forces in the community that cause the problem in the first place" (Syme, 2004).

At a fundamental level this may be as conceptually simple, and practically challenging, as ensuring non-racist practice. As Morrison and colleagues remind us: "We have a responsibility for reducing the potential for treatment experiences themselves, such as acute psychiatric admissions, to be traumatizing for service users" (Morrison et al., 2005). Tamworth Syndrome implies, and employs, ambivalence in Indigenous/non-Indigenous relations, as well as denial or minimisation of racist practice – the 'public secret' in operation.   Consequently, helping psychologists shift their practice becomes a significant challenge.

Finally, the implications of accumulative racism for psychology also include a factoring-in of both culture and the context of people's lives into whatever treatment or prevention regimes are going to be delivered (Marsella, 2001). The 'by-words' could, perhaps, be 'acknowledgement' and 'incorporation'. Given long-standing Indigenous mistrust of health services, hospitals, mental health practitioners, welfare workers and researchers, if one is going to work successfully with Aboriginal people it becomes crucial to not only acknowledge the past, but also the manner in which it plays out in the present, as well as remaining neither silent nor impotent in the presence of racism.

What are the Ramifications for the Education and Continuing Professional Development of Helping Professionals?

Health professionals require the skills to engage some of the complexities suggested by Tamworth Syndrome in a sophisticated, effective, manner. *Confronting* racism, however, is only the first step in *combating* it, in changing deep-seated attitudes and behaviours that have become 'normalised'. This raises the dilemma of how to design health professional training that can negotiate the complexity of racism. Ordinary, 'mainstream' racists bridle at the 'R' word: they have grievances, their own set of grievances. When such people say, "I'm not racist", in the sense of maintaining consonance between their sense of self and their beliefs and behaviour, they're right: in their flailing about in their anger, looking for someone to blame – or 'sink the slipper' into - they don't see themselves as being racist.

The work of the anthropologist Gillian Cowlishaw, in Outback NSW, assists us here. She reports two self-labelled populations in the town of Bourke: people self-define as either in the Aboriginal population or in the White (Cowlishaw, 2004). Such a simple binary is, in fact, nonsense, she suggests, because the two groups are comprehensively interrelated. Yet she reports difficulty amongst those who define themselves in the White camp in accepting the grievances of the blackfellas (Cowlishaw, 2004) – the implication being that no-one listens to *their* (White) grievances - genuine grievances about the latest service to be pulled out of the bush, or being treated like poor white trash or stupid rednecks. These grievances, then, are able to be co-opted in the service of racist ends, including the conservative political and media commentator accusation of *special treatment* for Indigenous (as against other, equally-deserving) Australians – a recipe for (a reverse) inequity, where: "… Indigenous blood guarantees you extra rights" (Albrechtsen, 2002).

Such accusations, on one level, are easily answered by reference to the need to tailor interventions, that dedicated approaches to Indigenous needs – or those of any other group – are, actually, about good *population health*. On a psychology curriculum and pedagogical level, however, unless we find ways to acknowledge the reality of the belief systems inhabited by both professional and client, unless we actually acknowledge people's *unacknowledged* grievances, then we will be ineffective. Unless we factor into our training that people feel they've been ignored, or treated like dirt, in a society they read as uncaring – in short, that we've both 'heard' and incorporated their reality - our educational and training initiatives will have limited, purely cognitive impact.

The final ramification of accumulative racism for education and professional development that actually enhances our practice is an acknowledgement of the breadth of challenge it offers: a challenge on four levels. The first is the discomforting nature of the material itself, and its threat to our personal beliefs and cultural worldview - it may, markedly, shift us out of our comfort zone. Transcultural models of training, for example, ask participating professionals to examine, and be constantly mindful of, their own cultural assumptions that they bring to the clinical or preventative encounter – assumptions that might never, previously, have been examined, let alone challenged.

Secondly, overcoming racism in therapeutic and community preventative encounters is also a professional challenge: the approach needed to overcome mistrust (McDermott, 2004) clashes with western models of professional distance and non-disclosure. Given the pervasiveness of racist experience, particularly in the vulnerable situation of seeking help for mental health / well-being issues, some, appropriate, disclosure on the part of the professional may be the only way to win an Indigenous client's trust (Gabb & McDermott, 2008). Clients and communities need to satisfy themselves of a practitioner's non-racist *bona fides*.

Thirdly, there is a serious organisational challenge involved in creating a culturally-safe environment. Changing the way an organisation goes about its business is a fraught process: fundamental change to the way an organisation works is a top-to-bottom process, potentially threatening and easily de-railed by an unsupportive funding body or the unacknowledged racism of a CEO.

Finally, the designing and implementation of education and training that effectively confronts the implications of accumulative racism is also a major political challenge. A major thrust of this paper is that a well-prepared mental health professional may still not be able to work effectively unless they address the political equation. With respect to Indigenous well-being in contemporary Australia, the political *is* the clinical. It substantially determines workforce training and support, strategic priorities, whether promising initiatives have existence beyond that of a one-off project and whether there is the will to make them sustainable

What 'cure' for Tamworth Syndrome? In part, it depends on the willingness of professionals to be 'public' professionals, employing an *extended* advocacy. We need to advocate, not only for *things,* but also for consciousness of the language deployed. Language controls what's possible (Aldrich, 2006): we need not to acquiesce to the status quo, but to re-set the parameters of the discourse. The death of racism has been greatly exaggerated. Alongside loss and trans-generational trauma, it needs to become an inalienable given in policy talk. Whichever policies or programmes are under discussion, we must build in the realities of the past and their contemporary consequences – as well as the reality of both societal and organisational racism as under-acknowledged confounders of success in improving Indigenous social, spiritual and emotional well-being. If such approaches are circumscribed through our lack of professional assertiveness, we violate our duty of care.

References

ABC News On-Line. (2008, January 9). *Outstation Manager Criticises Welfare Quarantining.* Retrieved May, 2008, from http://www.abc.net.au/news/stories/2008/01/09/2134938.htm.

ABC Radio On-Line. (2008, March). *No help for Aboriginal woman suffering stroke at crowded bus stop.* Retrieved March, 2008, from http://www.abc.net.au/worldtoday/content/2006/s1585925.htm

Albrechtsen, J. (2002, August 28). Blacks in a Race Against Equal Rights. *The Australian.*

Aldrich, R. (2006). *Flesh-coloured bandaids: Politics, discourse, policy and the health of Aboriginal and Torres Strait Islander Peoples 1972-2001,* Unpublished PhD Thesis, Faculty of Medicine, UNSW.

Apfelbaum, E. (2000). And now what, after such tribulations? Memory and dislocation in the era of uprooting. *American Psychologist, 55*(9), 1008-1017.

Atkinson J. (1997). Yuuyarag The Way of the Human Being. *Alaska Mental Health Consumer Web.* Retrieved May, 2008, from http://akmhcweb.org/ncarticles/Yuuyarag.pdf.

Boelen, P., & van der Bout, J. (2005). Complicated Grief, Depression, and Anxiety as Distinct Postloss Syndromes: A Confirmatory Factor Analysis Study. *American Journal of Psychiatry, 162,* 2175-2177.

Boelen, P., & van den Bout, J. (2006). A Cognitive-Behavioral Conceptualization of Complicated Grief. *Clinical Psychology: Science and Practice, 13*(2), 109–128.

Breggin, P. (2000) The NIMH Multimodal Study of Treatment for Attention-Deficit/Hyperactivity Disorder: A Critical Analysis. *International Journal of Risk and Safety in Medicine, 13,* 15-22.

Breggin, P.R. (2003). Psychopharmacology and Human Values. *Journal of Humanistic Psychology, 43,* 34-49.

Brunton, R. (1998). Betraying the Victims: the stolen generations report. *Institute of Public Affairs: IPA Backgrounder, 10* (1). Retrieved May, 2008, from http://www.ipa.org.au/files/IPABackgrounder10-1.pdf.

Cowlishaw, G. (2004). *Blackfella, Whitefella: the hidden injuries of race.* Blackwell Publishing.

Cripps, K. (2007). Indigenous Family Violence: From Emergency Measures to Committed Long-Term Action. *Australian Indigenous Law Review, 11* (2), 6-18.

Cunningham, J. (2002). Diagnostic and Therapeutic Procedures among Australian Hospital Patients Identified as Indigenous. *Medical Journal of Australia, 176*(2), 58–62.

Daniel, S. (2006). Public Secrets. *Vectors: Journal of Culture and Technology in a Dynamic Vernacular, Winter.* Retrieved March, 2008, from http://vectors.usc.edu/issues/04_issue/publicsecrets/

Davis, A. (2008). Vice-Chancellor's Oration, 2008: Recognizing Racism in the Era of Neo-liberalism. *Murdoch University.* Retrieved March, 2008, from
http://www.abc.net.au/news/opinion/speeches/files/20080318_davis.pdf.

Drexler, M. (2007, July 15). How Racism Hurts – Literally. *The Boston Globe On-line.* Retrieved May, 2008, from
http://www.boston.com/news/globe/ideas/articles/2007/07/15/how_raci sm_hurts____literally/

Dunn, K. M. (2003). Racism in Australia: findings of a survey on racist attitudes and experiences of racism. *Australian National University.* Retrieved May, 2008, from http://hdl.handle.net/1885/41761.

Duran, E., & Duran, B. (2005). *Native American Postcolonial Psychology.* Albany: State University of New York Press.

Durie, M. (1997). *PUAHOU: A Five Part Plan for Improving Maori Mental Health.* Paper presented at the Oranga Hinengaro Maori /

Maori Mental Health Summit 1997, Massey University, Palmerston North, NZ.

Gabb, D., & McDermott, D. (2008). What do Indigenous experiences and perspectives mean for transcultural mental health?: Towards a new model of transcultural teaching for health professionals. In R. Ranzijn, K. McConnochie, & W.Nolan (Eds.), *Psychology and Indigenous Australians – Effective Teaching and Practice* (pp. 65-82). Cambridge, UK: Cambridge Scholars Publishing.

Garvey, D. (2007). *Indigenous Identity in Contemporary Psychology: Dilemmas, Developments, Directions.* South Melbourne: Cengage Learning.

Gee, G. (2002). A Multilevel Analysis of the Relationship Between Institutional and Individual Racial Discrimination and Health Status. *American Journal of Public Health, 92* (4), 618.

Gratton, M. (2006, June 21). Abbott in Call for New Paternalism. The Age On-Line. Retrieved May, 2008, from http://www.theage.com.au/news/national/abbott-in-call-for-new-paternalism/2006/06/20/1150701552947.html.

Guerin, B. (2007). *Indigenous Psychology: A contradiction?* Paper presented at 'Psychology and Indigenous Australians: Teaching, Practice, and Theory –the Inaugural Annual Conference'. Adelaide, SA: University of South Australia.

Haebich, A. (2008a). *Spinning the Dream: Assimilation in Australia 1950-1970.* Perth: Fremantle Press.

Haebich, A. (2008b). Retro-Assimilation. *Griffith Review.* Retrieved March, 2008, from http://www.griffith.edu.au/griffithreview/campaign/atb/Haebich_ed15.pdf.

Hall, S., Bulsara, C., Bulsara, M., Leahy, T., Culbong, M., Hendrie, D., & Holman, C. (2004). Treatment patterns for cancer in Western Australia: does being Indigenous make a difference? *Medical Journal of Australia, 181(*4), 191-194.

Harris, R., Tobias, M., Jeffreys, M., Waldergrave, K., Karlsen, S. & Nazroo, J. (2006). Effects of Self-reported Racial Discrimination and Deprivation on Māori Health and Inequalities in New Zealand: Cross-sectional study, *Lancet, 367,* 2005–2009.

HeavyRunner, I. & Marshall, K. (2003). Miracle Survivors: Promoting Resilience in Indian Students, *Tribal College Journal, 14(*4).

Howard, J. (2006, January). Australia Day Address to the National Press Club. Retrieved May, 2008, from http://australianpolitics.com/news/2006/01/06-01-25_howard.shtml.

Human Rights and Equal Opportunity Commission. (2007). *Social Justice Report, Chapter 2*. Retrieved May, 2008, from http://www.hreoc.gov.au/social_justice/sj_report/sjreport07/chap2.html

Hunter, E. (1988). Indigenous Suicides in Custody: A view from the Kimberley. *Australian and New Zealand Journal of Psychiatry, 22*, 273-282.

Krieger, N. (2005). Embodiment: A conceptual glossary for epidemiology. *Journal of Epidemiology and Community Health, 59*, 350-355.

Lachlan and Evans Health Services. (1997). When will you understand us? Voices of Central West Aboriginal Women. In *The Aboriginal Women's Business Health Project Report; a needs assessment of Aboriginal Women's Health in the Central West*. Bathurst: Central West Public Health Unit.

Marmot, M., Siegrist, J., & Theorell, T. (2006). Health and the Psychosocial Environment at Work. In M. Marmot & R.G. Wilkinson (Eds.), *Social Determinants of Health* (2nd ed.). New York: Oxford University Press Inc.

Marsella, A. J. (2001). *Cultural diversity and cultural wellbeing: Nuances of a complex relationship*. Keynote Address at the First Diversity in Health Conference – Sharing global perspectives. Sydney Convention & Exhibition Centre, Darling Harbour, Sydney.

Mays, V., Cochran, S., & Barnes, N. (2007). Race, Race-Based Discrimination, and Health Outcomes among African Americans. *Annual Review of Psychology, 58*, 201-225.

McDermott, D. (2003). *Dorothy's Skin*. Wollongong, NSW: Five Islands Press.

—. (2004). *Ngara: Living in This Place Now*. Wollongong, NSW: Five Islands Press.

—. (2004). *You Can Leave Your Hat On (but take off that white coat): bridging cultural divides in Indigenous and multicultural health settings*. Seminar Presented at The George Institute, University of Sydney and the Centre for Culture and Health, UNSW.

—. (2006). Growing up brown in a white-shirted time. *Medical Journal of Australia, 185*(8), 464-466.

—. (2006). Unknown Family at the Taxi Stand. *Medical Journal of Australia, 184*(10), 519-520.

—. (Speaker). (2007, July 7). Deep Listening, Working with Indigenous Mental Distress. *ABC Radio National*. Retrieved May, 2008, from http://www.abc.net.au/rn/allinthemind/stories/2007/1967830.htm.

McDermott, D., Minniecon, R., Jackson Pulver, L., Clifford, A., Blignault, I. & Guthrie, J. (2008). *Bringing Them Home – Kinchela Boys' Home*

Aboriginal Corporation Strategic Plan. Sydney: World Vision Australia / Office of Aboriginal and Torres Strait Islander Health (OATSIH) - Department of Health and Ageing, Muru Marri Indigenous Health Unit, UNSW.

McKendrick, J. (1997). *Victorian Aboriginal Mental Health Network Submission to Bringing Them Home.* Retrieved March 21, 2007, from http://kirra.austlii.edu.au/au/other/IndigLRes/stolen/stolen21.html.

McKenzie, K. (2003). Racism and Public Health. *British Medical Journal, 326,* 66.

Memmott, P., Stacy, R., Chambers, C., & Keys, C. (2001). *Violence in Indigenous Communities: Full Report.* Canberra: Crime Prevention Branch, Attorney General's Department.

Morrison, A., Read, J., & Turkington, D. (2005). Trauma and psychosis: Theoretical and clinical implications. *Acta Psychiatrica Scandinavica, 112*(5), 327-329.

Murphy, R. T., Cameron, R. P., Sharp, L. & Ramirez, G. (1999). Motivating Veterans to Change PTSD Symptoms and Related Behaviours. *NC-PTSD Clinical Quarterly, 8(*2).

NACCHO/AHMRC Aboriginal and Islander Social and Emotional Well-Being Forum. (2003). NACCHO/AHMRC.

National Heart Foundation of Australia Expert Working Group. (2003). 'Stress' and coronary heart disease: psychosocial risk factors. *Medical Journal of Australia, 178* (6), 272-276.

New England Health. (1998, January – June). *Aboriginal Maternity Service Report.* New England Health

O'Dea, K. (2008). Loss of Mastery and Control Undermines NT Intervention. *CRCAH Intranews.* Retrieved April, 2008, from http://www.crcah.org.au/communication/Enews/Gwalwa-Gai13/gwalwagai13.html.

Paradies, Y. (2006). A Systematic Review of Empirical Research on Self-reported Racism and Health. *International Journal of Epidemiology, 35*(4), 888–901.

Paradies, Y., Harris, R. and Anderson, I.(2008). *The Impact of Racism on Indigenous Health in Australia and Aotearoa: Towards a Research Agenda, Discussion Paper No. 4.* Darwin: Cooperative Research Centre for Aboriginal Health.

Perry, B.D. (2001). The neurodevelopmental impact of violence in childhood. In D. Schetky, & E. Benedek (Eds.). *Textbook of Child and Adolescent Forensic Psych.* Washington: American Psychiatric Press.

Raphael, B., & Swan, P. (1997). The Mental Health of Aboriginal and Torres Strait Islander People. *International Journal of Mental Health, 26(3)*, 15.

Raphael, B., Swan, P. & Martinek, N. 'Intergenerational aspects of trauma for Australian Aboriginal People'. In Y. Danieli (Ed.). *International Handbook of Multigenerational Legacies of Trauma.* New York: Plenum Press, 1998.

Ranzijn, R., & Severino, G. (Eds.). (2007). *Psychology and Indigenous Australians: Effective Teaching and Practice - Report on the proceedings of the second national workshop on developing curriculum guidelines.* Adelaide, SA: University of South Australia.

Reconciliation and Social Justice Library. *National Report Vol.II – Institutional Racism.* Retrieved April, 2008, from http://www.austlii.edu.au/au/special/rsjproject/rsjlibrary/rciadic/national/vol2/70.html

Schore, A. (2002). Dysregulation of the Right Brain: A Fundamental Mechanism of Traumatic Attachment and the Psychopathogenesis of Posttraumatic Stress Disorder. *Australian and New Zealand Journal of Psychiatry, 36.*

Silove, D. (1999). The Psychosocial Effects of Torture, Mass Human Rights Violations and Refugee Trauma. *Journal Nervous and Mental Diseases, 187(44).*

Strand, J. A., & Peacock, T.D. (2002). Nurturing Resilience and School Success in American Indian and Alaska Native Students. *Educational Resources Information Center Digest.* Retrieved May, 2008, from http://eric.ed.gov/ERICWebPortal/custom/portlets/recordDetails/detailmini.jsp?_nfpb=true&_&ERICExtSearch_SearchValue_0=ED471488&ERICExtSearch_SearchType_0=no&accno=ED471488.

Swan, P., & Raphael, B. (1995). *Ways Forward: National Aboriginal and Torres Strait Islander Mental Health Policy – National Consultancy Report.* Canberra: Commonwealth of Australia, Australian Government Publishing Service.

Sydney Morning Herald On-Line. (2005, December 12). *PM Refuses to Use Racist Tag.* Retrieved May, 2008, from http://www.smh.com.au/news/national/pm-refuses-to-use-racist-tag/2005/12/12/1134235985480.html.

Sydney Morning Herald On-Line. (2006, December 15). *You're Not Welcome, Town Tells Refugees.* Retrieved May, 2008, from http://www.smh.com.au/news/national/youre-not-welcome-town-tells-refugees/2006/12/14/1165685828180.html.

Syme S.L. (2004, January 3). Social determinants of health: the community as an empowered partner. *Prevalence of Chronic Disorders.* Retrieved January, 2008, from http://www.cdc.gov/pcd/issues/2004/jan/03_0001.htm.

Syme, L. (2003). *The Social determinants of health: the community as an empowered partner.* Paper presented at The Community in Control Conference, Melbourne. Retrieved May, 2008, from http://www.ourcommunity.com.au/article/view_article.jsp?articleId=575

Tamworth's Rejection of Sudanese families "Racist". (2006, December 15). *The Age On-Line.* Retrieved May, 2008, from http://www.theage.com.au/news/national/tamworths-rejection-of-sudanese-families-racist/2006/12/14/1165685829692.html.

Trudgeon, R. (2000). *Why Warriors Lie Down and Die.* Darwin: Aboriginal Resource & Development Services Inc.

Tull, E. S., Sheu, Y-T., Butler, C., & Cornelious, K. (2005). Relationships between perceived stress, coping behavior and cortisol secretion in women with high and low levels of internalized racism. *Journal of the Native Medical Association, 97* (2), 206-212.

Van Der Kolk, B., et al. (1996). Dissociation, Somatization, and Affect Dysregulation: The Complexity of Adaptation to Trauma. *American Journal of Psychiatry, 153(*7).

Van Der Kolk, B. (1994). The Body Keeps The Score: Memory & the Evolving Psychobiology of Post Traumatic Stress. *Harvard Review of Psychiatry, 1*(5), 253-265.

Vasta, E., & Castles, S. (Eds). *The Teeth Are Smiling: The Persistence of Racism in Multicultural Australia.* St. Leonards, NSW, Allen and Unwin.

Westerman, T. (2003). *Development of an Inventory to Assess the Moderating Effects of Cultural Resilience amongst Aboriginal Youth at Risk of Depression, Anxiety, and Suicidal Behaviours. Doctor of Philosophy Thesis.* Perth, WA: Curtin University, School of Psychology.

Western Australian Aboriginal Child Health Survey (WAACHS). (2008). *WAACHS Survey, Vol. 2, Chapter 3.* Retrieved May, 2008, from http://www.ichr.uwa.edu.au/files/user17/Volume2_Chapter3.pdf.

'THE FINE LINE BETWEEN COMPENSATION AND TAKING ADVANTAGE': A DISCURSIVE ANALYSIS OF RACE PRIVILEGE

DAMIEN W. RIGGS AND MARTHA AUGOUSTINOS

Abstract

White Australians' acknowledgments of race privilege or complicity with colonialism continue to come under scrutiny for their 'confessional' role in speaking of racism only to yet again 'move on' from it. In a similar way, discourse analytic studies of racism continue to be criticised for their failure to produce 'real world' outcomes, and for their inability to 'shift' rather than merely 'describe' the existence of racism. Nonetheless, we suggest, there is considerable utility to be gained from an approach to combating racism that takes as its starting place an examination of white race privilege. In this paper we discuss how an application of discourse analysis to the examination of race privilege in the everyday talk of white Australians holds great potential for identifying the commonplace, indeed banal, ways in which race privilege is played out. The identification of such speech patterns, we suggest, has considerable utility for developing interventions into the function of race privilege, and for maintaining an explicitly political psychological focus on the actions of white Australians (towards Indigenous people in particular). This stands in opposition to the aforementioned simplistic voicing of the existence of privilege that often does very little to examine the attendant implications of privilege in very real life and practical ways.

Introduction

As a matter of protocol, we begin this paper by acknowledging, as two non-indigenous Australians, that we live and work upon the land of the

Kaurna people[1], and in so doing we recognise their sovereignty as First Nations people.

Making this acknowledgment, however, must in our opinion signify more than simply protocol. It must be connected to a praxis wherein Indigenous sovereignty is recognised not only as a fact that continues to exceed the claims to sovereignty made on the part of the Australian nation, but that there is an acknowledgment that Indigenous sovereignty is not something that non-indigenous people can speak for. As Fiona Nicoll (2000) states: "Indigenous sovereignty exists *because* I cannot know of what it consists; my epistemological artillery cannot penetrate it" (p. 370).

Yet there are certain things related to Indigenous sovereignty of which non-indigenous people *can* speak, namely the ways in which sovereignty continues to be denied by white Australia[2], and the ways in which such denial serves to accord considerable privilege to non-indigenous Australians. And thus it is to matters of racial privilege that we speak within this paper. In so doing our intention is not to create a protocol for confessing to racial privilege – this, we suggest, would do very little to actually engage in a praxis whereby the fact of Indigenous sovereignty is continually recognised as the ground from which non-indigenous scholars and activists write and work (Nicoll, 2004). Rather, our interest is to explore how racial privilege circulates in very concrete ways in the lives of non-indigenous Australians, with a particular focus on the experiences of those of us who identify or are identified as white Australians.

Locating ourselves firmly within the discipline of psychology, we provide one particular account of race privilege, based upon the framework of discursive psychology, which advocates for a politically engaged psychology capable of examining the actions of white Australians in non-individualising, non-internalising ways. Locating privilege in this way, we suggest, allows for an understanding of privilege as thoroughly located within social contexts wherein oppression and privilege circulate simultaneously, and where the management of privilege may be seen as something that white Australians are very much invested in.

---

[1] The Kaurna people are the traditional owners of the Adelaide Plains and surrounding region. The conference was held in Adelaide, the capital city of South Australia, which is located in the heart of Kaurna land

[2] While Australia is increasingly a multicultural country, the majority of the population is of European descent and the dominant culture is Anglo-European

Discursive Analyses of Racism

There now exists within the field of discursive psychology a considerable body of research focusing on racism (e.g., Augoustinos, 2002; Augoustinos & LeCouteur, 2004; Hook, 2006; Howarth, 2006; Riggs & Augoustinos, 2005; van Dijk; 1992; Wetherell & Potter, 1992). As is to be expected, the theoretical and philosophical leanings of discursive psychology, framed as they are by a critique of individualism, biologism and internalism, continue to receive a significant amount of negative attention within the mainstream of psychology (see articles in Manstead & Wetherell, 2005, for a summary of this). Such negativity dismisses discursive psychology as not sufficiently rigorous, unempirical, too subjective and thus failing to provide 'real world outcomes'.

In contrast, our claim within this paper is that discursive psychology is very much able to engage in analyses that do more than simply state that racism exists: we suggest that it can actually show us how racism functions and thus how it may be challenged. As it focuses specifically on the rhetorical functions of talk, and locates such talk within an interactional context, discursive psychology is equipped to identify the commonplace ways in which racism is enacted, and, more precisely in the context of this paper, the ways in which racial privilege is both managed and legitimated. As such, discursive psychology provides ways through which to understand how particular forms of language use, particular turns of phrase, particular metaphors, and the relational nature of language function to enable racist talk as a normative, rather than exceptional, way of making oneself understood.

Yet, as we have just suggested, discursive psychology, through its focus on language, does not simply document the language of racism: it can also elicit ways of shifting language use and highlighting the ways in which inequality is structured into language. This has particular implications for the challenging of racial privilege, as we elaborate throughout the remainder of this paper.

Race Privilege

It is important to recognise, of course, that examining the ways in which race privilege is enacted in the everyday talk of white people will not necessarily alter the institutionalised nature of racism. As Dorothy Roberts (2002) has suggested in the context of the US, recognising racial discrimination and enacting laws to combat it has not significantly reduced the economic disadvantage and social hostility experienced by African

American people (amongst other marginalised racial groups). Nonetheless, the endemic nature of racism requires multiple approaches in order to render visible its ongoing violence.

In Australia, the continuing forms of colonisation that take place result in dramatic disparities between the health and well-being outcomes of Indigenous and white Australians. Corollary to the disadvantages experienced by Indigenous people are the privileges accorded to white people, privileges that come as a result of the ongoing legacies of colonisation, dispossession and genocide. Understanding how racial privilege functions to legitimate colonisation, deny Indigenous sovereignties, and warrant white belonging in Australia is thus an important aspect of challenging racism, and in particular the ongoing failure on the part of white Australia to engage in respectful relationships with Indigenous people.

We can see racial privilege at work in the everyday ways in which white people benefit from living in a country that accords paramount consideration to the needs of white people (Riggs & Choi, 2006). In her work on white race privilege, Jenny Tannoch-Bland (1998) outlines 47 examples of how white people benefit from unearned privilege. Some of these include the assumption that as a white person:

- In Queensland[3], I can go into any public hospital and not have my recuperation hindered by my frustration that such infrastructure was funded from stolen wages[4] from my people (perhaps my own parents, siblings or myself) who are still waiting for the balance to be released by the Queensland government.
- If I am depressed, I can go to a counselor, psychologist or psychiatrist who shares my basic cultural assumptions and psychic world view, and who will not explain that I must change my belief and value system, forfeit my cultural identity, in order to exist in this society without a high level of pain.
- As an academic, I can, without penalty, be blissfully ignorant of any culture but mine (pp. 34-36).

Such examples of white race privilege work by normalising whiteness and thus justifying colonisation. Those of us who identify as white can

---

[3] One of the largest States of Australia, located in the north-east corner. Australia is comprised of six States and two Territories

[4] Many Indigenous Australians were never paid for the work they did to develop Australia, primarily in rural industries and domestic service. Currently there are many legal initiatives around Australia to try to recover these stolen wages

presume that our culture is the norm, that other people will see the world the way we do, and that our health will not be hindered (though will most likely benefit) from ongoing histories of oppression.

Some examples of racial privilege in the everyday talk of white Australians appear in discussions of race relations amongst white Australians that a) identify Indigenous people, but not white people, as belonging to a racial group; b) assume that a white model of subjectivity is appropriate for understanding the experiences of all people; c) claim that Indigenous people are always already subjugated 'objects of power'; and d) legitimate colonisation via particular constructions of Indigenous people and cultures. These four examples (amongst many others that could be identified) serve to normalise white hegemony through associating Indigenous people with notions of pathology. This assumed connection results in two main outcomes that we identify here as impacting negatively upon the health of Indigenous people: the justification of exclusionary practices, and the blaming of Indigenous people for poor health outcomes.

The forms of privilege we have outlined thus far function to legitimate white people's claims to belonging by reifying a particular model of subjectivity, namely the rational, autonomous individual of liberal humanism. Elizabeth Peel (2001) suggests that claims to liberalism are often used in highly variable ways to justify the status quo, and thus to legitimate oppression. Thus, as she suggests, whilst "liberal principles – such as meritocracy, freedom of the individual and so on – are often viewed as common-sense, cultural 'common places'" (p. 544), they are in actuality often deployed to condemn the rights of marginalised groups, and thus to reassert the freedom of particular individuals only. Liberalism is therefore "the perfect tool for the oppressor's use... [as it allows dominant group members] to sit on the fence, avoid taking sides [and] denounce polarization" (Sarachild, 1974, cited in Peel, 2001, p. 545). In relation to racism, this often results in dominant group members refuting the need for affirmative action strategies, through the suggestion that everyone has access to a 'level playing field' (Augoustinos, Tuffin & Every, 2005). The ways in which marginalised racial groups are denied access to the benefits enjoyed by dominant group members is thus seen as being due to what is constructed as either inherent pathology or a failure to achieve, rather than as a result of oppressive social structures.

We thus suggest that examining racial privilege is an important facet of challenging the rhetoric of equality, and its role in legitimating the benefits that white people gain as a result of living in a colonial nation. We will now elaborate this point through a brief analysis of some extracts of talk from a focus group with Australians focusing on white/Indigenous relations.

Analysis

Extract 1

Andrew: [In regards to Mabo[5]] ... You just have to be careful... a backlash ... in the sense that not too many people get very upset that 'why should they being having all these handouts'[6] in a sense.

John: ... if they're going to abuse it, particularly if they abuse it then if it comes up again that ... well people will say 'what are you going to do with it, last time... alcohol and what ever ... you've abused your position'.

Andrew: There is a fine line between them being compensated and them taking advantage of their position as it is felt to be. A lot of Anglo-Australians would umm are sort of are concerned about, they feel they are taking advantage; they're given much more than they need....

Mark: Like I've got an uncle that lives in Kempsey in New South Wales north coast[7] and they've got an Aboriginal, couple of Aboriginal groups up there and the government sort of got them housing and they burnt the houses to the ground so the government built them brick houses and um you saw them driving round in brand new Pajero four wheel drives or what not and you sort of get the impression that they sort of got all this and you see what they could do to it and they just don't seem to appreciate what they are given.

In this extract constructions of 'us and them' are used to highlight the differences between groups referred to by the participants as 'Anglo-Australians' and 'Aboriginals' in ways that render Indigeneity the problematic category. Thus 'Anglo-Australians' are depicted by the participants as being 'upset [that Indigenous people are] having all these handouts', and that Indigenous people are 'taking advantage; they're given much more than they need'. Such accounts of Indigenous people serve to position Indigenous people as 'taking advantage', rather than as being

---

[5] The Mabo settlement was a High Court finding handed down in 1992 which overturned the previous legal principle of 'Terra Nullius' (land unoccupied by people) and asserted the traditional ownership of land continuously occupied by local Indigenous peoples since 1788. It sparked what is still a continuing unrealistic fear among many non-Indigenous Australians that their properties would be taken back by the traditional owners.
[6] Social security benefits, including educational support specifically for Indigenous people.
[7] New South Wales is a large state situated in the eastern part of Australia, between Queensland and Victoria

justly compensated for the impact of colonisation. Thus as Andrew suggests, 'there is a fine line between them being compensated and them taking advantage of their position'. Statements such as these work to position white people as a) not to blame for Indigenous disadvantage (indeed Indigenous people are seen as having 'money thrown at them' – as being privileged) and thus b) that there are not implicit advantages to being recognised as white in Australia.

Interestingly, however, despite the participants' continued focus on Indigenous people as 'taking advantage' or 'getting all this [stuff]', we can nonetheless read these accounts for what they do not mention, namely the fact that it is a particular dominant group (i.e., white Australians) who are 'giving out' benefits to Indigenous people. Both Mark and Andrew note that Indigenous people are 'given' things, denoting at the very least a group of people who are in the position to 'give'. The implication of this is not only that there must be a reason for such giving (i.e., colonisation), but that this particular group has the power and indeed privilege through which to give. This point about those who are in the position of 'giving' is also signaled by Mark's suggestion that there is a lack of appreciation. His reference to appreciation in the context of 'giving' signals the importance of that which is given, and the privileged position from which such appreciation is expected.

In this extract we can therefore see some of the ways in which the advantages that white people hold simply by being white are ignored, and instead Indigenous people are depicted as receiving 'all these handouts', handouts that are seen as unwarranted. The privilege held by the white participants (and the white government they refer to) is nonetheless evident in the extract in the subtle ways in which the participants orientate to notions of 'giving' and 'appreciation'.

In the second extract, participants move on from talking about 'handouts' and instead talk about land rights claims:

Extract 2

Mark: Something the media failed to bring out – the sort of aid – you've been given all this chunk of land and that it was sort of 'save the backyards' kind of mentality and a lot of people got scared... the truth of the matter was that unless they had continual contact with their land they didn't have a claim under that decision[8] so I think that people failed to realise that and that scared a lot of people.

---

[8] The Mabo decision referred to previously

Andrew: Umm and I was surprised 'cos I guess you read about... some group that was about to make a claim on Adelaide and it really freaked me out this is bullshit.

John: They've already claimed part of Brisbane[9], haven't they a claim....

In this extract Mark introduces the topic of land rights by locating sovereignty rights as 'aid'. Such a depiction of Indigenous people fails to acknowledge ongoing histories of colonisation by constructing the white Australian nation as generously giving aid or assistance to Indigenous people, rather than land rights following on from the fact that title to land was never ceded by Indigenous people. Constructing land rights as 'aid' allows Mark and his fellow participants to ignore their own privileged location as white Australians and instead focus on Indigenous people as 'freaking out' or 'scaring' white Australians.

Of note in this extract is the varyingly repeated expression of surprise. If we are to accept the veracity of these claims, rather than read them as disingenuous forms of denial aimed at claiming a lack of knowledge on the part of the participants in regards to land rights, then it is possible to see the privilege of whiteness at work within the extract. In other words, the very fact that the participants can appear so surprised by claims to native title is a result, we would suggest, of the ways in which white Australians are often able to ignore issues that we do not see as pertaining to us: being blissfully unaware (at least until we are 'surprised' and 'freaked out') is one of the privileges that results from identifying as white in Australia.

Also in relation to the hegemony of whiteness and its resultant privileges, Mark introduces a point of clarification about land rights decisions in order to disclaim the need for 'a lot of people [to get] scared'. By referencing a High Court finding that denied land rights on the finding of 'no continual contact', Mark is able to demonstrate to his fellow participants that such claims are often inherently untenable. Yet, as Aileen Moreton-Robinson (2004) suggests, this is only the case if white interpretations of land ownership are accorded priority. In contrast to Mark's privileged claim to the authority of white laws, then, it is important to emphasise that Indigenous law and relationship to country continues to exceed the claims made on behalf of the white nation, at the same time as the nation continues to deny rights to Indigenous people in very concrete ways.

---

[9] The capital city of Queensland

As with the first extract, this second extract highlights the subtle ways in which we may see examples of race privilege being enacted in the specificities of talk. In addition to our overall claim that white Australians hold considerable privilege on a daily basis, it is thus possible to see how this privilege is played out in everyday conversations.

Conclusions

As we have suggested throughout this paper, talking about racial privilege within Australia holds particular implications for how we understand the psychological relationships that exist between white and Indigenous Australians. Rather than focusing on internalised or individualised accounts of such relations, we have provided one account of the role that race privilege plays in particular constructions of Indigenous people.

This leads us to suggest that rather than only working to develop ways in which the discipline of psychology can better support or engage with Indigenous people, it is also important to look at the ways in which white people talk about Indigenous people, and how this often reflects our privileged location. As we have suggested here, it is necessary to examine how oppression or social exclusion is produced in relation to privilege, and how this results in health disparities between Indigenous and white Australians. Such an approach may thus engender an understanding of racialised power that refuses a simplistic notion of dominance/subordination, and which instead examines the complex ways in which all Australians are positioned in a relationship to colonisation and the ongoing denial of sovereignty. Challenging racism and race privilege is thus about much more than just pointing out offensive statements or 'including' marginalised groups within the discipline of psychology. It is also about contributing to an understanding of the mundane ways in which privilege is enacted, and developing ways of rendering language use visible to white Australians and exploring the implications of particular ways of understanding our selves and our relations to others.

Whilst such a focus on racial identities may read in places as a rather deterministic account of racism, it is thus not one that precludes social change. Rather, our suggestion is that social change can only occur once white people are able to recognise how racial subjectification works, and how it produces white identities that are always already invested in racial privilege (Riggs & Augoustinos, 2004, 2005). Being accountable for this investment is not the same as being stymied in attempting to challenge racism and race privilege. Instead, it is to understand how any challenge to racism by white people is always produced in a relation to ongoing histories of colonising violence.

Acknowledgments

Thanks to the late Precilla Choi for working with Damien on an earlier version of the ideas contained in this paper.

References

Augoustinos, M. (2002). History as a rhetorical resource: Using historical narratives to argue and explain. In A. McHoul & M. Rapley (Eds.) *How to analyse talk in institutional settings: A casebook of methods* (pp. 137-147). Continuum International: London.

Augoustinos, M., & LeCouteur, A. (2004). Apologising to Indigenous Australians: The denial of white guilt. In N. Branscombe & B. Doosje (Eds.) *Collective guilt: International perspectives* (pp. 552-609). Cambridge: Cambridge University Press.

Augoustinos, M., Tuffin, K., & Every, D. (2005). New racism, meritocracy and individualism: Donstraining affirmative action in education. *Discourse & Society, 16*, 315-339.

Hook, D. (2006). 'Pre-discursive' racism. *Journal of Community and Applied Social Psychology, 16*, 207-232.

Howarth, C. (2006). Race as stigma: Positioning the stigmatised as agents, not objects. *Journal of Community and Applied Psychology, 16*, 442-451.

Manstead, T. & Wetherell, M. (2005). Special issue: Dialoguing across divisions. *The Psychologist, 18*, 542-554.

Moreton-Robinson, A. (2004). The possessive logic of patriarchal white sovereignty: The high court and the Yorta Yorta decision. *Borderlands e-journal 3*. Retrieved July 3, 2007, from http://www.borderlandsejournal.adelaide.edu.au

Nicoll, F. (2004). 'Are you calling me a racist?' Teaching critical whiteness theory in Indigenous sovereignty. *Borderlands e-journal, 3*. Retrieved July 3, 2007, from http://www.borderlandsejournal.adelaide.edu.au

Peel, E. (2001). Mundane heterosexism: Understanding incidents of the everyday. *Women's Studies International Forum, 24*, 541-554.

Riggs, D.W., & Augoustinos, M. (2004). Projecting threat: Managing subjective investments in whiteness. *Psychoanalysis, Culture & Society, 9*, 219-236.

Riggs, D.W., & Augoustinos, M. (2005). The psychic life of colonial power: Racialised subjectivities, bodies, and methods. *Journal of Community and Applied Social Psychology, 15,* 461-477.

Riggs, D.W., & Choi, P.Y.L. (2006). Heterosexism, racism and psychology: Challenging or colluding with privilege? *The Psychologist, 19,* 288-291.

Roberts, D. (2002) *Shattered bonds: The color of child welfare.* New York: Basic Books.

Tannoch-Bland, J. (1998). Identifying white race privilege. In The Foundation for Aboriginal and Islander Research Action (Ed.) *Bringing Australia together: The structure and experience of racism in Australia* (pp. 33-38). Queensland: The Foundation for Aboriginal and Islander Research Action.

van Dijk, T. (1992). Racism and argumentation: 'Race riot' rhetoric in tabloid editorials. In F.H. van Eemeren, et al. (Eds.) *Argumentation illuminated* (pp. 242-259). Dordrecht: Foris.

Wetherell M., & Potter, J. (1992). *Mapping the language of racism: Discourse and the legitimation of exploitation.* New York: Columbia University Press.

MOVING LEARNING FROM THE HEAD TO THE HEART: TEACHING AND LEARNING INDIGENOUS CONTENT IN APPLIED PSYCHOLOGY AND SOCIAL HEALTH COURSES

MICHELLE DICKSON

Abstract

The Applied Psychology and Social Health programs (Department of Psychology, Macquarie University, NSW) provide postgraduate training to psychology interns undertaking a Psychology Registration program and to counsellors completing counselling training in Indigenous Health, Child and Family or Alcohol and Other Drug work.

Students explore a range of learning experiences focused on developing understandings of Indigenous health and well-being, while developing culturally appropriate skills and strategies to work with Indigenous clients and their communities. The growth of these learning opportunities depended upon a collaborative research process inclusive of Indigenous Community priorities and academic priorities. These priorities have formed a framework for the development of a range of opportunities for learning: it is not enough to tick a box or sign a certificate, the learning needs to connect head and heart.

Our course content continues, each time it is delivered, to refine itself, acknowledging that engaging students in culturally appropriate ways of learning and working is more than setting readings and sitting through lectures. Through interactive workshops, group work and shared reflective learning tasks, psychology students look at the meaning of their learning, while exploring the impact their learning will have on their future work as counsellors and psychologists.

I will begin by sharing my own story, to locate myself in this paper. Locating myself is important because much of the work we do at Macquarie University in Psychology is around locating yourself, locating in community. Much of the work involves stories and yarning[1].

I am a Darkingjung/Ngarigo woman. Darkinjung country is in the Central Coast of New South Wales and Ngarigo country in the Snowy Mountains area. I am a mother of four children and am undertaking PhD research with Indigenous health workers. I am the Director of post-graduate courses in Applied Psychology and Social Health at Macquarie University in New South Wales. My family, like many other Indigenous Australian families, live with legacies of past government policies, policies that saw the separation of families and communities, policies that often forced loving parents to hide their children in an effort to keep families together. This process impacted very deeply on my own family for generations and I think has enforced a certain way of living for us. It was through sharing of stories in our family that I developed a true sense of my own identity and the identity of my family members. They continue to play a key part in my professional life, and I take that with me in my teaching and my research.

My maternal grandmother's yarning played a vital role for me early on when I listened to her telling stories about teaching her kids how to play hide and seek when certain government officials knocked at the door. The kids would know 'it's hide and seek time now'. The kids were told it was just part of a game, but what my grandmother was doing was keeping safe the things that were really important to her. She knew that the pale-skinned kids in our family for a couple of generations had been sent off to other states and far-away places as a result of the Stolen Generations government policies.

Listening to her stories about that and about other bits of her life helped me to form a mental understanding of what she did as a strong Indigenous woman and helped me to understand the importance of stories and of keeping some stories close - in the heart and head - and other stories quite public. The following quote, from my Grandma Rose, sets the foundation for our Applied Psychology and Social Health students, and I thank Grandma for that: "Give me a few minutes and we'll talk but sit and have a cuppa and I'll tell you a story".

This is the foundation of how we work with our students: trying as best we can to sit with them and really hear their stories, really listen to

---

[1] The term 'yarning' is used by Indigenous (and increasingly non-Indigenous) Australians to refer to the practice of engaging in conversation, to establish trust and a comfortable conversational space that enables learning and sharing to occur.

their learning needs and learning goals, and hear about what experience they might have already had in working with Aboriginal families and communities. If they have none, we talk about what they feel they need in order to fulfil their professional growth.

The postgraduate courses in Social Health and Applied Psychology provide training to two groups of students: psychology interns who are undertaking a psychology registration programme, and counsellors who are completing counselling training, not necessarily as part of registration but to work as counsellors in Indigenous health, drug and alcohol work, or family and child work. For myself, growing the courses has been a little bit like a pregnancy, a metaphor that will be continued through this paper.

Originally the courses were established by a colleague, Dr Daphne Hewson, who was exploring ideas around the professional development needs of both trainee counsellors and psychology interns who may be looking at an alternate pathway to psychology registration beyond 4th year[2]. Later Daphne worked with another colleague, Terry Widders, to further develop the Indigenous health work strand. The birth of both courses did not start in the normal way, with a curriculum document focusing on particular standards or academic requirements. Instead, we looked at the professional development needs of our students - what do they need to work in an appropriate and respectful way? - and yarning about that process resulted in a solid academic curriculum document. We looked at needs first and moved on from there.

In our courses students explore training in a range of areas including drug and alcohol dependency, child protection, Indigenous health, trauma and narrative therapy. They explore a range of learning experiences that focus on developing understandings of Indigenous health and wellbeing and aim to develop culturally appropriate skills and strategies to work with Indigenous clients in their communities. The span of learning opportunities that we build into the courses means that our Indigenous content is never considered an add-on. Quite the reverse: it is the core component of the courses. The Indigenous content is totally embedded, not just an occasional workshop, and that is really important. For us that was a priority and it remains a priority. It's on that basis - that the Indigenous content is built into every workshop - that the students attend. Hence we are constantly connecting from head to heart.

---

[2] In Australia, in order to become registered as a psychologist a student needs to complete a four-year accredited program of study in psychology followed by either two years of postgraduate (Masters) professional education or two years of supervised practice under the supervision of an accredited psychologist

Some people might not have completed a full three year psychology undergraduate degree. Some people - and this is particularly important for our Indigenous students - might not have completed an undergraduate degree at all, so we've developed an alternate entry pathway for people who have been working in a counselling capacity for a number of years. We look at what they may have done at University, their work experience, and other learning - and by other learning we take into account what Western approaches would call non-traditional learning, but it also includes what Indigenous people would call traditional learning experiences.

The two courses have 60% articulation so that students can switch from one stream to another if they wish. Students commonly enjoy the experience of the postgraduate certificate or diploma so much that they then articulate through to the Masters level. Those who have either completed four years undergraduate training in psychology or the full year of the Applied Psychology course can either enrol in a postgraduate diploma in Social Health, go on to psychology registration, or enrol in the Postgraduate Diploma of Applied Psychiatry. Since much of the content of the Social Health and the Applied Psychology courses is in common, graduates from either program can fulfil the New South Wales Registration Board's requirements for registration. We also offer a Postgraduate Certificate in Applied Psychology, articulating into a Postgraduate Diploma in Applied Psychology, and there is also an articulated pathway for people who want to go on to the Masters program in Social Health.

The development of our course options was like nurturing a pregnancy, in all of its stages. Like all good pregnancies, various stages of course development were really crucial. We had to take care that we got things right and that we set down the grounds that were nurturing and supportive, and this is where we looked at our Indigenous content very closely. We repeat this process almost every time we present the courses. We take great pains to keep in touch with what's happening out in the front line. We constantly connect with community[3] on issues around health and wellbeing. If there are particular needs in terms of knowledge and skills, at the beginning of semester we look at our Indigenous content and possibly move things around to meet those frontline needs. Making sure that we've got the content right is a demanding and time-consuming process, but vitally important.

---

[3] The term 'community' is commonly used by Indigenous Australians to refer to their local Indigenous community

In developing our Indigenous content, community consultation is the most essential component. It's really important to keep in touch with communities not only close to us in the Sydney area but also communities that feed us students. It's also important to meet the needs of our frontline Indigenous workers. We talk a lot to Indigenous health workers who will be working with our non-Indigenous students, whether they are registered psychology students or psychology counsellors, because the teamwork approach is really important. We also consult with peak bodies to ensure that our curriculum, teaching and assessment, and administration are always culturally appropriate. Looking at scholarship opportunities for students is also important, including scholarships for Indigenous students to access postgraduate places, but it's also important to increase the opportunities of non-Indigenous students to undertake courses with a significant amount of Indigenous content.

The research process that contributes to the development of our courses is focussed on qualitative ways of exploring strengths and needs. We have held, and continue to hold, interactive workshops inviting students, staff members, frontline workers, peak bodies, and academics from Macquarie. We workshop ideas around how well we're doing, what we can do better, and what can we continue to do well. We try and take a strengths-based approach, but in saying that we acknowledge that we learn a lot from the challenges we face. Those workshops are really important for continually refining the Indigenous content. They also remind us that head learning must always be connected to heart learning in order for students to take what they're learning and do something with it effectively in practice.

Listening to people's voices is really important to us. We take a narrative approach, which allow us to finds ways of engaging our students that connects their learning and knowledge from head to heart. It allows space for people to explore their professional journeys, and this includes space for lecturing staff as well as students. We use a narrative approach for all the stakeholders in our courses to make sure that what they are learning when they engage with our Indigenous content is valuable head knowledge but, even more importantly, valuable heart knowledge.

Returning to the pregnancy metaphor: there's always a labour in pregnancy, and we do have challenges that we have to face and wrinkles to be ironed out. Meeting those challenges is important because they are what keep our programs alive. Essential elements for keeping the Indigenous content appropriate and working well include ongoing staff development, for our administrative staff as well as our teaching staff.

Maintaining open communication about the content in our courses is really important. We invite students to evaluate every workshop they attend. The evaluation framework is open enough for the students to be brutally honest about what they like and what they don't like, and we take that on board and make changes as a result of that.

Another thing keeping us alive in terms of Indigenous content is linking teaching and learning to community needs, and fitting with community needs means being flexible. For instance, if we have community workers or guests in as co-lecturers or workshop facilitators and we get a phone call at five minutes to nine that something has happened in the community which involves that lecturer, we need to be flexible and respectful enough to say, 'Of course, our thoughts are with you, we'll see you when you can come.'[4] It's important to be respectful and have that flexibility, which is not easy in an academic context, especially when timetabling staff. It's quite a commitment, but one that we really have to honour.

As mentioned earlier, Indigenous content is not considered an add-on in the courses, but embedded throughout each unit, and there are many common units that both the Applied Psychology and Social Health students share. The core unit is Counselling and Professional Practice. Right from the first day we get students thinking about working with Indigenous cultures, asking themselves questions individually in the form of a reflective journal, and doing group work around what they need to know, sharing ideas about what they think they already know, and sharing stories about experiences they might have had working in the community or learning in communities. Most importantly, throughout this unit our focus is on the students identifying for themselves what they need to develop professionally. It's empowering for the students to take this on board in their core unit, and at the end of semester it's interesting to reflect on their journals and look back at what they thought was important when they started the course. At the end of the course they often have a totally new agenda for themselves.

For the Social Health Perspectives unit, we have a colleague who conducts an Indigenous sensitivity workshop, and all of our students work with her for at least three-quarters of a day, although it generally goes on for longer than that. We also have a debriefing session on this workshop

---

[4] An important aspect of Australian Indigenous culture is that the cultural obligations of community workers will usually take priority over their non-community obligations. Hence, government departments and other organisations are increasingly building in the need to attend important community events, such as funerals, as part of their working conditions

that helps to put the content of the workshop into the student's development plan as a psychology intern or counsellor.

We include workshops on counselling with Indigenous clients in communities, building on the basic principles of respect and culturally appropriate ways of working. Counselling in the communities is a high level skill. We also have other workshops on working with non-dominant cultures that connect some learning and thinking from the previous two or three workshops and includes case-based Indigenous work. For this unit we deliver four full-day workshops with a very large slab of Indigenous content which connects from day one right through to day four.

In all of the other units apart from those I've already mentioned there's an Indigenous content or component, such as case studies of Indigenous programs and initiatives in the communities and in professional networks, or interventions that are appropriate to the students' professional needs. For instance, one of our specialisations is the Alcohol and Other Drugs unit. In all these units a range of approaches is taken. Whether the Indigenous content is about Indigenous-based case studies, Indigenous health programs, or profiling a particular Indigenous initiative - for example, circle sentencing[5] which is part of the New South Wales Government's drug crime diversion programme - whatever it is, diversity is embedded, so that students get exposed to a range of ways of thinking about and working with Indigenous clients in their own community. Similarly, in the Children and Families Unit, where the focus is on child protection and working with children in families, sometimes we might look at case-based approaches, or sometimes particular interventions that have been developed by Indigenous colleagues, but again we cover a good range of issues and content.

With regards to our psychology registration programs, in addition to the common Indigenous content mentioned already there are some specific initiatives, for instance for teaching psychometric assessment. We do that in the form of workshops that are done in small groups so that students get small group supervision hours while they're learning this. They look at culturally appropriate ways of testing and psychological

---

[5] Circle sentencing involves taking a sentencing court to the local community, where the magistrate and the community sit in a circle, discuss the matter and arrive at an appropriate sentence. Community members include the offender and victim and their families and respected members of the local Indigenous community. Australian circle sentencing is based on Canadian experience. In New South Wales the scheme is invoked once the alleged offender has pleaded or been found guilty (Reference:
http://www.aic.gov.au/topics/indigenous/interventions/alternatives/circle.html)

assessment. We look at a whole range of tests, not only for Indigenous cultures, but for other cultures as well, and it's quite interesting to get feedback around this process. Commonly we get feedback such as, 'When I signed up for psychological assessment I didn't realise I'd get so much cross-cultural knowledge.' It's great to get that kind of feedback in a unit that could be otherwise seen as fairly narrow in focus.

The next section describes a typical assignment that we set our students, which includes a group meeting time of about two hours, in which they work with other students. By this time they have already done the Indigenous sensitivity workshop and have had a debriefing workshop. They go off together and watch Jane Elliot's *Australian Eye*[6]. They then come together as a group to discuss the issues that they focussed on, and they audiorecord that discussion. They submit the group's audiotapes and also an individual list of comments where each student reflects on their journey with Indigenous learning and the knowledge that they have gathered through the workshops they have done off site. This gives them the chance to write about their head learning – reflecting on set readings that they have to do – and also to reflect on their heart learning through their participation in the workshop. They combine those in this assignment, and at the end they are asked to think about how that all fits in terms of the needs of Indigenous clients and how they can work with them from a counselling perspective.

We strongly emphasise skills training underpinned by theoretical knowledge. Students start off by reading about working with Indigenous clients - that's their head knowledge starting - but we move the reading into skills development through experience or workshops, so it quickly becomes a combination of head, heart, and guts actually.

We use problem-based learning: case scenarios, and case discussions for which we bring in expertise from the field. We use some of our academics at Macquarie, but we also bring in frontline workers, community workers, to share their teaching and learning. We always remain open to sharing professional stories, and sometimes personal stories if that is appropriate. We try to create an environment for our students in which they do their head learning through readings and attending formal classes and their heart learning by sharing their stories and making connections through their professional experiences.

To conclude, in one of the feedback forms this comment came from a student: "As well as helping me to grow on a professional level, this class

---

[6] A documentary about the experiences of participants in a workshop who are randomly divided into two groups – brown eyes and blue eyes – and experience the effects of physically-based discrimination at first hand

and its participants has given me a new outlook on life and what's important to me." So for the students, studying the Indigenous content is not just the reading and it's not just attending class, it's having the experience of being a member of a learning group, a learning community. This student's comment is about what they learnt from each other as much as from the learning strategies that we teachers devised.

WHAT DO INDIGENOUS EXPERIENCES AND PERSPECTIVES MEAN FOR TRANSCULTURAL MENTAL HEALTH? TOWARDS A NEW MODEL OF TRANSCULTURAL TEACHING FOR HEALTH PROFESSIONALS

DIANE GABB AND DENNIS MCDERMOTT

Abstract

Transcultural mental health draws upon many academic disciplines, including psychology, psychiatry and sociology. The resulting transcultural paradigm requires a focus on the culture of both client *and* practitioner in order to unpack the complex interpersonal interactions which make or break successful health communication and potential intervention. While a transcultural focus has assumed, in Australian health settings, a multi-ethnic and multicultural position determined by the complexities of an immigrant population, little attention has been paid to equally complex and important transcultural encounters between Indigenous and non-Indigenous Australians. Indeed, anecdotal evidence points to a reluctance or a timidity to include Indigenous issues at all. This paper widens the transcultural paradigm to include Indigeneity amongst the panoply of Australian heritages usually addressed. It examines how effective professional education programs might best be developed. These require a working partnership with Indigenous practitioners to illuminate the factors - historical, cultural, political and psychological - underpinning Indigenous health issues, and to share contemporary Indigenous lived experience with non-Indigenous counterparts. Finally, this paper moves from an exploration of innovative pedagogy and facilitation to the implications for models of transcultural teaching.

Introduction

In Australia, as in many other former colonies, there is an enduring crisis of poor health and shortened longevity among Indigenous peoples. Yet, the personal histories, post-colonial legacies and cultural perspectives of Aboriginal and Torres Strait Islander clients challenge many clinicians, whose professional training has done little to inform them in these crucial areas. Using the transcultural mental health paradigm, we present a model of transcultural teaching for health professionals that addresses key aspects of value systems and knowledge needed for operating in both cognitive and affective domains of learning that are essential for working effectively with Indigenous clients. Such necessity arises from widespread anecdotal evidence of personal and national ignorance about Indigenous life and history, and solid evidence for the persistence of interpersonal racism and systemic discrimination against Indigenous Australians (Paradies et al., 2008), despite a competing national ethos and practice of tolerance (McDermott, 2008). Therefore, since 2003, we have collaborated on and facilitated professional development programs for clinicians who have, or will have, Indigenous clients within their practice, and it is our experience in designing and facilitating these programs that informs the teaching content of this paper.

Transcultural Mental Health

A transcultural mental health paradigm illuminates our understanding of mental health and illness by focusing on the cultural perspectives and world views of both client and clinician. These, in turn, provide the bases for the explanatory models of mental illness that are part of all human communities. The transcultural clinical relationship of trusting, treating and healing requires a capacity for self-reflection on behalf of the clinician: how does he or she appear to the client, in terms of interactive behaviours, attitudes and cultural values? What is his or her level of communication - or miscommunication? This construct owes much to the formulations of culture-centred counselling models developed in North America (Pedersen & Ivey, 1993; Sue, Ivey, & Pedersen, 1996; Sue & Sue, 1990). These were applied in multicultural settings where clinician and client came from different cultural backgrounds, usually immigrant or refugee backgrounds in the case of the clients. A similar focus on indigenous culture in the work of John Berry in Canada, with Aboriginal North Americans, and later Aboriginal Australians in the 1970s, threw light on the dynamics of Indigenous and non-Indigenous encounters from a cultural perspective (Berry, 1970, 1975).

The development of social psychiatry, and then transcultural psychiatry - informed by anthropology and sociology - ultimately resulted in a method of 'cultural formulation' in the process of assessment in the Diagnostic and Statistical Manual of Mental Disorders (DSM) IV (American Psychiatric Association, 1994). In USA, Arthur Kleinman's work on the cultural meaning of illness and care in the 1970s and 1980s was seminal in moving from an older one-way anthropology/psychiatry view: e.g.,–*isn't this condition an intriguing cultural phenomenon?* --- to --- *we as clinicians are an equally significant part of the clinical encounter* (Kleinman, 1977, 1980; Kleinman & Good, 1985). In Canada, Kirmayer formalised the development of transcultural psychiatry by establishing a university department at McGill University, Montreal. He advanced the discipline further by the inclusion of Native American explanatory models of illness (how people make sense of the cause and course of an illness) and idioms of distress (how they manifest and/or describe their distress) (Kirmayer, Simpson, & Cargo, 2003). This development was closely paralleled by Marsella at the University of Hawaii with research into cultural concepts of mental health and the treatment required from different cultural perspectives (Marsella, 1979, 1989). Work in the UK also added a great deal to the knowledge and practical application of a transcultural mental health approach to the mental health and illness experience of ethnic minorities, and the effects of racism and marginalisation on members of these minorities (Bhugra, 2004; Littlewood & Lipsedge, 1989). In Victoria, Australia, from its establishment in 1989, the Victorian Transcultural Psychiatry Unit (VTPU) developed post-graduate and professional development programs on transcultural immigrant and refugee mental health for clinicians; in 1997, VTPU began collaborating with Indigenous health professionals on professional development workshops for clinicians from the Resource Unit for Indigenous Mental Health, Education & Research (RUIMHER) of the University of Melbourne (Gabb, Piu & Thorpe, 2000). In South Australia, Nicholas Procter in his innovative 'Reciprocity in Education' model brought immigrant and refugee groups together with mainstream health professionals in frank and open transcultural dialogue about how each group experiences the other (Procter, 2001).

Transcultural Paradigm

The transcultural paradigm is the 'equation' formed when individuals of different cultures interact. It is applicable to any interaction between people of different cultural backgrounds and world views. It focuses the attention on complex interpersonal interactions which may make or break successful communication. In the field of health, in particular, such communication may be critical to effective intervention. The notion of 'culture' is not based only on ethnicity or nationality; there are other forms of culture, such as rural culture, the culture of medicine and the culture of colonialism[1]. The transcultural paradigm requires that equal attention and respect be paid to the culture of both parties in the interaction. This enables each side to learn something of 'the Other', and this can only be done by revealing something of 'the Self'. Therefore, in a health setting, there has to be a subtle shift in the clinician/client dynamic, despite the obvious disparities in clinical expertise and status; in effect each party is acting upon cultural knowledge - such as the biomedical model of medicine, or centuries' old folk medicine or particular cultural understandings of methods of assessment and treatment - which the other does not have, but may urgently need, for a successful outcome.

Scope of a Multicultural Focus

In Australia, and other countries with similar histories of colonialism and the dispersal and neglect of Indigenous peoples, there have been long-standing immigration policies to 'grow' populations and build nations. The multi-ethnic and multicultural societies that these policies produce, however, require an affirmative approach to achieve equality of opportunity and access to all government services (Victorian Health Promotion Foundation, 2007). This is especially critical in regards to health. The urgent mental health needs of immigrants and refugees have all been a focus for action in USA, Canada, UK and Australia (Reid & Trompf, 1990; National Mental Health Strategy, 2000; Spector, 2004). In population terms, in all of these countries, the *mainstream* in large cities is now *multicultural* (*The Age* Newspaper, 2007; Australian Bureau of

---

[1] The work of Anthony Marsella cautions us that 'culture' should not be considered as monolithic and static: rather, it should be twinned, routinely, with 'context' (Marsella, 2001: *Cultural diversity and cultural wellbeing: Nuances of a complex relationship,*   Keynote Address at the first Diversity in Health Conference – Sharing global perspectives, 28-30 May, 2001, Sydney Convention & Exhibition Centre, Darling Harbour, Sydney, Australia.

Statistics, 2007). In fact, a number of Australian locales now exemplify a 'normal' multiplicity and 'overlapping-ness' termed, in the British context, 'super-diversity' (Vertovec, 2006).

In terms of attention to Indigenous health, the USA and Canada have shown a commitment to First Nations' health and mental health by recognising the political and historical factors underpinning poor Indigenous health, and by insisting on mandatory professional standards of cultural competence in assessment, treatment and management (Kirmayer, 2003). Also acknowledging political and historical wrongs of the past, Aotearoa/New Zealand has based its creation of biculturalism firmly on the foundation of the Treaty of Waitangi (1840), which has led to the growth of a bicultural nation, culturally and linguistically. New Zealand has developed 'cultural safety', which is a practice that "extend[s] beyond cultural awareness and cultural sensitivity" (New Zealand Psychologists Registration Board, 2006). Culturally safe practice involves a re-configuration of power in the professional-client encounter (Aekins, 2006). It is premised on client guidance as to how the professional's skills can be applied – in effect, client determination of how the service can be delivered - so as not to compromise, or threaten, a person's cultural identity. It also requires that practitioners undertake a potentially challenging process of reflection on their own cultural identity and its impact on their praxis. In some health jurisdictions in New Zealand, training in cultural safety is now mandatory: in nursing training this has been the case since 1992-4 (Ramsden, 2002). In others – such as mental health – practitioners must meet mandatory standards of cultural competence (Ministry of Health, NZ, 2003).

Indigenous and Non/Indigenous Encounters in Health and Mental Health

As clinicians and educators in the field of health and mental health in Australia, we note from our experience that, overall, very little attention has been paid to the dynamics of transcultural encounters within health settings between Indigenous clients and their non-Indigenous clinicians. Transcultural mental health units, funded by state health departments in Australia over the last 20 years, are generally not expected or encouraged to include Indigenous health issues within their scope of expertise and research. In Victoria, however, the Victorian Transcultural Psychiatry Unit (VTPU) has responded to the demand from clinicians who wish to receive knowledge and skills to best serve Indigenous clients in collaboration with Indigenous health personnel. Nevertheless, this work remains unfunded. Government sources insist that peak Indigenous health organisations fulfil the training role alone. The cultural awareness / cultural sensitivity approach most commonly employed, however, remains outside the transcultural paradigm, as it is essentially a stand-alone 'show and tell' model which is not able to explore *a transcultural encounter* and the personal and traditional values that are involved on both sides of the equation.

In fact, throughout Australia, educating mainstream health professionals about Indigenous life and health is not usually carried out within the transcultural paradigm. Instead a typically 'old style' anthropological approach within in-service training and professional development curricula has been used; one where Indigenous people are objectified. This has the effect of emphasising the 'Otherness' of the culturally alien. Indeed, it may reinforce entrenched feelings of fear and racism. Accordingly, anecdotal evidence from clinicians tells us that many clinicians are uncertain as to how to approach Indigenous clients in a way that develops trust and successful treatment opportunities through respectful and culturally competent clinical encounters. All too frequently, clinical encounters are experienced negatively by both parties, and more often than not the client does not return for subsequent visits. Again, the anecdotal evidence from clinicians is strong: most report little or no training on Indigenous issues and mental health. Generally they report a poor knowledge of local Indigenous communities and available services (Saric, 1998). Nevertheless, in many parts of urban and rural Australia, in varying numbers, many will have Indigenous clients – whether recognised as such, or not. Some have experienced occasional cultural awareness programs presented by Indigenous liaison workers, but these are often given without clinical or educational support, so, while of general interest, they are often unfortunately discounted as superficial or lightweight in terms of the educational expectations of clinicians.

In 1997, the Resource Unit for Indigenous Mental Health Education and Research (RUIMHER) under the auspices of the University of Melbourne was developed within the Department of Psychiatry. For five years there were a number of notable achievements emerging from a continuation of earlier research into Victorian Indigenous health (McKendick & Charles, 2001; McKendrick & Thorpe, 1991; McKendrick et al., 1992; Thorpe & McKendrick, 1992), together with transcultural educational programs for non-Indigenous professionals in collaboration with VTPU educators. When administrative problems arose, however, RUIMHER was de-funded and not replaced. In 2007, a possible training partnership between VTPU and the Victorian Aboriginal Community

Controlled Health Organisation (VACCHO) was suggested; however, policy and funding issues have proved barriers to this proposal.

Using a Transcultural Model: Key Aims

As clinicians and educators, we could see that by developing a partnership where one of us is Indigenous and the other is non-Indigenous, we could create an environment where it is authentic and legitimate—and safe—to open up the difficult questions that a 'show and tell' approach can never really do. This makes it possible to engage participants in not only *cognitive* learning, but also *affective* learning, i.e. the tapping into deeply-held feelings, beliefs and prejudice, which may be very confronting. By taking this approach, and balancing the Indigenous/non-Indigenous transcultural equation, our aim for our workshop participants is to find ways of working effectively with Indigenous clients, in conjunction with exploring further opportunities for learning from both Indigenous health professionals and local elders, who are the repository of salient local knowledge that is not, usually, available anywhere else.

Using a Transcultural Model: Key Methods

Using a workshop format, participants are encouraged to share their own experience, both personal and clinical. Key content items are presented in a variety of ways: in short team-teaching presentations, in facilitated large and small group discussions, in case studies for role play and discussion, in exercises for personal self-reflection, and by creating opportunities (when appropriate) for linking non-Indigenous health and Indigenous professionals, often for the first time in some localities.

Using a Transcultural Model: Key Content - I

Where're You From? Who's Your Mob?

These casual-sounding lines have a particular utility and potency in focussing participants on the importance of establishing a human connection between Indigenous clients and their non-Indigenous clinicians. They are also the first step in actualising an innovative aspect of our integrated model: *cultural ease.* This notion combines an acknowledgement of the validity of Indigenous inter-personal axioms, the development of a familiarity with key Aboriginal protocols and, eventually, a seamless incorporation of Aboriginal 'ways' into one's professional repertoire: in essence, an Indigenisation of praxis.   Trialling, then discussing, an exercise based on one such protocol creates an experiential base for the personally and professionally challenging suggestion of using Aboriginal 'ways' in one's professional work. In particular, it introduces elements of a particular Indigenous practice, 'deep listening'. 'Deep listening' is a principle of inter-personal relations central to the cultures of Aboriginal nations across the continent.   Found under a variety of names – such as *Dadirri* and *Ngara* - that reflect the diversity of those cultures, it is, yet, an obligation in common to contemplate, in real time, everything that you hear – to self-reflect as you listen, and then, tellingly, to *act* on what you've registered.

A first step, then, is to situate yourself in an Indigenous universe, to let your *Self* be known, to become both familiar and transparent. This, of course, is challenging to western models of professional distance. *'Where're you from' / Who's your mob?'* is about revealing something about yourself that cuts through the professional exterior to the ordinary person underneath.   Disclosure, of course, needs to be appropriate – sufficient to dissolve one or two layers of historic Indigenous mistrust, yet respectful of therapeutic boundaries. Thus, traditional clinical misgivings about showing something of the Self may be allayed by developing the skill of "taking off your white coat, while keeping your professional hat on" (McDermott, 2004). We make the point that this type of clinician flexibility is not only germane to working within the transcultural paradigm, but also essential to developing the 'meta-skill' of real, rather than 'check-list' cultural competence (McDermott, 2006, after Durie, M., private communication, 2005)

A next step in a multicultural, multi-ethnic population like Australia's is that we need to be able to explore our personal and collective ethnic and geographical origins, before and after first European contact. This can be done as an introductory workshop exercise using a time-line to show where participants place ancestors, family members or themselves in terms of migration history or Indigenous history (Gabb, 2000). This may also add to the depth of personal introduction made possible in the 'deep listening' experience.

Exploring key values (both personal and professional) using the seminal research done by Hofstede on value systems (Hofstede, 2001) forms a natural progression from the introductory exercises described above. Hofstede's research shows patterns of cultural values that vary significantly from culture to culture, despite the large number of survey participants in fifty countries being drawn from the ranks of a large multinational company – and with very similar levels of education. Of particular relevance to clinical work, are Hofstede's 'cultural dimensions' which illustrate the differences in world view and personal values between 'individualism' (societal focus on the individual) and 'collectivism' (societal focus on the group), and between 'small power distance' (fluid distribution of power) and 'large power distance' (fixed distribution of power). This framework for understanding cultural dimensions may be applied to any cultural value system, traditional or contemporary, so it is highly useful in any transcultural work.

Using a Transcultural Model: Key content - II

Contexts of Indigenous Lives

As our participants are usually from health-related professions, this part of the program opens up an examination of Indigenous Australia's health status, before making international comparisons with other Indigenous groups with similar colonial histories. We contrast critiques of utilising Indigenous-specific (and Indigenous-appropriate) approaches to service delivery – often disparaged in the Australian context as 'special treatment' – with the lessons of good population health practice: of dealing with the health and related social needs of any given population facing particular health issues with pertinent and dedicated responses. Introducing the notion of a population health approach leads to a discussion of the social determinants of Indigenous health and illness, and poses the question: 'Why are there such health disparities between Indigenous and non-Indigenous populations?' It also fosters an examination of certain stereotypes of Indigenous life, such as the misuse of alcohol and other drugs.

How do You get Cured of Spiritual Sickness?

In this section the focus shifts to what happens to a people's spirit—collectively and individually—when they are engulfed by a cycle of trauma: invasion and colonisation, dispossession, complex grief, loss, the 'Stolen Generations' of children removed from their families by government policy, trans-generational trauma, racism and discrimination. This leads to an opening up of Indigenous perspectives on past and current health status and the way in which health is understood in a holistic way, with holistic concepts of prevention and treatment, and what these might mean for participants' clinical work.

What Is the Nature of Cultural Learning?

We now turn attention to a self-reflective focus for our non-Indigenous clinician participants, by asking them to imagine for a moment the time when their own people were once indigenous, in a far away past that is rarely ever contemplated. Participants are offered some questions for quiet self-reflection (see box below). The questions touch on a person's early learning about Aboriginality and how concepts of race and difference may have been dealt with within the family of origin. When the group resumes, the discussion centres around what we have all lost by losing an indigenous life, one where we were once closely attached to the land, physically and spiritually. And then this begs the question: what have we gained by moving to a migratory life over thousands of years? Questions then arise concerning: what do we value, what do we fear, and what is the relevance of culture to health? These also make it possible to revisit the issue of why can we not just treat everybody the same.

Questions for Self-Reflection

Where do I fit into Australia's history and society?
Where am I from? Where are my ancestors from?
What do I value?
What do I fear?
What did I learn as a child about 'us' and 'others' [people culturally and racially different]—at home?—at primary school?—at secondary school?
What did I learn about Indigenous Australians?
What places have special significance for me?
Long ago my ancestors must have been indigenous somewhere---what would that distant life have been like?
If we are no longer indigenous, what have we lost (long ago)?
What have we gained?
Are there any traces or echoes of that ancient life?

Positive Approaches to Clinical/Prevention Issues with Clients and Communities

Clinicians attend professional development programs because primarily they are looking for opportunities to perform their work more successfully. Therefore it is important to give them concrete indicators as to how to proceed in developing their services, and what aspects of the clinical encounter may have worked against encouraging and retaining an Indigenous clientele, and worked against producing positive health outcomes. We introduce a series of case scenarios for small group discussion, after which each group brings to a plenary session working conclusions as to the problems each case represents and what measures may be adopted for positive intervention. This leads to a discussion on how to incorporate culture and the context of Indigenous life into treatment and prevention strategies, which may be represented as an integrated model incorporating *cultural awareness*: being aware of your own and others' cultural backgrounds and values; *cultural competence*: being able to use knowledge and skills to work successfully and confidently with clients culturally - and, possibly, linguistically - very different to yourself; *cultural safety*: being able to create a health intervention experience where power dynamics in the health encounter are addressed and clinician cultural underpinnings are also a focus; and *cultural ease*: being confident in expecting that Indigenous culture is represented and celebrated as the bedrock upon which all other migratory cultures in the modern nation state have taken root, with a concomitant move towards incorporation of Indigenous protocols and 'ways' into the professional repertoire. This last construct also infers a recognition of the timelessness and universality of all Indigenous cultures in the world, out of which all contemporary ethnic cultures have ultimately emerged over millennia, and thus may help in reversing the still-evident cycle of contempt and destruction, one that has tainted and constrained even health professionals' interactions with Indigenous Australians (Hunter, 1993).

Working Effectively Across the Cultural Divide

This is about maintaining a transcultural mindset: this means keeping in mind that *the culture of the clinician is as important a focus as that of the client*, in that we cannot be culturally neutral in any clinical encounter. We need to promote opportunities to note and discuss the similarities and differences to other parts of our transcultural working experience with our colleagues. In a multicultural community, it is a given that clinicians regularly work with people whose cultural background and ethnicity are unfamiliar to them. We need to be aware of our own responses, whether positive, negative or something in between; then we need to ask ourselves: where did that response come from? How, what and where did I learn about 'Otherness'? Are there stereotypes that I have in mind? What must it be like being the 'other'? In practice, how does this work in terms of interpersonal encounters and relationships (Estable, et al, 1997)? This last point is best demonstrated by using a well-chosen case study presented as a scenario for discussion or a role-play which can be 'edited' in successive 'takes' to show different approaches and predict outcomes.

How to make a Difference?

Busy clinicians want something concrete to take with them from a training session. A succinct summary of key ideas, skills and principles from the content area of the training are these:

- *Strengthen the resilience of Indigenous people*: we can support 'cultural resilience' – connection to culture, country and spirituality - which may prevent or ameliorate adverse outcomes, and we can promote individual resilience by working to reduce the magnitude, chronicity and arbitrariness of major life stressors.
- *Incorporate 'deep listening' (and other Aboriginal protocols and 'ways'):* an approach that demands simultaneous listening and reflection, of listening non-verbally, of listening to the silence in between (or *of*) client communication(s). It is a technique for client/clinician communication that lifts the traditional clinical boundaries of self-disclosure a little, so that a level of rapport can be achieved between the Indigenous and non-Indigenous members of the dyad. Using it in practice is again most effectively demonstrated with a case-study/role-play.
- *Keep a 'de-Othering' perspective:* actively practice inclusion and reduce inadvertent organisational marginalisation ('us' and 'them') - use the internal technique of 'placing yourself in another's shoes' and minimise the impact of difference in communication styles with flexible communication skills, incorporating aspects of content, speech register, seating and silence. Being alive to, and combating, 'invisible' racism (both interpersonal and systemic) markedly 'de-Others' a service.
- *Activate cultural competence and cultural safety in the workplace:* an organisational challenge which may require clinicians to act as catalysts, even 'champions'.
- *Build environments for change:* bringing about change requires a move beyond simply diagnosing and treating, to encompass actions capable of significant impact on one or more of the social determinants of health.
- *Employ 'extended' advocacy:* which may involve time, commitment and further challenge. Clinicians need to keep in

mind that, in regard to improving Indigenous outcomes, *the political is the clinical.* Pursuing one's professional duty of care to Indigenous clients and communities involves seeking sustainable, population specific - and genuinely appropriate – programs, and supporting a trained workforce to implement them. Undeniably, this involves considerable professional and political risk.

Strategies for Effective Professional Education Programs

From our five years' of collaborating in producing educational programs for clinicians, we know that busy people require short, sharp, interactive workshops. They need a detailed program outline in advance, take-home readings, and PowerPoint notes. Key adult education principles are essential: acknowledging and encouraging the sharing of personal and professional experience. Discussions work best in pairs or small groups; the results are then brought to the whole group in plenary sessions. We invite local Indigenous elders and health workers to participate; this gives opportunities for future contact between individuals and starts to build a relationship between the local non-Indigenous health organisation and the Indigenous community. Careful facilitation and introductions help to make people feel comfortable, in what for many is a challenging and sometimes unsettling activity.

Where appropriate, the use of powerful or meaningful visual images can greatly enhance words and text. For example messages about racism from old cartoons in the print media, or 1950s school books, often elicit a powerful and affective response that incites further discussion.

Each session should be anonymously evaluated for each discrete topic. We use a Likert scale (of 1-5, 'strongly disagree' to 'strongly agree'), and invite written comments about what worked and what did not, along with suggestions for further sessions.

Finally, the value in Indigenous/non-Indigenous team teaching cannot be underestimated and is something that should be made use of wherever possible. This enables the facilitators to model mutual respect and authentic sharing of each other's areas of knowledge and experience.

Innovative Pedagogy and Sensitive Facilitation

We find that with sensitive facilitation, and the creation of a safe environment, participants will share opinions, concerns, theoretical knowledge, and their own emotional responses. They are also more likely to ask the 'hard questions' they may not have had the opportunity to ask before. By using Paul Pedersen's multicultural training model of awareness, knowledge and skills (Pedersen, 1994), we are able to break down 'awareness' to elicit different responses: e.g., *I know of these issues, I'm aware of my emotional response/ sorrow, discomfort/ fear, I remember my family's attitude to Aboriginal people*, or *I now know how little I learned in school.* We aim to establish a spirit of 'taking you along with us' instead of mounting a blank challenge. This is important because the Australian ethos of tolerance (and a 'fair go') makes people sensitive to 'anti-racism' topics. Rather than employing some of the confronting tactics used in anti-racism training in USA, we find encouraging self-reflection on challenging issues leads to a willingness to discuss in pairs or small groups the experience of early attitudinal learning, and what implications there may be for personal and professional encounters.

Implications for Transcultural Teaching: A New Model

Transcultural teaching for health professionals requires that the study of 'clients in the fishbowl' should be abandoned, as in that model there is no account taken of the culture and values of the clinician, who forms part of the clinical equation. We need to create opportunities for learning and for discussing difficult or confronting topics, often based in sensitive areas around perceptions of race and ethnic background. We need to promote how, in our professional lives, to hear the real narratives surrounding a person's lived experience; to make this happen we have to be prepared to engage in dialogue with our clients about who we (the clinicians) really are and what our cultural 'take' brings to the clinical encounter. We therefore 'equalise' the equation of client and clinician, which within an Indigenous context acknowledges the powerful meaning of placing both participants in the context of their genealogy and their locality, opening the way to honest and transparent communication. To most effectively underpin the clinical encounter, we must encourage ideas that make services more visible, more accessible and more supportive. In order to achieve all this, we must nurture the cultural confidence of clinicians, a capacity essential for working in any community.

References

Aekins, V. (2006). Northland Polytechnic / Tai Tokerau Wananga. *Nursing Journal, 10*, 13-17.

American Psychiatric Association (1994). *Diagnostic and Statistical Manual of Mental Disorder, Fourth Edition (DSM IV)*. Washington, DC: American Psychiatric Association.

Australian Bureau of Statistics (2007). *Year Book of Australia 2006*. Canberra: Australian Bureau of Statistics.

Berry, J. W. (1970). Marginality, stress and ethnic identification in an acculturated Aboriginal community. *Journal of Cross-Cultural Psychology, 1* (3), 239-52.

—. (1975). Ecology, cultural adaptation and psychological differentiation: Traditional patterning and acculturative stress. In R. Brislin, S. Bochner, and W. Lonner (Eds.), *Cross-Cultural Perspective on Learning*. New York: John Wiley & Sons.

Bhugra, D. (2004). Migration and mental health. *Acta Psychiatrica Scandinavia, 109*, 243-258.

Estable, A., Meyer, M. & Pon, G. (1997) *Teach Me To Thunder – A Training Manual for Anti-racism Trainers*. Ottawa: Canadian Labour Congress.

Gabb, D. (2000). Development of transcultural mental health education by the Victorian Transcultural Psychiatry Unit. *Synergy*, 2000 Summer, Multicultural Mental Health Australia.

Gabb, D., McKendrick, J., Piu, M. & Thorpe, L. (2000). *Sharing the load: transcultural mental health professional development using an Indigenous and non-Indigenous team approach*. Victorian Transcultural Psychiatry Unit & Resource Unit for Indigenous Mental Health Education and Research.

Hofstede, G. (2001). *Culture's consequences: Comparing values, behaviors, institutions and organizations across nations*. (2nd Edn.). Thousand Oaks, CA: Sage.

Hofstede, G., & Hofstede, G. (2005). *Cultures and organizations: software of the mind* (2nd Edn.). New York: McGraw Hill.

Hunter, E. (1993). *Aboriginal health and history – Power and prejudice in remote Australia*. Cambridge, UK: Cambridge University Press.

Kirmayer, L. (2007). Psychotherapy and the cultural concept of the person. *Transcultural Psychiatry, 44*, 232-257.

Kirmayer, L., Simpson, C. & Cargo, M. (2003). Healing traditions: culture, community and mental health promotion with Canadian Aboriginal peoples. *Australasian Psychiatry, 11*(1), S15-S23.

Kleinman, A. (1977). Depression, somatisation, and the "New Transcultural Psychiatry". *Social Science and Medicine, 11,* 3-9.

—. (1980). *Patients and healers in the context of culture.* Berkeley: University of California Press.

Kleinman, A. & Good, B. (Eds). (1985). *Culture and depression – studies in the anthropology and cross-cultural psychiatry of affect and disorder.*

Lalumiere, C. (2007). Roots of resilience. *McGill Reporter.* http://www.mcgill.ca/reporter/38/10/kirmayer

Littlewood, R. & Lipsedge, M. (1989). *Aliens and alienists: ethnic minorities and psychiatry* (2nd Edn.) London: Unwin Hyman Ltd.

Marsella, A. J. (1979). Culture and mental disorders. In A.J. Marsella, R. Tharp and T. Ciborowski (Eds.), *Perspectives on Cross-Cultural Psychology.* New York: Academic Press.

—. (1989). Culture and mental health. In A.J. Marsella & G. M. White (Eds.), *Cultural conceptions of mental health and therapy.* Dordrecht, Holland: D. Reidel Publishing Company.

McDermott, D. (2004). *You Can Leave Your Hat On (but take off that white coat): bridging cultural divides in Indigenous and multicultural health settings.* Unpublished seminar presentation, The George Institute, University of Sydney and the Centre for Culture and Health, UNSW, September, 2004

—. (2006). *The What, Why and How of Koori Well-Being: Understanding and working successfully with Indigenous mental distress,* Unpublished seminar presentation, Australians for Native Title and Reconciliation (ANTaR), Victorian Aboriginal Community Controlled Health Organization (VACCHO) and Victorian Transcultural Psychiatry Unit (VTPU), St. Vincent's Hospital, Fitzroy, Melbourne, 5th December, 2006

—. (2008). What Cure for Tamworth Syndrome? The Accumulative Experience of Racism, Blackfella Well-Being and Psychological Practice. In R. Ranzijn, K. McConnochie, & W.Nolan (Eds.), *Psychology and Indigenous Australians – Effective Teaching and Practice* (pp. 19-42). Cambridge, UK: Cambridge Scholars Publishing.

McKendrick, J. & Charles, S. (2001) *Report of the Rumbalara Aboriginal Mental Health Research Project.* Rumbalara, Victoria: Woongi Cultural Healing Group, Rumbalara Aboriginal Co-operative Ltd.

McKendrick, J., Cutter, T., Mackenzie, A. & Chiu, E. (1992). The pattern of psychiatric morbidity in a Victorian urban Aboriginal general practice population. *Australian and New Zealand Journal of Psychiatry, 26,* 40-47.

McKendrick, J. & Thorpe, M. (1991). *Koori views on mental health problems.* Melbourne: Victorian Aboriginal Health Service.

McKendrick, J. & Thorpe, M. (1998). The legacy of colonalisation: trauma, loss and psychological distress amongst Aboriginal people. *Grief Matters,* September, 4-8.

Minas, H. & McKendrick, J. (1994). Psychiatry in a multicultural setting. In S. Bloch & B. S. Singh (Eds.), *Foundations of Clinical Psychiatry.* Melbourne: Melbourne University Press.

Ministry of Health, New Zealand (2003). *Health Practitioners Competence Act.* Retrieved November 2007, from http://www.moh.govt.nz/hpca

New Zealand Psychologists Registration Board (2006). *Standards of Cultural Competence for Psychologists Registered under the Health Practitioners Competence Assurance Act (2003) and Those Seeking to Become Registered,* p. 4, http://www.psychologistsboard.org.nz/pdfs/HPCA%20PDFs/Cultural %20Competence%20May%2006.pdf, accessed November 2007

Paradies, Y., Harris, R. and Anderson, I. (2008). *The Impact of Racism on Indigenous Health in Australia and Aotearoa: Towards a Research Agenda,* Discussion Paper No. 4, Cooperative Research Centre for Aboriginal Health, Darwin, 6-7.

Pedersen, P. (1994). *A handbook for developing multicultural awareness* (2nd Edn.) Alexandria, VA: American Counseling Association.

Pedersen, P. & Ivey, A. (1993). *Culture-centred counselling and interviewing: a practical guide.* Connecticut, USA: Praeger.

Procter, N., Amirghiasvand, M., Eaton, A., Engelhardt, R. & Moutakis, A. (2001). *Sadness and the heart of acceptance: The reciprocity in education project.* Conference paper; Diversity in Health – Sharing global perspectives: Conference, Sydney Convention & Exhibition centre, Darling Harbour, Sydney, 28-30 May, 2001.

Ramsden, I. (2002). *Cultural safety and nursing education in Aotearoa and Te Waipounamu.* Chapter Seven. Retrieved from http://culturalsafety.massey.ac.nz/thesis.htm

Saric, R. (1999). *Exploring practitioner perspectives on Aboriginal client/patient issues in mental health settings.* Unpublished dissertation, Graduate Diploma in Mental Health Sciences (Transcultural Mental Health), University of Melbourne.

Sue, D. W. & Sue, D. (1990). *Counseling the culturally different: Theory and practice.* New York: Wiley.

Sue, D. W., Ivey, A. E. & Pedersen, P. B. (1996). *A theory of multicultural counselling and therapy.* Pacific grove, CA: Brooks/Cole.

The Age Newspaper, October 2007. Melbourne, Victoria.

Vertovec, S. (2006). *The emergence of super-diversity in Britain.* Centre on Migration, Policy and Society: Working Paper No. 25, COMPAS, University of Oxford. Retrieved from, http://www.researchasylum.org.uk/?lid=154

Victorian Health Promotion Foundation (2007). *More than tolerance: Embracing diversity for health – Discrimination affecting migrant and refugee communities in Victoria, its health consequences, community attitudes and solutions. A summary report.* VHPF September 2007.

Wise, A. (2007) *Multiculturalism from below: Transversal crossings and working class cosmopolitans.* Paper presented at COMPAS Annual Conference, Oxford.

'DOING OUR OWN WORK':
RE-WORKING WHITENESS IN PSYCHOLOGY

TRACEY POWIS

Abstract

When engaging with questions of Indigenous/non-Indigenous relationships, my attention has been drawn to a space in relationship for non-Indigenous people to 'do our own work' around racism and social injustice. This notion seems to me to resonate with an understanding of the importance of both supervision and personal counselling for people working within 'the helping professions'. It also seems to be quite ordinary to having and holding relationships in general. Nevertheless, as a discipline, I thought psychology should be well equipped to enable non-Indigenous people working within it to 'do their own work' around their (racialised) identities and the legacies of colonisation for their own subjectivities and for their relationships. In my experience I found this both accurate and severely misleading. In this paper I set out to share stories from my experiences and connect these with questions raised at a workshop, to articulate some of the ways in which dominant "psy-knowledges" (Rose, 1991) may enable and constrain non-Indigenous people in 'doing their own work'. I tried to trace a process by which I came to understand the question of 're-working whiteness' in terms of re-working epistemological commitments that inform the contemporary field of psychology within Australia.

I acknowledge the Kaurna people as traditional custodians of the land on which the conference was held, and I also acknowledge those who have gone before in enabling the discursive space within which to present conferences like this. For me, this includes Indigenous writers, and the Aboriginal communities I visited with as a PhD student in psychology, where 'whiteness' assumed a tangible, embodied, form for me. And whilst I choose not to speak for my imagined reader I wonder at the people and histories that brought us together – the people/s who tuned a reading/listening ear to the particular rhythms and murmurs that can be felt and heard at the intersections of "psychology and Indigenous Australians": to them, and you, I also pay my respects.

I'd like to begin by sharing a song with you. 'Not a White Country' is a song by Leroy Johnson, a Barkinji Wiimpitja man from Wilcannia NSW, whom I met when still a fresh-from-school PhD student, and whose songs intersect with my stories, as do the songs and stories of many others who I met through my PhD. Reproduced here with permission, 'Not a White Country' enables me to give voice to experiences that might otherwise be subsumed in the silences that mark *terra nullius[1]* as an existing, persistent fiction in this country many now call Australia.

As you read these lyrics, listen for the deep resonance of his voice, the strength and the softness that fits so well with a melody more reminiscent of a ballad than any other genre my cultural frames-of-reference might supply. The song, and how it is sung, are inseparable. Whilst a written text might seem poorly equipped to do justice to this, it might also represent an invitation to tune in to other senses as a part of our reading practices.

Not a White Country – Leroy Johnson

They walk on by
They don't look at me
I'm forgotten people in my country
I'm on the streets
I'm on the land
Invisible, to their average man

But rise up
Don't sit back
Take the future get your pride back
Rise up, you will see
It's a sunburnt land it's not a white country

When I think back
To what we saw
I don't understand what it all was for
Rounded up
Always pushed back
You can't be here boy,
Don't you know you're black
Rise up
Don't sit back,
Take the future get your pride back
And rise up, you will see

---

[1] The legal doctrine that held that Australia was unoccupied by human beings at the time of British colonisation

The time is now for you and me

And rise up
Don't sit back
Take the future get your pride back
And rise up
You will see
It's a sunburnt land it's not a white country

I look around
And feel the ghosts
Of our old people
What means the most
This land of ours
Our very lives
Belongs to us not them
And it's worth the fight

So rise up
Don't sit back,
Take your future
Get your pride back
And rise up
You will see the time is now for you and me

And rise up
Don't sit back
Take the future get your pride back
You will see it's a sunburnt land it's not a white country
It's a sunburnt land it's not a white country (rep times 3)
It's not a white country
It's not a white country
It's not a white country

For me, to speak with this song is also to remember – to be reminded of those relationships that precede and follow me in everything I do; and to be reminded of the impossibility of telling my own stories, without also speaking of and with others. Telling my stories through some form of dialogue – with this song, for instance – seems congruent with my experience of speaking as a relational process, despite the monologic form frequently required in academic contexts.

So I listen to this song and, in hearing Leroy sing of being invisible, I catch a fleeting glimpse of my own subjectivity as inhabited by 'they'. I wonder at how it is possible that such a process of invisibilisation can occur that I could walk in this country, in such oblivion…

And then I'm also suddenly aware that it's through listening to Leroy, through engaging with this song, that I notice myself as a culturally-located subject, make a connection between the histories he sings of, and requisite histories to my own subjectivity. So there's something about the invisibilising effects of whiteness that I want to draw out, and there is also something about the ways in which those processes (and my own subjectivity as inscribed by them) are invisible to me. And that I am privy to such fleeting glimpses, whispers, and gestures toward, my own subjectivity through relationships with others, evokes difficult questions for me:

- How to do whiteness, differently, when it is invisible?
- How to take responsibility as a speaking subject, when my own subjectivity is hidden from me?
- And what are the implications of this for my relationships with others?[2]

In my experience, these questions are not encountered as singular epiphanies, as grand moments on the road to Damascus: rather, they recur for me, return to me, in the ordinariness of every day. When I experience questioning as "repeated citations" (Davies, 2006) perhaps what is sought is not an answer, as much as a politics of response.

So I have been reflecting lately on how to address these questions. As I wonder at my response, I am reminded of Michelle Dickson's work (2008), where she spoke of bringing together the head and the heart. I have had the joy of working with Michelle, and continue to learn from our connection; certainly, finding ways to represent both head and heart in the stories I share has been important to me. And psychology does not give generously a language of the heart: when I hear it speak of 'the heart' at all, it is to produce 'it' as an object, and then to disconnect it from 'the head' (and body, and voice, and soul).

So it seems as though if I am going to address questions of whiteness and 'doing our own work', I am necessarily addressing questions of subjectivity and representation within psychology. And I do so as a member of academic communities bound by disciplinary connections to psychology and necessarily, then, to disciplinary histories of complicity

[2] Aware of the burgeoning literature constituting a 'field' of 'whiteness studies', I use 'whiteness' hesitantly; my relationship to the concept is embedded, in particular, in readings of Aileen Moreton-Robinson's work (e.g., 2004; 2003; 2001; 2000). The writing of Sarah Ahmed (2004) also speaks to the uneasy relationship I hold...

with colonisation (Dudgeon & Fielder, 2006; Dudgeon & Pickett, 2000; Garvey, 2001; Gridley, Davidson, Dudgeon, Pickett & Sanson, 2000; Rigney, 1999). When I consider the extent to which psychology has come to assert a warranting voice over subjectivity (Gergen, K., 1989) in contemporary social discourse, it occurs to me that a reflexive approach to these questions may also constitute an ethical way of holding membership to those communities.

Consistent with notions of reflexive engagement, I want to turn to other work[3] that has enabled me to ask these questions – that supports me in finding a place from which to listen to Leroy's song and hear invisibility…

Here I could talk *about* narrative therapies and narrative psychology and feminist psychologies and post-structuralism, but what those really mean to me are communities of people who have been working questions of marginalisation and politics through working different theoretical spaces and epistemological commitments, and doing this long before me – enabling me to come to this place. I can't dwell explicitly in dialogue with all their voices here though, so it will have to suffice that I acknowledge the contingency of my speaking position with others, and the ways in which they also brought me to a place where I heard Leroy singing.

And some time after hearing Leroy sing 'Not a white country' for the first time, I was reading Mark Freeman (1993) writing about subjectivity and narrative in psychology. And I was particularly interested that he used aspects of Jill Ker Conway's autobiography *Road to Coorain* in his own work. I really identified with what he borrowed of her story of 'coming to consciousness' of Indigenous histories in Australia, and the effect that had on her understanding of her-self. Jill writes of coming to an awareness of pre-existing histories that contradict the nation-building myths of Australia – Indigenous histories, Indigenous presences that necessarily invoke 'counter-narratives' of Australian history as colonisation. Engaging with her stories, Freeman writes that "When this *history* became part of her *story*, her life itself took on new and more complex dimensions" (p. 301).[4]

---

[3] The other work that I turn to here belongs more to white institutional traditions…although my encounters with those works, and readings of them, are also inextricable from Indigenous traditions and the relations in which we are already entangled…can the capacity to 'work' those questions be considered separately from the relationships whereby the questions are asked?

[4] I might use this reading, too, as an example (differently) of the ways in which 'white' intellectual traditions are not separable from relationships that precede them…

This reading moves me to again experience any one of those countless moments where I've felt a whiteness of my own subjectivity, received a reminder that my speaking position is always, already *implicated*: one of those moments where life does indeed seem to become more complex and where I find psychology inadequately resourced for some means of apprehension that will not perpetuate and re-inscribe the same historical processes I am speaking from and simultaneously against. It's hearing Leroy sing of looking around and feeling ghosts, and being moved to wonder at the ghosts I am pre-occupied by...how to account for our own ghosts in the stories we take up and tell with/in psychology: to students, to each other, to our children?

To account for the ways in which history and 'self' are entwined, does psychology need to rethink its subject? It seems as though if we are speaking in the context of a relationship between psychology and Indigenous Australians, we are necessarily engaging with questions of history – disciplinary histories, yes, and also (already, always) cultural histories. Of Jill Ker Conway's experiences, Freeman writes that "What Conway had come to articulate through these experiences was precisely a set of counter-narratives...which in turn required that she rewrite not only her past, but her very self."

Might the 'self' that is necessarily re-written be not only individual subjects, but (necessarily) the form that subjectivity takes within psychology? Without that, psychology as a discipline sounds relatively inarticulate (to me) in apprehending relationships between history and self. What are the implications for my relationships in the specific context of being a white woman, and a psychologist, engaged in work with Indigenous communities?

Pausing with these questions, I am reminded of the Psychology and Indigenous Australians workshop held in Adelaide in 2006. I was sitting and listening to Aunty[5] Rosemary Wanganeen interweave her stories with her grief and loss model. I remember being so moved by how evocatively, sensitively and gracefully she moved in dialogue between 'personal', 'cultural', 'professional', 'theoretical'...how I heard her presentation resound against an absence of those connections in psychology's story-telling practices. Yet it was such an intricate and beautiful pattern, and how powerfully it articulated themes that have been evoked throughout this conference too – of survival, of wisdom, of multiple layers of grief and loss, of intergenerational trauma, of the imperative to engage with

---

[5] Aunty and Uncle are terms of respect commonly accorded to Indigenous Elders even if one is not related to them. Non-Indigenous Australians also commonly use these terms

histories of colonisation. What I heard Aunty Rosemary saying last year, and have heard again here, is that we carry our histories with us. And the emphasis here is on 'we'.

The moment that has such significance for me, that I am reminded of here, is the moment where she turned her telling around and offered it to us as a listening audience, as a profession, as participants in a relationship – an invitation to unpack the histories we carry with us. What are our legacies of colonisation, of the imperialist/capitalist threads with which colonisation is woven? What griefs, what losses, do we bear? And she asked, "What is so frightening about unpacking your past?"

> An aside: as I revisit this question, it's not fear that predominates (which is not to exclude fright from my embodied remembrances of response) but discomfort: the idea of unpacking our past, of doing our own work that touches on another question – how to do this without (re)filling conversational spaces with white voices, white anxieties? Without reproducing a disparity in the allocation of resources tangible and intangible? Again, a gesture towards a politics of response…and I wonder what speaking from a place of discomfort enables, a place not highly valued in a social context pre-occupied with valuing unequivocal knowledge. Does speaking from a place of discomfort enable at least a modicum of hesitation in patterns of gubba[6]-Indigenous relationships…?

Recollecting Aunty Rosemary brings me to Darren Garvey, speaking after, and of, her presentation at that same workshop. Darren represented her journey visually: Indigenous history mapped onto a distance of roughly three metres, white presences on this sunburned land occupying a fingernail-width space within that, psychology teetering on the tiniest fringe, of roughly a quarter-fingernail-length. Three metres of cultural knowledge and pride, he spoke of, set against a fingernail of this Other…

I remember turning to my colleagues and wondering aloud – how many metres would I have to go back, before I could connect with even a fingernail's worth of cultural tradition that might evoke pride for me? And after the workshop I took this wondering back to Sydney, and into conversation with Leroy who raised his eyebrows and nodded and asked, in his inimitable style: you couldn't go back three metres though, could

---

[6] Non-Indigenous. Whilst 'gubba' might be an increasingly common term, it is not generic. Different Indigenous language groups have sustained their own terms for 'whitefella', and gubba should be read here as locating the author in specific relationships (loosely described, but not decided, by the borders of NSW).

you? You haven't been around that long – where *do* you fellas come from, anyway?

There are many layers to this conversation: what was most salient for me at the time, was that in that moment I felt humbled by an apprehension of similarities *and* profound differences in the form that 'our' historical work might assume: in the space and the silence that ensued, I touched the edges of humility, and realised – in the time it took for me to give my experience this name – how little space we give humility in conversations within psychology. To the extent that the ordinariness of our conversations within psychology precedes us in conversations with colleagues, clients, communities…what are the implications for our relationships at the intersections of psychology and Indigenous Australians?

When I first shared these stories at the conference, I did so as a visitor: a visitor with histories of connections to other parts of this country we now call Australia, and connections to Aotearoa New Zealand, from which my original conference paper was transformed. I located myself within a space of dislocation, articulating whiteness in the specificity of different relationships. For me, metaphorising my position as a visitor enables space in which I might experience surrender in relation to others – to be in the position of accepting and reciprocating the hospitality that inheres in a personal relationship.

As a visitor to specific pre-existing relationships within Adelaide, I was visiting, too, a particular political time/space: the (then) incumbent government's 'Northern Territory Intervention' was occupying prominent place within local and international media. I joined with the conference wondering what space, if any, would be given to this, and what the limits of my speaking position were. I both wanted to speak, and felt impelled to do so through silence. I recall struggling to determine, during the many conversations I shared in and overheard, when silence seemed to speak as collusion and when it seemed to speak a respectful response. Whilst I might experience fear and discomfort at the implications of 'getting it wrong' I also experience a sense of something else…something blissfully inarticulate, connected to a sense that the 'outcomes' and 'implications' are not mine (alone) to speak…

Acknowledgements

I'd like to thank Erika Te Hiwi and Robbie Busch for helpful comments on initial drafts of this paper and for conversations through which it took shape.

References

Ahmed, S. (2004). Declarations of Whiteness: The Non-Performativity of Anti-Racism. *Borderlands e-Journal, 3*(2) (accessed November, 2007)

Davies, B. (2006). Re-thinking 'behaviour' in terms of positioning and the ethics of responsibility. In A.M. Phelan, & J. Sumison (Eds.) *Provoking absences: Critical readings in teacher education.* Netherlands: Sense Publishers.

Dickson, M. (2008). Moving learning from the head to the heart: Teaching and learning Indigenous content in Applied Psychology and Social Health courses. In R. Ranzijn, K. McConnochie, & W.Nolan (Eds.), *Psychology and Indigenous Australians – Effective Teaching and Practice* (pp. 55-64). Cambridge, UK: Cambridge Scholars Publishing.

Dudgeon, P., & Fielder, J. (2006). Third Spaces within Tertiary Places: Indigenous Australian Studies. *Journal of Community & Applied Social Psychology, 16,* 396 – 409.

Dudgeon, P., & Pickett, H. (2000). Psychology and Reconciliation: Australian Perspectives. *Australian Psychologist, 35*(2), 82 – 87.

Freeman, M. (1993). *Rewriting the self: History, memory, narrative.* New York: Routledge.

Garvey, D. (2001). Boongs, Bigots, and Bystanders: Indigenous and Non-Indigenous Experiences of Racism and Prejudice and their Implications for Psychology in Australia. In M. Augoustinos & K.J. Reynolds (Eds.) *Understanding Prejudice, Racism, and Social Conflict.* (pp. 43 – 57). London: SAGE.

Gergen, K (1989). Warranting voice and the elaboration. In J. Shotter & K. Gergen, (Eds.) *Texts of Identity.* London: Sage Publications Ltd.

Gridley, H., Davidson, G., Dudgeon, P., Pickett, H., & Sanson, A. (2000). The Australian Psychological Society and Australia's Indigenous People: A Decade of Action. *Australian Psychologist, 35*(2), 88 – 91.

Moreton-Robinson, A. (Ed) (2004) *Whitening Race: Essays in social and cultural criticism.* Canberra: Aboriginal Studies Press.

Moreton-Robinson, A. (2000). Troubling Business: Difference and Whiteness Within Feminism. *Australian Feminist Studies, 15*(33), 343 – 352.

—. (2001). *Talkin' Up to the White Woman: Indigenous Women and Feminism.* St. Lucia, Queensland: University of Queensland Press.

—. (2003). "I still call Australia home": Indigenous belonging and place in a white postcolonising society. In S. Ahmed, C. Castaneda, A.M. Fortier & M. Sheller (Eds.), *Uprootings/Regroundings: Questions of Home and Migration,* (pp. 23 – 41). Oxford: Berg.

Riger, S. (1992). Epistemological debates, feminist voices: Science, social values, and the study of women. *American Psychologist, 47*, 730-740.

Rigney, L-I. (1999). Internationalization of an Indigenous Anticolonial Cultural Critique of Research Methodologies: A Guide to Indigenist Research Methodology and Its Principles. *Wicazo Sa Review, 14* (2), 109 – 121.

CRITICAL DISCURSIVE METHODS AS A RESOURCE IN EDUCATION AND ANTI-RACISM: POTENTIALS AND PITFALLS

DANIELLE EVERY

Abstract

A key part of undergraduate education for cultural competence is developing critical perspectives on race and racism. As an educational and research tool critical discursive theory and methodologies are invaluable for developing such critical thinking. However, whilst critical discourse analysis is useful for deconstructing power relationships and hegemonic representations of the other, it is less effective as a tool for developing counter discourses and practices. Although critical discourse analysis is integral to identifying instances where such counter theories, discourses and practices reproduce, rather than challenge, racialised inequality, there is the potential for this to lead to a form of paralysis: if the discourses in common use for anti-racism are also problematic, what are the alternatives? This paper examines some of the potential theoretical and methodological ways out of this paralysis that allow for the creation of more effective, less problematic, anti-racism discourses.

I wish to start by acknowledging the Kaura people, the traditional owners of the site of the conference.

Reflexivity is a very important aspect of the critical psychological project of decolonisation. It is possible to assume that if we are engaged in critical psychology, then we are not engaging in an uncritical psychology; in other words, to assume that we are challenging, rather than perpetuating, colonisation. But simply labelling what we do as critical does not eliminate this possibility.

Ahmed (2004) draws attention to the need for constantly re-examining critical research and practice. Critical perspectives have contributed a great deal towards understanding racism and colonisation. However, at times critical psychology has also failed to engage with white privilege (Riggs & Selby, 2003), or has continued to marginalise Indigenous voices (Moreton-

Robinson, 2000), or has become caught up in methodological debates at the expense of a commitment to political and social action (Painter & Blanche, 2007). Reflecting critically on the critical is thus an essential aspect of the decolonisation of psychology. This paper therefore interrogates critical theory and research and the usefulness of critical discourse analysis for anti-racism.

This focus on critical discourse analysis reflects my interest and experience with this method. And the engagement with theory and method reflects my position as a researcher, rather than a practitioner. This is not an attempt to privilege the method of critical discourse analysis as the best, or only, way of doing critical research. The focus on racism reflects my belief that the key to decolonisation and reconciliation is recognising and challenging white racism (McCartney & Turner, 2000). Critical discourse analysis can be particularly useful for this. In this paper, I concentrate on research on white racism and the construction of white privilege. Finally, the focus on the role of critical discourse analysis in anti-racism reflects my aim to translate research into action. Although I use anti-racism in the singular here in this paper, really it's more accurate to talk about anti-racisms. Anti-racism takes many forms. It's a diverse project that can encompass many strategies, often conflicting, and is driven by different agendas, for different purposes. In this paper I am contributing to the examination of what Terry Kessaris (2006) calls white on white anti-racism - white anti-racism in media, politics and everyday conversations that opposes the racism of other white people.

Before looking at the issue of critical discourse analysis and anti-racism in more detail I need to define what I mean by critical psychology and critical discourse analysis.

I use the term critical psychology to distinguish a body of work that interrogates psychology's relationship with neo-colonialism, racism, capitalist exploitation, and neo-liberal market ideologies. This work attempts to upset psychology's ideological complicities and create spaces for resistance. Critical psychology challenges empiricist, white and male-centred research and practice. It aims to reconfigure psychology as a socially relevant, progressive practice along new epistemological, theoretical and methodological lines (Painter & Blanche, 2007).

Critical discourse analysis is the method that is used for the interrogation of these ideologies (de la Rey, 1997). A critical discursive analysis examines talk and texts for the ways in which identities and events are constructed employing culturally available discursive resources. These constructions are examined for their political and social effects: for example, who do they benefit, and who they marginalise? This analysis demonstrates the ways in which power is reproduced and maintained, and the ways in which ideologies become hegemonic and other voices marginalized. As I argue later in this paper, a critical discourse analysis should also aim not only to examine the workings of oppression, but also contribute to its transformation.

Critical discursive work has contributed significantly to understanding contemporary forms of racism, especially as these are articulated and enacted in the mundane, everyday rituals of Australian life. Traditionally, psychologists have sought to understand racism as an aspect of personality or cognition. In contrast, critical discursive psychologists understand racism as a social practice, as an aspect of discourse and communication. Discursive research on the language of racism has examined the social construction of identity, and how majority group members use culturally available discursive resources to justify and legitimate current social practices.

Margaret Wetherell and Jonathan Potter (1992) were among the first to use critical discourse analysis to examine the reproduction of racism in language. They analysed interviews with white New Zealanders[1], as well as psychological and sociological texts on race and racism. They revealed the culturally available resources drawn upon in these interviews and texts to marginalise and deny Maori land rights, protests, and claims of prejudice and racism. These arguments employed liberal discourses, such as equality and meritocracy, to avoid the label of 'racist', and to give the appearance of being logical and right.

In Australia, critical discursive work has examined the representation of Indigenous Australians in media, politics and everyday talk and the ways in which these undermine Indigenous leadership and justify paternalism, inequality, disadvantage and racism. For instance, Martha Augoustinos (2001) demonstrated the ways in which versions of history are used to present colonisation as unproblematic and to deny that white Australians are responsible for the effects of colonisation. Terry Kessaris (2006) examined the covert racism in Australia that commonly occurs as part of everyday, shared, social activity amongst white Australians. This work identified benevolence, silence and a sense of entitlement as some of the ways in which white Australians perpetuate racism and colonisation, and justify oppression and inequality.

Other researchers have identified: the ways in which white Australians seek to avoid being labelled 'racist' by presenting their arguments as

---

[1] The four million people in New Zealand are predominantly Anglo-European in origin, but 15% are Maori, the Indigenous peoples, and there are significant numbers of Pacific Islanders (6%) and other ethnic groups

logical, practical common sense (Rapley, 2001); the privileging of agricultural land owners over traditional ownership in anti-land rights arguments (LeCouteur, Rapley, & Augoustinos, 2001); and the use of notions of progress, technology and modernity to present Indigenous Australians as responsible for the effects of colonisation (Augoustinos, Tuffin, & Sale, 1999).

Critical discourse analysis has also been used to expose the ways in which colonisation and racism are reproduced in anti-racist contexts. This analysis of anti-racism has critically examined the construction of racism as an individual problem, the limitations of the discourses of multiculturalism, constructions of Australia/ns as 'basically not racist'; and the reproduction of whiteness in discourses of reconciliation.

The construction of racism as an individual problem has been effective in obscuring the widespread nature of racism across institutions and social structures. This construction provides support for interventions that are based on changing the attitudes of a few rotten apples rather than more significant and far-reaching changes to social and institutional practices (Henriques, 1984; LeCouteur et al., 2001).

Multiculturalism is similarly limited in its anti-racist effects. Ghassan Hage (1998) and Jon Stratton (1998) find that this ostensibly 'liberal' discourse reproduces white dominance by constraining diversity to the cultural, rather than political and economic spheres. Martha Augoustinos has also observed the lip service paid to the participation of Indigenous Australians in economic and political spheres, which is glossed over by a focus on the acceptance of 'cultural diversity' and 'cultural preservation' (Augoustinos, Tuffin, & Rapley, 1999). These analyses make an important point that discourses of cultural inclusion, which may be presented as anti-racist, do not allow for, and actively exclude focussing on, political and economic issues.

Constructions of Australia and Australians as 'not racist' are prevalent in anti-racist discourse. This is often employed as an appeal to the Australian public to return to their true, non-racist nature. Whilst this can be a political strategy for keeping an audience on side, it also has the effect of perpetuating the claims that racism is not a problem in Australia. It also contributes to a national denial of racism as a practice in which all Australians participate (Every, 2006).

The work of Chris Sonn and Meredith Green (Green & Sonn, 2006) demonstrates the ways in which white dominance and privilege can be reproduced in the context of talk about reconciliation. Simply failing to acknowledge whiteness in anti-racism reproduces its power. They also examine specific reconciliation discourses and the ways in which they reproduce whiteness. For example, they identify a discourse of 'expert analysis' in which white reconcilers position themselves as knowledgeable about, and able to 'solve', Indigenous issues. This reproduces a longstanding paternalistic discourse and focus on the Indigenous 'other' by white experts. They also identified a discourse of 'cultural connection' in which their interviewees constructed romantic notions of Indigenous culture, the incorporation of which was essential to reconciliation. As Green and Sonn argue, such a discourse reproduces the dominant prioritising of white culture (Green & Sonn, 2005).

These critical analyses of anti-racism are invaluable for problematising a too neat distinction between racism and anti-racism. They reveal the ways in which anti-racist discourse may draw upon and reproduce racism. The exploration of whiteness and anti-racism demonstrates that reconciliation requires an interrogation of whiteness, without which deeply problematic anti-racist discourses remain invisible and unchallenged. This critical research makes the important point that even seemingly liberal discourses often reproduce and maintain inequality, rather than challenging it.

But, as well as exposing the oppressive effects of anti-racism, can critical discourse analysis also inform alternative anti-racist discourses and practices? Can critical discourse analysis be used constructively, as well as critically? Whilst critical discourse analysis rightly challenges many of the discourses and practices of white anti-racism, alternatives are not always explored. There is a kind of analysis going on here that effectively disrupts the many ways in which oppression may be legitimated, but in doing so, it does not then go on to engage with the issue of how it could be done differently.

Speaking from personal experience, I found this contributed to feelings of paralysis and hopelessness. At the end of writing my doctoral thesis on anti-racism, I felt as though I had very effectively pulled anti-racism apart, but in doing so, I thought I had also destroyed any hope of an effective anti-racism. I was very disillusioned with discourse analysis as a potential tool for developing, as well as critiquing, anti-racism. I know I'm not alone in this experience. Paralysis is also an issue for educators introducing critical perspectives on racism and whiteness. Ross Williams (2000) and Gillian Cowlishaw (1999), reflecting on the responses of students and others to critical examinations of whiteness, have noted the prevalence of discomfort, paralysis and helplessness. Chris Sonn has also reported that a lot of students at some stage experience a temporary paralysis of some sort (in Ranzijn & Severino, 2006).

What we do with these responses, how we deal with them, is an important aspect of the process of learning. In a workshop aimed at developing curriculum guidelines for incorporating Indigenous content in psychology undergraduate education, work groups identified a need to structure a way to deal with discomfort, embarrassment and guilt – not to 'manage feelings' but to use them as a way of shifting positions and moving forward (Ranzijn & Severino, 2007). This is also an important aspect of reconciliation and anti-racism.

One response to paralysis is a critical discourse analysis that not only deconstructs, but also seeks to explore alternative discourses and practices. What would such an analysis look like? Firstly, it's important that critical discourse analysis is employed as part of a commitment to anti-racism and decolonisation. Ian Parker (1992) has argued that the political impact of critical discourse analysis depends on its commitment to analysing oppression. I would go further, and say that the political impact of critical discourse analysis depends on its commitment to contribute to changing, as well as analysing, anti-racist discourses. A core aim of this research would be to engage with critical analyses of anti-racism as well as propose alternatives.

Some research has already begun to focus on alternative anti-racist discourses. Meredith Green and Christopher Sonn critically analyse reconciliation discourses, but also examine ways in which these problematic discourses might be shifted to become spaces of resistance. Taking up the two examples of problematic discourses I outlined earlier, they suggest that white reconcilers may be able to negotiate a different way of being connected to Indigenous people and communities that doesn't rely on romantic constructions as in the 'cultural connection' discourse. Likewise, within the 'expert analysis' discourse the enthusiasm for making sense of issues Indigenous people face may be shifted away from the Indigenous subject and towards an analysis of dominance, power and privilege (Green & Sonn, 2005). Steve Kirkwood, James Liu and Anne Weatherell (2005) also use discourse analysis as a way of developing arguments that challenge racism in New Zealand. They suggest that for white New Zealanders, the Treaty of Waitangi[2] offers a discursive resource for constructing the subject position of a 'partnership' with Maori that legitimises the positions of both groups.

Bernard and Pauline Guerin's work on racism in everyday conversations has also focussed on using discourse analysis to contribute

---

[2] The Treaty of Waitangi, signed in 1840 between the Maori peoples and the British colonisers, was designed to protect Maori rights to their land while also enabling British settlement

to anti-racism. They propose that a community's discursive resources can be actively altered to provide rejoinders for racist comments. They have used this work to develop a discursive resource sheet for refugee advocacy, which was handed out at a refugee event organised by the authors (Guerin, 2003).

The issue of materiality is also important in relation to developing resistance. Discourse analysis has been criticised for its privileging of discourse; for ignoring the materiality of oppression. Desmond Painter and Martin Blanche (2007) make this point. They argue that discourse analysis in the UK, and also in Australia, which borrows from the UK tradition, has tended to become heavily involved in identifying the rhetorical aspects of racism and oppression, but has been less concerned with the nexus between discourse, space and place. However, whilst the issue of materiality remains a significant one for discursive theory and research, it's not inevitable that discourse analysis concentrates only on discourse.

The critical discursive work of Kevin Durrheim and John Dixon (2001) in South Africa is a good example. Their research is concerned with the ways in which Apartheid and post-Apartheid discourses structure communal spaces such as beaches and restaurants. Their work highlights the importance of place in the reproduction of racism:

> This analysis of the materiality of discursive practices opens up new possibilities for discourse analysis and political action. A focus on the inscription of racism on space and time offers different ways of thinking about resistance, not only in terms of changing discourse, but also for intervening in the structures this discourse makes possible.

A critical discourse analysis that contributes to anti-racism must also be localised and detailed. Kevin Dunn's research on the geography of racism makes it clear that racism manifests in multiple ways in different places, intersecting with factors such as class (Dunn & McDonald, 2001). Bernard and Pauline Guerin's research, employing detailed, longitudinal interviews and observation, points to the subtle manifestations of prejudice that are not necessarily readily discernible through one-off interviews. This kind of work demonstrates the importance of localised, rather than universal, interventions against racism, and the importance of localised and detailed research as a foundation for anti-racist discourses and practices (Guerin, 2005).

An emphasis on the historical contexts of anti-racism is also useful for developing discourses and practices of resistance. Although there is only a relatively small body of work on this issue, it demonstrates the long history of anti-racism, its multiple facets and manifestations, and makes available resources for anti-racist activity that have been forgotten or marginalised (Bonnett, 2000; Lloyd, 1998).

Finally, using critical discourse analysis for changing discourse also requires that these new discourses are made available. Green and Sonn (2006) make this point, as does Parker (1992): changing the available discursive resources requires spaces in which these can be developed, practiced and elaborated. I mentioned earlier Bernard Guerin's intervention: handing out fliers at a refugee advocates' rally that set out potential discursive resources for challenging anti-refugee policies. Educational spaces, such as those opened up by the project to decolonise psychology (Ranzijn & Severino, 2006, 2007) offer a particularly useful forum for generating, using and disseminating counter discourses.

Although there remain many barriers and difficulties for developing effective anti-racism, the constructive critical discourse analysis that I've outlined here offers some possibilities for coping with paralysis, and a potential foundation for critical anti-racist action. It's an issue on which I'm constantly re-examining and refining my ideas.

References

Ahmed, S. (2004). Declarations of whiteness: The non-performativity of anti-racism. *Borderlands ejournal, 3*. Retrieved 7/6/07, from http://www.borderlandsejournal.adelaide.edu.au/vol3no2_2004/ahmed _declarations.htm

Augoustinos, M. (2001). History as a rhetorical resource: using historical narratives to argue and explain. In A. McHoul & M. Rapley (eds), *How to analyse talk in institutional settings* (pp. 135-145). London: Continuum.

Augoustinos, M., Tuffin, K. & Sale, L. (1999). Race talk. *Australian Journal of Psychology, 51*, 90-97.

Augoustinos, M., Tuffin, K., & Rapley, M. (1999). Genocide or a failure to gel? Racism, history and nationalism in Australian talk. *Discourse & Society, 10*(3), 351-378.

Bonnett, A., 2000. *Anti-racism.* London: Routledge.

Cowlishaw, G. (1999). Black modernity and bureaucratic culture. *Australian Aboriginal Studies, 2*, 15-24.

de la Rey, C. (1997). On political activism and discourse analysis in South Africa. In Ann Levett, Amanda Kottler, Erica Burman & Ian Parker (Eds), *Culture, Power and Difference Discourse Analysis in South Africa* (pp. 198-204). London: Zed Books,

Dunn, K. M., & McDonald, A. (2001). The geography of racisms in NSW: a theoretical exploration and some preliminary findings from the mid-1990s. *Australian Geographer, 32*(1), 29-44

Durrheim, K., and Dixon, J. (2001). The role of place and metaphor in racial exclusion: South Africa's beaches as sites of shifting racialization. *Ethnic and Racial Studies, 24* (3), 433 - 450

Every, D. (2006). *The politics of representation: A discursive analysis of refugee advocacy in the Australian parliament.* Unpublished PhD thesis, University of Adelaide.

Green, M. J., & Sonn, C. C. (2006). Problematising the discourses of the dominant: Whiteness and reconciliation. *Journal of Community and Applied Social Psychology, 16*, 379-395.

Green, M. J., & Sonn, C. C. (2005). Examining discourses of whiteness and the potential for reconciliation. *Journal of Community and Applied Social Psychology, 15*, 478-492.

Guerin, B. (2003). Combating prejudice and racism: New interventions from a functional analysis of racist language. *Journal of Community and Applied Social Psychology, 13*, 29-45.

—. (2005). Combating everyday racial discrimination without assuming racists or racism: New intervention ideas from a contextual analysis. *Behaviour and Social Issues, 14*, 46-70.

Hage, G. (1998). *White Nation*. Annandale, NSW: Pluto Press.

Henriques, J. (1984). Social psychology and the politics of racism. In Julian Henriques, Wendey Hollway, Cathy Urwin, Couze Venn and Valerie Walkerdine (Eds), *Changing the subject: Psychology, social regulation and subjectivity* (pp. 60-89). London: Routledge.

Kessaris, T. N. (2006). About being Mununga (Whitefulla): Making covert racism visible. *Journal of Community and Applied Social Psychology, 16*, 347-362.

Kirkwood, S., Liu, J. H., & Weatherall, A. (2005). Challenging the standard story of Indigenous rights in Aotearoa/New Zealand. *Journal of Community and Applied Social Psychology, 15*, 493-505.

LeCouteur, A., Rapley, M., & Augoustinos, M. (2001). 'This very difficult debate about Wik': Stake, voice and the management of category memberships in race politics. *British Journal of Social Psychology, 40*, 35-57.

Lloyd, C., 1998. *Discourses of Anti-Racism in France*. London: Ashgate.

McCartney, T., & Turner, C. (2000). Reconciliation happens everyday: Conversations about working alliances between black and white Australia. *Australian Psychologist, 35*(2), 173-176.

Moreton-Robinson, A. (2000). *Talking up to the white woman: Indigenous women and feminism.* St. Lucia: University of Queensland Press.

Painter, D. and Blanche, M. T. (2007). *Critical Psychology in South Africa: Looking back and looking forwards.* Downloaded 7/6/07 from http://www.criticalmethods.org/collab/critpsy.htm

Parker, I. (1992). *Discourse dynamics: Critical analysis for social and individual psychology.* London: Routledge.

Rapley, M. (2001). How to do X without doing Y: accomplishing discrimination without 'being racist - 'doing equity'. In M. Augoustinos & K. Reynolds (Eds.), *Understanding prejudice, racism and social conflict* (pp. 231-250). London: Sage,

Ranzijn, R., & Severino, G. (Eds.). (2006). *Psychology and Indigenous Australians: Effective Teaching and Practice - Report on the proceedings of a workshop on developing curriculum guidelines.* Adelaide, SA: University of South Australia.

Ranzijn, R., & Severino, G. (Eds.). (2007). *Psychology and Indigenous Australians: Effective Teaching and Practice - Report on the proceedings of the second national workshop on developing curriculum guidelines.* Adelaide, SA: University of South Australia.

Riggs, D. W., & Selby, J. M. (2003). Setting the seen: Whiteness as unmarked category in psychologists' writings on race in Australia. In M. Katsikitis (Ed.), *Proceedings of the 38th APS Annual Conference* (pp. 190–195). Melbourne: Australian Psychological Society.

Sonn, C. (2006). Indigenous Issues are Really Important and Should be Compulsory": Challenges and Issues for Teaching Indigenous Issues. In R. Ranzijn & G. Severino, (Eds.). *Psychology and Indigenous Australians: Effective Teaching and Practice - Report on the proceedings of a workshop on developing curriculum guidelines.* Adelaide, SA: University of South Australia.

Stratton, J. (1998). *Race daze.* Sydney: Pluto Press.

Wetherell M., & Potter, J. (1992). *Mapping the language of racism: Discourse and the legitimation of exploitation.* New York: Columbia University Press.

Williams, R. (2000). Why should I feel guilty? Reflections on the working of guilt in white-Aboriginal relations. *Australian Psychologist, 35*(2), 136-142.

KEYNOTE ADDRESS: FINDING OUR RELATEDNESS STORIES: PSYCHOLOGY AND INDIGENOUS HEALING PRACTICE

JUDY ATKINSON

Abstract

This is a Story of relatedness. Finding our Stories of Relatedness is necessary for us to understand who we are: who we are as Indigenous Australians, seeking healing from layered traumatisation; and who we are as psychologists working in the field of mental, emotional and psychosomatic distress. The philosophies, theories and practices of psychology and Indigenous therapies have bridges we need to walk across. Until we take the time to sit with each other, to listen and learn from each other, someplace on those bridges, we cannot find and know our Stories of relatedness. Knowing our Stories of Relatedness; Respecting our Stories Of Your Relatedness: Renewing our Stories Of Relatedness (Martin, K. 2007), provides the opportunity to find common ground.

You may ask: can there be a renewal of relatedness between Indigenous peoples and psychology? Has there ever been relatedness between Indigenous peoples, and Indigenous worldviews, and the relatively new science of psychology as it is defined within the world of the professional psychologists – those who teach practice and theorise psychology?

I say there is a possibility, and a responsibility of renewal, and this will occur as this fast growing infant called psychology begins to find its own Story, its own origins, its evolutionary past so it can see where it is going into the future. This will occur in the day-to-day activities of teaching, practice, theory. However it will occur more fully when we sit together to share our Stories: Your Story and My Story builds our changing worldviews; and in the sharing, we come to know how closely related we are, while we also value and give honour to our diversity.

My first duty is to acknowledge the Kaurna People, the Traditional Owners and custodians of the land upon which the conference was held. I do this not just to pay respect, but to bring our attention to all those who have contributed to our present life circumstances. We come together within environments natural, and built, social, and educational, that allow us to sit together and learn from each other. The collective contribution of their many Stories help us make meaning of our communal, interrelated experiences.

I presently live in Bundjalung country: the northern rivers region of New South Wales. I work at Gnibi – the College of Indigenous Australian Peoples (CIAP), Southern Cross University.

There is a Story I want to share about Gnibi, which I will use to make other points in this larger Story I am exploring. By Story, I refer to a personal or collective history, a narrative or description of life events, which allow us to make meaning of our lives.

When I commenced work at the College of Indigenous Australian Peoples, I asked many people what was the meaning of the language name CIAP was known as, at that time. I was given many different interpretations. I became confused. We must know who we are. I went to the old people, the Elders of the Bundjalung Nation[1]. I was told that the language spelling and meaning ascribed to the name of the College was wrong. I asked if the College of Indigenous Australian Peoples should be given a new name.

The name they gave is *Gnibi*. *Gnibi* is the Bundjalung name for the constellation of stars known as the Southern Cross. The term *Gnibi* refers to the Black Swan and the spiritual association between *Gnibi* (the constellation) and Bundjalung country and Peoples.

The day CIAP presented its five year strategic plan, and our new name, to the University executive, one of our Elders came forward to speak, and he admonished us: "Stop talking about the culture, and the language. Teach it and live it." Afterwards, I went up to my room. As I reflected on the words of this Elder, I absentmindedly picked up a book. The book fell open to page 232, and at the top of the page was a new chapter heading: Wise Women and Men of high Degree. The first three words of the chapter were 'The Black Swans'. The Elders had chosen wisely. We at Gnibi, with a name that has meaning, are getting on with our jobs to become wise women and men of *High Degree*. I acknowledge the

---

[1] The language group that consists of the traditional owners of a particular part of Australia is often referred to as a Nation, to reflect their traditional and ongoing sovereignty, which has never been ceded to the colonisers

Widjabel people of the greater Bundjalung nation, custodians of the land on which Lismore campus of Southern Cross University is built.

In this presentation I explore the intersection between psychology and Indigenous healing practice. Psychology is defined as the scientific study of the human and animal behaviour of an organism in its environment, more particularly, the human mind, and mental states. Indigenous Healing Practice refers to customary or natural processes that cure, mend, make well or regenerate the functioning system of interdependent parts that comprise living entities.

Circles of Sharing, Learning and Healing

The Circle of Healing

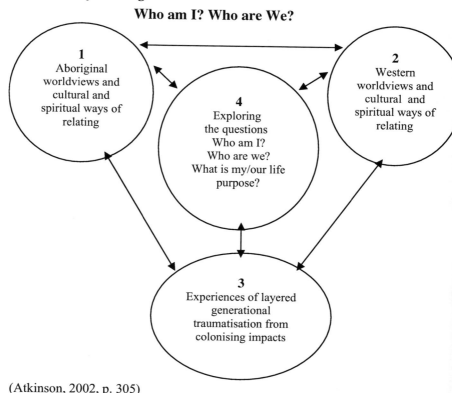

(Atkinson, 2002, p. 305)

The diagram above comprises four circles. Circles one and two are the worlds that were and are. Circles three and four are the work that is being done and that has to be done for healing to happen. The first circle represents the Aboriginal (Indigenous Australian) world-of-relating before colonisation. There is a need to name the cultural strengths and weaknesses of those times, and bring the valuable cultural strengths into the present. The second circle represents the Western world-views and colonising impacts. Colonisers brought both good and bad. Aboriginal peoples need to know what to keep and what to discard from what has been introduced by the invaders and immigrants.

Circle three represents the layered transmission of trauma across generations and the experiences of this traumatisation that has largely formed who we are today. In all our pain, we must give value to these experiences, renaming the knowledges and the strength derived from such experiences as profound learning. In the day to day work of engaging with people for counselling or healing, I find this is the circle where most people start. Unfortunately many people are caught in this circle, in cycles of painful abuse and self-abuse; in conflicts of identity, and a devaluing of their Aboriginal cultural and spiritual heritage.

Circle four represents the educational work that has to be done, and the integrity, knowledges and skills that are available to facilitate people moving from victim/perpetrator/survivor to be creators of a future free of violence. The educational work of circle four, which must be done by all Australians, is to achieve optimal health or well-being which exists:

> ...When a person experiences Self as an integrated whole that encompasses the body, the emotions, the mind and the spirit. This state of health experienced as a pervasive sense of well-being can only occur through connection with other Selves –'without you there can be no me'. To become whole the Self needs to be experienced and expressed from the inside and recognised from the outside. Hence the critical context for both health and healing is the interpersonal (Self-Other) relationship (Fewster, 2000, pp.1-2).

In this circle, the self-other relationship is explored, and negotiated, as individual Stories are found and shared, to make a collective Story. As the present is explored, each person also visits the past and the future. Circle four represents the culturally safe places that must be created for the trauma stories to be told, the safe environments where people can give context to their lives through the narration of their experiences, making sense of their own realities, and, in the demanding process of healing, find a shared and new way forward. Circle four represents the healing places where people can sit in ceremonies of mutual care, in *dadirri*[2] (Ungunmerr, 1993), and return to the work to which Stanner (1979) refers, the important business of *uniting hearts and establishing order.* While this is the vital work that faces all humankind, it is the foundational cornerstone of Aboriginal cultural responsibilities. Rose (2000) alludes to these responsibilities as she explores the worldviews of the Yarralin[3]:

> Our lives are part of an oscillation which has preceded and will succeed us. This sense of cosmic vastness can lead to a sense of our own insignificance. Yarralin people rarely understand human life in this way. The end point of sequential time is now. All that preceded us and all that comes after depend on us. What we do matters so powerfully that to evade our responsibilities is to call down chaos (p. 217).

Many Aboriginal people believe the chaos in our lives has resulted from lack of attention to our relationship responsibilities.

During my PhD field work, which investigated the violence - trauma stories of a group of Aboriginal people in Central Queensland, I realised that people moved through different talking circle themes, as they explored their stories of pain and of healing. They would often start at any one of the three outer circles in the above diagram, however would move in and out of the centre circle, which became the place of healing. In the Story-making and Story-telling, as people moved from one circle of learning to another, they came to see how violence, experienced as trauma, fragments people's sense of identity, fracturing the loving and enduring connections of family and community that provides structure to human lives. At the same time, it was also clear that, in the sharing and learning together, healing was possible.

For some, the word healing is problematic. However for the group with whom I was working, the word had a depth of both yearning and meaning. Healing, for them, acknowledged their layered unexpressed pain, and healing came with an awakening to their unmet inner needs. Hence the word healing, derived from the Old English word *haelen*, 'a return to wholeness', could be described as the curative process of becoming well from the fragmentation and fracturing, as they made sense of the stories that held their pain. The word healing symbolised their choice to do work that would help them feel and become well. Within the circle, healing was the educational process of learning about the self at a deep level, about

---

[2] Inner deep listening to another person, quiet still awareness
[3] An Aboriginal community located 382 km south-west of Katherine, Northern Territory.

what has made the person *who they are,* and which opened the possibilities of *who they can become,* with the life choices that emerge as they come to know and accept themselves. In the sharing between people, listening to, and learning from each other, they found a way through their pain, re-conceptualising their Stories, creating different narratives as they reclaimed power over their lives.

Such processes are fundamental cultural tools that have been part of Aboriginal Australian, indeed Indigenous cultures generally, in ceremonial relatedness, being-in-the-world of relationships.

The diagram provides a re-conceptualisation of the crisis Aboriginal peoples face today in light of the critical need to address issues of violence in all its forms, as part of commissioned government reports in Queensland, Western Australia, New South Wales, Northern Territory, and South Australia, and in the media focus and saturation of the issue[4]. The centre circle allows us to name this critical time as both a challenge, and an opportunity. The challenge is Aboriginal people's ability to take the courage to begin to address the fracture in family and community relationships, and the opportunity is to show Australians generally that such reconciliation can be done. The diagram is built on the assumption that healing involves education at its most fundamental level for individuals, and within family and community circles.

What is appropriate now is that Indigenous peoples demonstrate the way forward from the chaos that has evolved from colonial conquest, on this continent and elsewhere. This is also the opportunity for the discipline called psychology to walk across the bridge to learn from and give support to Indigenous Healing Practice.

The First Circle - Relatedness and Being Well

Our greatest need is relationship, where rules for proper behaviour provide safety and security in our relational activities. Karen Martin challenges us to more fully define our worldview through: ontology (the nature of being and what we believe to be real in our world); epistemology (the knowledge that informs how we think about that reality); and methodology (how we understand, define, and redefine our ontological selves). In her research Martin asks the same questions we did in our circles: Who are we? Where do we come from? What are our relationships

---

[4] There has been a huge amount of media interest in Indigenous affairs, especially the situation of remote Aboriginal communities in the central and northern parts of Australia, since 2006

with the entities that make up our world, *People, Land, Animals, Plants, Skies, Waterways* and *Climate* (Martin, 2002). Immediately we see the difference between western psychology, with its study of the human and animal behaviour – more particularly, the human mind, and mental states – and Indigenous healing practice which recognises the interdependent nature of relational activities.

Martin defines relational activities as relatedness: 'This relatedness occurs across contexts and is maintained under certain conditions that are: physical, spiritual, political, geographical, intellectual, emotional, social, historical, sensory, instinctive and intuitive' (2006). Martin discusses three activities of relatedness which are affirmed in Story-work: Ways of *knowing* our stories of relatedness; ways of *being in respecting* our stories of relatedness; ways of *doing in renewing* our stories of relatedness (Martin, 2002 – my emphasis).

How does this relate to wellbeing? Each child is born out of relatedness, sometimes a fractured distressed relatedness, more often a vibrant life affirming relatedness. All children, whether born from a fractured relatedness or a loving relatedness, should enter the world with rights, the right to be in safe shelter, fed, loved, cared for, guided, and taught to engage in activities where they are respected for who they are in a relational world. As the child is nurtured, and grows, the child learns responsibility, and from responsibility emanates the principle of reciprocity: I give – you give – we share, we grow together. The process and the principle has not previously been part of the relationships between western trained psychologists and Indigenous healing practitioners, but rather one of hierarchy and privilege. Various groups, on both sides of the divide are now walking across the bridge, to develop better ways of working together.

The closest word for health within Aboriginal languages is *well-being*. The word *punyu,* from the language of the Ngaringman[5] from the Northern Territory, sometimes translated as *well-being*, explains the concept and functions of *being-well. Punyu* encompasses *person* and *country* and is associated with being:

> strong, happy, knowledgeable, socially responsible (to 'take a care'), beautiful, clean, safe - both in the sense of being within the lore and in the sense of being cared for (Mobbs 1991, p. 298).

> 'In Ngaringman cosmology the known universe constitutes a living system the goal of which is to reproduce itself as a living system. Each part of the

---

[5] Ngaringman country is in the north-west corner of the Northern Territory

cosmos, country, Rainbow Snake, animals, people, etc is alive, conscious, and is basically either punyu or not punyu. That which is punyu is not just alive but also contributing to life (Mobbs, 1991).

Rose explains that *'When people and country are punyu the flow of energy keeps both strong, healthy, and fruitful'* (Bird-Rose, 1987). *Punyu* and being well connect People - Place – Lore into a whole. Being well would therefore be an 'achieved quality, developed through relationships of mutual care' (Bird-Rose, 1987). This is the whole-of-life view and it also includes the cyclical concept of life-death-life (National Aboriginal Health Strategy Working Party 1989: x). How does this translate to an urban situation? Mobbs suggests that '"being well" means having harmonious social relationships with kin, with others who are not kin, and even with strangers' (Mobbs 1991, p. 289).

Aboriginal sciences[6] would say that each plant, animal and human has a story of some unique way of being in the world. By Story-mapping, tracking their stories (listening to – observing – gathering the disciplined bodies of knowledge about them) our own lives may be informed and enriched. And we more deeply connect to our relatedness.

The Second Circle – Western Approaches to Children Rearing

Alice Miller (1983) documented the culture of child rearing in the societies that colonised Australia, and other Indigenous nations, from the 15th Century onwards. The cultural practices and beliefs that influenced child rearing had clear impacts on generations of people, and informed the ways in which the colonisers interacted with the colonised.

Culture is the set of beliefs, values and rules for living that are distinctive to particular human groups. It is passed down across generations in the complex of relationships, knowledges, languages, social organisations and life experiences that bind diverse individuals and groups together. Culture is a living process, being cyclical and dynamic in nature. It changes over time to reflect the changed environments and social interactions of people living together.

Cultural mores influenced the way in which the colonisers interacted with those they colonised, resulting for example, in the removal of Aboriginal children from their families, to be placed in institutions of the state. Within the class structures and culture that determined such

---

[6] Science: a disciplined body of knowledge.

policies, it was normal cultural practice to place children in institutions. At the upper end of the class scale, the children of the British upper class were sent to English public boarding schools. At the lower end of the class scale, the children of the dispossessed Irish were forced into workhouses, as, for example, the ravages of the potato famine decimated families and dislocated people from the lands of their birth. At both extremes such children grew into adulthood having been socialised and enculturated into particular beliefs and behaviours, at one level a belief in superiority, and at the other extreme a fractured felt sense of inferiority. In both extremes, children experienced both a fracturing of their spirit, and a socialisation which would ensure the continuation of such beliefs and practices. In both instances many surviving children have stories of the brutality they survived in these institutions.

In her book *For Your Own Good: Hidden Cruelty in Child-rearing and the Roots of Violence*, Miller (1983) lists five interactive ingredients that contribute to the development of a violent individual or society:

- being profoundly hurt as a child – or as a people;

- being hurt, but being prevented from experiencing or expressing the pain of that hurt;

- having no one in whom we can confide our true feelings, not being heard, or acknowledged in our pain;

- having a lack of education or knowledge, therefore being unable to intellectualise the abuse;

- having no way we can transform our pain without repeating the cycle of abuse on our own children, ourselves and others.

The Third Circle - Layered Generational Traumatisation from Colonising Impacts

Australia was 'settled' under the 'savagery' of world wide colonisations. It was designated a penal colony, with the transportation of convicts from the stinking prison hulks moored in the River Thames. It resulted in the subjugation and traumatisation of Indigenous Australian peoples, in large-scale epidemics, massacres, removals of whole populations to detainment camps called reserves, removals of children, splitting apart of family groups, physical and cultural genocide, layered in their traumatic impacts across generations.

Baker (1983) names three distinct yet interactive periods of colonization. The first period was the physical violence of the frontier – *invasion, disease, death, destruction;* the second was the structural violence - *enforced dependency - legislation, reserves and removals;* the third was psycho social dominance - *cultural and spiritual genocide.*

Cultural and spiritual genocide attacks the very heart, the locale of *who we are* more so than physical violence. People come to believe that they themselves are of no value, that their cultural practices and traditions are inferior and hence so are they, that they are non-persons with no value (Atkinson, 2002). Consequently they may *'build their own prison and become simultaneously prisoner and warden'* (Baker, 1983, p. 40).

It is this layered trauma on which I want to focus now. From within this context, the healing that is the yearning within individuals, and in families and communities, provides opportunity for psychologists and Indigenous therapists to work together for a common good. In this, I provide a particular focus on the rights of the child.

Children and Trauma

Children are shaped by their early life experiences. A child is not a one dimensional entity but multidimensional. Experiencing happens at many levels: vital, social, mental, emotional, physical and environmental. A child's organising nature is felt in the moment when they are safe. A child senses they are safe at their vital core, and this sensing allows the organism to organise, developing the foundation of resiliency for future life events.

Research by social scientists has shown that children growing up in safe homes and communities with nurturing, predictable and attentive caregivers view the world as a relatively safe, exciting place to explore and learn. Research also shows that consistent, nurturing and enriching experiences help children develop in optimal ways, thereby increasing their chances for health, happiness, productivity and creativity. Positive early life experiences not only facilitate the development of the child's cognitive capacities but also stimulate the child's physical, social, emotional and behavioural development.

Many children, however, do not have all of the opportunities to help them meet their potential. Numerous reports over recent years (for instance, Aboriginal and Torres Strait Islander Women's Report on Violence Queensland 2000: Putting the Picture Together; inquiry into response by government agencies to complaints of family violence and child abuse in Aboriginal communities, Western Australia 2002; Breaking the Silence Creating the Future addressing child sexual assault in Aboriginal communities in NSW 2006; Report of the Northern Territory Board of Inquiry into the Protection of Aboriginal Children from Sexual Abuse [Ampe Akelyernemane Meke Makarle *Little Children are Sacred*] 2007), highlight the critical situation for Aboriginal children, their families and communities. From these reports, it is clear many Aboriginal children experience violence at various levels.

Violence against children is listed as physical, sexual, psychological, neglect (as a passive form of violence), and systems abuse. All these experiences are traumatic, and will have particular crisis potential according to when the experience occurred. The degree of traumatisation is significant to other factors such as different times in the lifecycle, who violated the child, and environmental and relationship factors critical to growth.

Macksound et al. (1993) list a number of other factors and experiences that may contribute to being profoundly hurt as a child. This is the violence that may be happening in the child's surrounds, which also has profound effects on the child. Children who witness the violent death of a parent or close family member or friend are traumatised. Children who see violence against a close family member, a parent, a friend, are traumatised. Forced separation from parents and displacement from home, participation in violent acts, witnessing parental or close-carer fear reactions to violence, all are elemental in child traumatisation. Extreme poverty and starvation are also traumatising experiences for children (Macksound et al., 1993). Across generations the vast majority of Aboriginal children have experienced one or more of these. In some communities some children have had multiple compounded traumatic experiences and the impacts are cumulative over time and place.

The same children are unable to experience the pain of the hurt, because of a number of factors. They cannot share what they have seen, heard and felt, because family/community members are in crisis themselves. Parents who are in crisis themselves cannot hear the Story the child needs to tell, for often the child reflects the unbearable pain of the adult. The child's terror is their own terror, the child's cries their own. They cannot use their arms to provide safe protection to the child because they cannot provide safe protection to themselves. They cannot provide a nurturing and caring environment for the child because they cannot provide a nurturing and caring environment for themselves.

Children do not become used to violence. They adapt. Trauma experiences become part of child play and behaviour however (Herman 1992). Children will repetitively re-enact trauma in such play, which can be so literal that if a person observes it, they can guess the trauma with few other clues (Herman 1992). In fact adults as well as children often feel driven to re-create the moment of terror, and this has the capacity to create further layers of traumatisation under some circumstances. Such re-enactment can become criminal activity.

A crisis occurring to a child has a different impact to a trauma experienced by an adult (Herman 1992). A crisis in the life of an adult may change the person, eroding the structure of the personality already formed (Herman 1992). It is a threat to an already formed identity (Tedeschi). This formed identity is endangered, but it is still a formed identity. When a child experiences trauma, the crisis is more likely to be integrated into a forming identity that is then carried throughout life, establishing the thinking, perceiving and reacting to life situations into the future (Tedeschi, p. 18). It is more than social learning. 'Repeated trauma in a child forms and de-forms the character, often fragmenting the personality'. The pathological[7] environment of childhood abuse forces the development of both extraordinarily creative and destructive capacities (Herman, p. 96) in children and the emerging adult.

The impact of trauma on a child may interfere with the emergence of moral concepts, resulting in behaviour that is overly regulated by considerations of good or bad, or alternatively manifestly amoral. Even when such behaviour is dysfunctional, it still has function, has meaning, in the relevancy of the dysfunctional situation in which they are enclosed. They still hurt and experience conflicting, flooding feelings of terror and excitement when violence erupts whether they are experiencing it or expressing it. The experience is still traumatising and trauma becomes compounded, compacted and complex. These compounding experiences, both in the short and long term hurt children, and consequently the emerging adult, in ways that we do not yet fully understand. (Extract from the Aboriginal and Torres Strait Islander Women's Task Force on Violence Report 2000, written by myself).

Bessel van der Kolk, in his recent research on the developmental impact of childhood trauma, writes: "Childhood trauma, including abuse and neglect, is probably the single most important public health challenge … a challenge that has the potential to be largely resolved by appropriate prevention and intervention" (van der Kolk, 2007, p. 224). Psychology, working with Indigenous community workers / healers has much to contribute to prevention and intervention programs. Trauma represents 'an emotional state of discomfort and stress resulting from memories of an extraordinary, catastrophic experience which shattered the survivor's sense of invulnerability to harm' (Figley, 1985, p. xviii). Trauma ruptures our connections to ourselves, physically, emotionally mentally and vitally. It fragments our relationship with others, in our family, social group, generation, and culture. It also fractures our relationship to nature,

---

[7] Pathological – emotion – consciousness – feeling – passion - impression

instinctually, and environmentally. The shock in trauma cannot be integrated and digested as are normal events and can cause re-enactment. The person may then be caught in a 'trauma vortex'.

All human beings have a personal functioning baseline, which will vary according to previous events, and the person's resiliency capacity. At the time of a distressing, potentially traumatic event, a person has a capacity to activate a resource - discharge response, a survival mechanism. At the next event with a potential trauma outcome, the person continues to be able to resource and discharge, however, dependent on a person's compensatory management survival energy, a person may lose their capacity to resource, discharge and move on. Hence the trauma vortex, and the development of psychological and physical symptoms.

In Australia, the stories of the Aboriginal child removals have been extensively documented in the report *Bringing Them Home,* the result of the National Inquiry into the Separation of Aboriginal and Torres Strait Islander Children from Their Families (1997). This report says the inquiry was 'not raking over the past' for its own sake, but that 'the past is very much with us today, in the continuing devastation of the lives of Indigenous Australians' – the trauma vortex (ibid: 3). The report details 'multiple and profoundly disabling' layers of abuse in the lives of all those affected, causing 'a cycle of damage from which it is difficult to escape unaided' (ibid:177):

- separation from primary carer
- effects of institutionalisation
- physical brutality and abuse
- repeated sexual violations
- psychological and emotional maltreatment
- loss of cultural and spiritual knowledge and identity
(ibid:177-228).

The results are a group of profoundly hurt people living with multiple layers of traumatic distress, chronic anxiety, physical ill health, mental distress, fears, depressions, substance abuse, and high imprisonment rates. For many, alcohol became the treatment of choice, because there was no other treatment available. "If they hadn't used alcohol they probably would have committed suicide. ....Having flashbacks of traumatic events can cause such psychic pain that the person might start to drink heavily or use other psycho-active substances" (ibid: 199).

For others, acting out the alienation and violence they had experienced meant a cycle of offending and re-entering other institutions of containment, juvenile detention centres and prisons.

Anger is a normal human response to a violation of the self. For some, however, the anger becomes disabling, unable to be expressed in safety to others or self because they live in places that are not safe:

> One of the effects that Eric identifies in himself is that, because of the violence in his past, when he himself becomes angry or confused, he feels the anger, the rage and the violence welling up within him. ..... Eric's symptomatology is obviously severe and chronic. It is clear that he deals with many deep emotional wounds that do not clearly fit [a Post Traumatic Stress Disorder] diagnostic classification. His deep sense of loss and abandonment, his sense of alienation, and his gross sense of betrayal and mistrust are normal responses to a tragic life cycle (ibid: 180).

Van de Kolk lists long term health and social outcomes of trauma on children:

- Violation of child's sense of safety and trust, of self worth, with a loss of a coherent sense of self,
- Emotional distress, shame, grief, self and other destructive behaviours
- Unmodulated aggression, difficulty negotiating relationships with caregivers, peers and marital partners
- Clear link between suicide, alcoholism and other drug misuse, sexual promiscuity, physical inactivity, smoking, obesity
- More likely to develop heart disease, cancer, stroke, diabetes, skeletal fractures, and liver disease
- People with childhood histories of trauma make up almost our entire criminal justice population (van der Kolk 2007, pp. 224-241)

This is more than a bridge of opportunity, for psychologists and Indigenous therapists or healers, to come together, to work with each other. Clearly this is a moral imperative, and the tools we must use are embedded in diverse and relevant streams of psychology and well as Indigenous healing practice.

Circle Four - The Centre of Learning and Healing

In the centre circle, people come together to explore the age old questions: Who am I? Who are we? What is our life purpose? These are not only personal questions, deserving of deep reflection and discussion, but collective, communal questions of social and cultural groups, across countries and nations, that must be explored and answered. These are questions human beings have asked of themselves across millennia.

Sitting in the circle, men and women - young and old - from diverse cultures and backgrounds, have found more common ground than dogma that divides.

I now address three separate principles for action, inviting Indigenous therapists and healers to work together with psychologists and educators.

Firstly, we understand that all cultures and peoples have similar patterns of behaviour in support of early childhood development. It may be that some of us may talk about '*neuro-developmental process in early childhood*' and others may talk about '*early childhood education*', while others may talk about '*growing up kids*'. But all children, in all cultures have similar needs in their early brain development (0 to 6 years) for enrichment and healthy growth. Developmental psychology teaches us the following, which we must build on, embracing cross-cultural programs designed to meet urgent needs.

Neuro-Developmental Rationale for Sequential Enrichment

The critical need in Indigenous Australia today is to invest in our kids, to help establish, in every community, programs for early childhood. The chart below outlines not just an early childhood approach using the creative arts, but embodies an approach for working with childhood trauma. There is work here for child psychologists working with Aboriginal therapists and educators.

Second, in response to the five points made by Alice Miller, which contribute to layers and levels of violence in individuals, and societies, we respond from both an educational and therapeutic approach. Or in the language we use at Gnibi, educaring.

The word education comes from the latin *educere* - to rear up, to nurture the children, to draw out from, to lead, to show the way.

Table 1: *Neuro-Developmental Rationale for Sequential Enrichment*

Developmental age	Sensitive Brain Area	Critical Functions	Primary Goal of Development	Optimising Experience	Enrichment Activities
0 - 1	Brainstem	Regulation of arousal	State regulation Flexible stress responses	Rhythmic and patterned sensory input Auditory or tactile	Massage Rhythm Touch Therapy
1 - 2	Midbrain	Integration of multiple sensory inputs Motor regulation	Sensory integration Motor control Affiliation	More complex movement Simple narrative	Music Movement Touch Therapy
1 - 4	Limbic	Emotional states Social language: Interpretation of social information	Emotional regulation Attachment Empathy	Complex movement Narrative Social experiences	Dance/Play Therapy Art Therapy Nature discovery
2 - 6	Cortex	Abstract cognitive functions Social/ emotional integration	Abstract reasoning Creativity	Complex conversation Social and emotional experience	Storytelling Drama Exposure to performing arts

© George Laws Earthchild Community Education and Enrichment

An educaring approach begins with establishing cultural safety and security. Cultural safety refers to: "an environment that is spirituality, socially and emotionally safe, as well as physically safe for people;... It is about shared respect, shared meaning, shared knowledge and experience of learning together" (Robyn Williams, 1999, p. 213). Cultural safety,

"extends beyond cultural awareness and cultural sensitivity. It empowers individuals and enables them to contribute to the achievement of positive outcomes. It encompasses a reflection on individual cultural identity and recognition of the impact of personal culture on professional practice" (Mary-Ann Bin-Sallik, 2003, p. 21).

In response to having been hurt as a child, we encourage people to find and tell their individual and collective stories, building on the strengths and resilience that they have drawn on previously to survive. This is a narrative therapy approach.

In response to having been hurt, but prevented from experiencing or expressing the pain of that hurt, we help people make sense of their stories, understanding through a cogitative behavioural therapy approach (CBT) that we do not have to be locked into survival scripts that keep us in those hurt places.

In response to the need to acknowledge our true feelings, not being heard, or acknowledged in our pain, we use the somatic therapies, helping to heal the body memories.

In response to a lack of education or knowledge, we provide an educational approach that will help us intellectualise what has happened to us, both individually and collectively, exploring theories about trans-generational trauma, and the trauma therapies.

Finally, the creative arts allow us to transform our pain - art is healing.

Third, and finally, we must collectively invest in education. Education has many layers and levels. Education is a powerful tool for social change. It is essential for personal and professional development. It enables and nurtures community enrichment and growth. It is an essential force for liberation.

At Gnibi, we have established *the Healing CIRCLE* foundation. C.I.R.C.L.E stands for Collaborative Indigenous Research Centre for Learning and Educare. The Healing CIRCLE also works within circles of learning:

- grounded within community, at community request, in response to community needs, an Indigenous Crisis Educaring Response Team (ICERT) brings education to the community, and in turn learns from our engagement with them;
- within the university, at the undergraduate level, with an undergraduate degree in trauma and healing;
- within the university, at the postgraduate level, a masters by course work degree in Indigenous Studies (wellbeing); and
- through a combined course work / research Professional Doctorate.

While we have a number of Indigenous and non-Indigenous students undertaking research degrees at both masters and PhD level, we decided last year to focus our postgraduate research work in the area of professional doctorates. We need quickly, and urgently, research documents that provide evidence to policy makers. Government has defined its need for evidence-based-policy. Evidence-based-policy can only come when people are working on the ground, responding to critical needs as they manifest.

We have students working in diverse regions of Australia, and with their work we will be able to chart what works across that diversity while also being able to name what does not work or needs more attention.

One Aboriginal woman is researching community change in a rural community in New South Wales, who, after a major crisis, invited us in while also initiating government intervention. This intervention is being driven by the community, and the research approach, in process evaluation research, critiques the crisis that motivated community action: action into practice; practice into evidence; evidence that informs policy.

It is clear again, that relationships between psychologists and Indigenous peoples are vital, not just within the area of teaching, but in research. Partnerships are important, if only because qualified, skilled Aboriginal Australians need working relationships with others who know that success in any given activity cannot be judged by size, rather it must be judged by its effect on the lives of those participating. An Aboriginal woman's work in a rural town in NSW, even if she does not hold a degree in psychology, is important. Principles are more important than programs and people are more important than organizations. The principle of working together in relatedness can create bridges between psychology and Indigenous healing practice that have benefits beyond our limited vision.

Conclusion

I began this paper with the Story about the finding of a new name for Gnibi. In that finding we were challenged to become 'wise women and men of High Degree'.

I outlined circles of sharing, learning and healing, four places for deep discussion and reflective practice, coming finally to the centre circle, showing the work we are doing at Gnibi to embed Indigenous healing practice in university education. In all our work we are informed by psychological theory and teaching, however we build on the Story-work that was started as Aboriginal women began to search for solutions to the issues affecting their lives and the lives of their children.

Karen Martin reminds us that

> Stories have power and give power. Stories are our law. Stories give identity as they connect us and fulfil our sense of belonging. Stories are grounding, defining, comforting and embracing. Stories vary in their purpose and content and so Stories can be political and yet equally healing. They can be shared verbally, physically or visually. Their meanings and messages teach, admonish, tease, celebrate, entertain, provoke and challenge (Martin, 2002).

Martin's relatedness theory also applies to the relationships between psychologists and Indigenous healers and therapists. Psychology and Indigenous healing practitioners must also work together to develop new ways of attending to Indigenous pain and distress, and in research that turns action into practice and practice into evidence. Teaching practice should be informed by what is happening on the ground, for the text books have not yet been written. They are being formed as we sit in the circle, and when we invite others to sit with us we expand our knowledge and skills so that our knowledge is deepened and expanded.

We can paraphrase Tolle (2002, p. 85) - *The teacher and the taught together create the teaching.* In our relatedness, we need to ask: who is the teacher and who is the taught, the psychologist or the Indigenous healer? I would suggest we both are, and more, as we sit together in circles of sharing, learning and healing.

References

Aboriginal and Torres Strait Islander Women's Task Force on Violence. (1999). *Aboriginal and Torres Strait Islander Women's Task Force on Violence Report.* Brisbane: Queensland Government.

Atkinson, J. (2002). *Trauma Trails – Recreating Song Lines, The Transgenerational effects of Trauma in Indigenous Australia.* Melbourne: Spinifex Press.

Atkinson, J., & Graham, J. (2002). Recreating the Circle of Well-being: A Tool for Changing the Health of Communities and Health Professional Education and Practice. In D. Neylet & J. Higgs (Eds.), *Change Imposed & Desired*, ANZAME conference publication July 5th 8th 2002 (pp. 39-56). Sydney: Faculty of Nursing, University of Sydney.

Baker, D. G. (1983). *Race, Ethnicity and Power*, London: Routledge & Kegan Paul.

Bin-Sallik, M-A. (2003). Cultural Safety: Let's Name It! *The Australian Journal of Indigenous Education, 32,* 21-28.

Fewster, G. (1999). Turning My Self Inside-Out: My Theory of Me. *J of C&YC, 13*(2), 35-54.

—. (2000). When the Subject Becomes the Object: The Art of Bringing life into Classrooms. *J of C&YC, 14*(1), 75-88.

Figley, C. (1985). *Trauma and Its Wake: The Study and Treatment of Post Traumatic Stress Disorder.* New York: Brunner/Mazel.

Gordon, S., Hallahan, K., & Henry, D. (2002). *Putting the Picture Together: inquiry into response by government agencies to complaints of family violence and child abuse in Aboriginal communities.* Perth: Western Australia Department of Premier and Cabinet.

Herman, J. (1992). *Trauma and Recovery: From Domestic Abuse to Political Terror.* HarperCollins: London.

Macksoud, M., Dyregrov, A., Raundalen, M. (1993). Traumatic War Experiences and Their Effects on Children. In J.P. Wilson & B. Raphael (Eds.), *International Handbook of Traumatic Stress Syndrome* (pp. 623 – 633). Plenum Press: New York.

Martin, K. (2001, 10–13 July). *Ways of knowing, ways of being and ways of doing: Developing a theoretical framework and methods for Indigenous re-search and Indigenist research.* Paper presented at The Power of Knowledge and Resonance of Tradition, Indigenous Studies Conferences, Canberra, Australia.

—. (2003). Ways of Knowing, being and doing: A theoretical framework and methods for Indigenous and Indigenist re-search. *Journal of Australian Studies, 76,* 203–214.

Matsumoto, D, & Juang, L. (2004). *Culture and Psychology.* United States: Thomson Wadsworth,

Miller, A. (1983). *For Your Own Good: Hidden Cruelty in Child- rearing and the Roots of Violence.* New York: Noonday.

Mobbs, R. (1991). In Sickness & Health: The sociocultural context for Aboriginal wellbeing, illness and healing. In J. Reid & P. Trompf (Eds.), *The Health of Aboriginal Australians.* Sydney: Harcourt Brace Javanovic.

National Aboriginal Health Strategy Working Party (1989). *A National Aboriginal Health Strategy.* Canberra: Commonwealth of Australia.

Rose, D. B. (1987). Consciousness and Responsibility in an Australian Aboriginal Religion. In W. H. Edwards (Ed.). *Traditional Aboriginal Society.* Adelaide: Macmillan Press.

—. (1996). *Nourishing Terrains: Australian Aboriginal Views of Landscape and Wilderness.* Canberra: Australian Heritage Commission.

—. (2000). *Dingo Makes Us Human: Life and Land in an Australian Aboriginal Culture.* Cambridge, UK: Cambridge University Press.

Stanner, W. E. H. (1979). *White Man Got No Dreaming: Essays 1938-1973.* Canberra: Australian University Press.

Ungunmerr, M. R. (1993). Dadirri. In J. Hendricks and G. Hefferan (Eds.). *A Spirituality of Catholic Aborigines and the Struggle for Justice* (pp. 34 – 37). Brisbane: Aboriginal and Torres Strait Islander Apostolate Catholic Archdiocese of Brisbane,

Van de Kolk, B. (2007). Developmental impact of Childhood Trauma. In L. Kirmayer, R. Lemelson, & M. Barad (Eds.). *Understanding Trauma: integrating biological, clinical and cultural perspectives.* Cambridge MA: Cambridge University Press.

Williams R. (1999). Cultural Safety – what does it mean for our work practice? *Australian and New Zealand Journal of Public Health, 23*(2): 213-214.

KEYNOTE ADDRESS: THE VALUE OF UNIQUE SERVICE PROVISION FOR ABORIGINAL AUSTRALIANS: THE BENEFITS OF STARTING FROM SCRATCH

TRACY WESTERMAN

Abstract

Indigenous Psychological Services (IPS) is a private company based in Western Australia that was established in 1999 for the purpose of providing tertiary mental health services for Aboriginal people. This paper describes the ideology behind the development of IPS, the approach being that cultural factors have a primary rather than distal role in determining mental health outcome for Aboriginal Australians. Cultural factors are important in engagement and assessment as well as intervention strategies. Unfortunately attempts to redress the disadvantage experienced by Aboriginal Australians with regard to equity in access to effective mental health services have been plagued by the absence of empirically based therapeutic frameworks that have determined their efficacy across populations of Aboriginal people. For an Aboriginal psychologist the balance becomes: at what point does the need for an evidence base outweigh the realities of protecting the cultural security of client information, particularly that which is directly implicated in client wellbeing?

The paper explores issues relating to culturally appropriate clinical intervention and assessment as primary barriers for equity in access to mental health services for Aboriginal people, and covers the following areas:

1. Problems with identification and treatment of mental health problems amongst Aboriginal people
2. The Indigenous perspective on mental health in terms of causality and its manifestation within the perspective of how to approach working with Aboriginal people

3. Suggestions for prevention efforts that address the risk factors that have been associated with Aboriginal mental health.

The paper demonstrates the value of a unique approach to service provision to Aboriginal clients through a number of empirically validated models of intervention that have been tested at the population level across a number of Aboriginal groups.

I would like to acknowledge our traditional owners, both past and present.

The field of Indigenous mental health is in its infancy and plagued by ambiguity. Many people have a great desire to work more effectively with Indigenous people, but struggle to know how to. This paper aims to give some guidelines to help people like that.

My traditional people are the Nyamal mob who are located between Port Hedland and Marble Bar in the north-west of Western Australia. I grew up in a little place called Useless Loop with a population of about 100. I first lived in a house at seven years of age. We lived in a tin shed that dad had built, and when he bought a caravan and connected the caravan up to the tin shed, that was our house. At about 16 years of age, I decided I wanted to study psychology. It was quite an interesting thing to do, to come home and tell my very traditional Aboriginal people that that's what I wanted to do. About nine years ago, after working in the area of government welfare services for seven years, I started a company called Indigenous Psychological Services (IPS) when I completed my PhD on the psychological assessment of Aboriginal people.

When I first started to go back to my community I was 21 years of age, with a Masters Degree in Psychology and no idea at all. I was a baby psychologist. My first job was out in the central desert communities in Western Australia. In the community in which I worked, there were enormous substance abuse problems. There were people with cans of petrol around their necks, and that was their day-to-day experience, just sniffing petrol. I remember feeling quite overwhelmed by that, but also feeling quite inspired that as an Indigenous person they wanted to come and see me for healing. However, I felt often that I was really struggling to know how to respond to some of the things that were being directed at me. For instance, a traditional Aboriginal male who was charged with the sexual assault of a 12-year-old girl from the Aboriginal community was sentenced to two months in prison on the basis that he argued that the girl was promised to him as part of the traditional marriage aspect of

Aboriginal culture[1]. As another example - these scenarios are actual dilemmas that I worked on myself and I use the information with permission - an Aboriginal man was on trial for the murder of his traditional wife. I was an expert witness for this particular case. He said that on the days leading up to the event he was being sung[2], and this involved auditory hallucinations. He had no history of violence. Was this a psychotic episode or a culture-bound phenomenon?

What I was trying to do was to make sense of mainstream teaching in a culturally specific way without any guidance about how to achieve that. Aboriginal people continue to experience what I refer to as 'the big three' when it comes to access to psychology-specific services: misdiagnosis, over-diagnosis, and under-diagnosis of mental health issues. When I first went back out to my community with my psychology degree, I thought I was going to be able to help everybody that came along. Since then, the main focus of my work has continued to be trying to undercover the causes of 'the big three'. I am at my core a very solutions focused person. I am not a big fan of just talking about what is wrong and thereby creating paralysis within the profession. I am a much bigger advocate of identifying the causes of 'the big three' and then finding solutions, ultimately evidence-based scientific and cultural best practice to address these causes. So far, my journey has enabled some resolutions or solutions to 'the big three'.

The first cause I will illustrate via a fairly sobering example that I came across and continue to come across to this day - cultural triggers to mental illness are often not identified in mainstream assessment. My first example of this was a young lady who was referred to me by the community after she had made a suicide attempt. I spoke some words with her and used my mainstream[3] suicide risk assessment tool and started doing work with the community and with her. Despite our best efforts she started to become more and more unwell. After a period of time we identified that the reason why she made a suicide attempt was

---

[1] The term 'promising' refers to the traditional practice in which, around the time of the birth of a new baby girl, the community decides, on the basis of strictly defined rules of kin relationships, which man she will marry when she comes of age

[2] The term 'being sung' refers to the belief that sorcery can be used to inflict physical or psychological harm, usually as 'payback' (retribution) for an offence, such as a crime or for violating traditional law

[3] The term 'mainstream' is commonly used in Indigenous contexts to distinguish the dominant Western methods of assessment, interventions, etc, from those designed for Indigenous contexts

because she had fallen in love with someone who was the wrong way for her, that is, with someone who was of a completely wrong skin group for her[4].

As an Aboriginal person, and as a psychologist, my 'shame' was that I just completely missed it. How was this possible? The reality is, that there is actually no requirement, when you're conducting an assessment, to engage at the level of cultural belief or identity with every Aboriginal client you see. Therefore, we are left to make assumptions about the relative importance of culture for every Aboriginal client, with an absence of guidance around this as in relation to the assessment process. The fact is that there are a myriad of cultural differences within our culture. It permeates every aspect of our assessment, from engagement to intervention to counselling skills, to the whole myriad of automated behaviours that practitioners bring in to the process of assessment, counselling, and intervention. So, why is it that we pay so little attention to providing evidence-based practice around these realities?

In the assessment of Indigenous Australians we also need to have a greater understanding of the concept of bias or error. What is often underplayed is the role that practitioners have in contributing to an inordinate amount of assessment and test bias when they are involved in assessing clients from a different cultural background. The reality is that there are actually two main reasons why clients present the way they do. One is they have a mental illness – for example, they have depression, anxiety, psychosis etc. The other factor that contributes to client presentation at assessment is what is known as 'extraneous factors', that is, those things that as a practitioner we often unwittingly bring into the assessment process which can result in a client's presentation being a response to these differences. For Aboriginal people, factors such as being from a different cultural background and being of a different gender to your Aboriginal client are known contributors to bias or error in assessment.

Attention Deficit Hyperactivity Disorder (ADHD) is a further example of how cultural differences can result in diagnosis being confused, and cultural differences being seen as deficits in functioning. I have recently commenced a post doctoral fellowship in ADHD in Aboriginal people. What we have found has been that some of the primary Aboriginal child

---

[4] Marrying 'the wrong way' in the traditional context refers to marrying someone from a group you are not allowed to marry into according to the traditional kin relationships. The system of deciding who was appropriate for someone to marry was evolved over thousands of years. It helped to maintain a stable society with defined roles and avoided many potential problems, including in-breeding.

rearing strategies, such as raising their children to explore their environments without restrictions and without boundaries, often results in a greater 'yardstick' for impulsivity and particularly agitation. From the perspective of Aboriginal child rearing, these behaviours that are encouraged in an Aboriginal environment are seen as strengths, since this is how Aboriginal kids learn independence and practical competence from a young age. However, in mainstream, Eurocentric environments, these behaviours are seen as deficits more than strengths. So 'independent' becomes 'off task' – and God help you if you are off task!

There are many things that we bring to the client-practitioner relationships that can account for a difference in presentation. I work a lot in suicide prevention. Sometimes the Aboriginal community may say, 'This person's a really high risk.' Then, when we send them into a mainstream mental health service they'll often say, 'They're not at risk.' There's often a real mismatch between how the person is in their culture and what they're assessed as from a mainstream perspective.

There are many things that we see as normal within our culture that are seen as abnormalities from the mainstream perspective. A classic example is people experiencing visits from deceased loved ones. That's normal for our culture. Say you need to decide whether something is delusional, which is part of how to assess psychoses. Somebody can't be delusional if the culture believes that it's possible. Since the Aboriginal culture believes it's possible for spirits of deceased loved ones to visit us, it doesn't meet the criteria for delusions based on cultural understanding. What is normal behaviour is culturally relative.

In IPS we do lots of work around psychological assessment. When I went into court for the case about the young guy who believed that he had been sung, I made a decision when I saw very mainstream-looking people who had never come in contact with Aboriginal culture in their life. I thought, 'I can either sit here and talk about being sung, or I can focus on trying to make sense of the behaviour', which is basically what I did. But then I said to them, 'Look, it actually doesn't matter whether you believe that being sung is possible. It doesn't matter. It actually doesn't even matter whether you believe it's possible. What matters is that *we* believe that *he* believes it'. He was a very traditional man, with no exposure to mainstream judicial systems and processes, so therefore he lacked the sophistication to be able to manipulate that system in a way to try to excuse culture as a reason for his violent behaviour.

We do a lot of training for people who work in Indigenous contexts, as many as a thousand people a year. We have four mental health specific packages focussing on the retention of Indigenous clients and four

Indigenous specific intervention programmes. We have done a lot of research. We're trying to create an evidence base where historically there has never been one. People don't really know what works with Aboriginal people. People will share their stories of what they have found works, but what we're aiming to do is to provide population level information so that people can then have a degree of confidence around what works across whole populations of Aboriginal people. We develop a model, then we test it out on hundreds of people. We're developing a consistent systematic approach across Indigenous culture, working with community groups and prevention programmes on a community level. We also do some work around organisational cultural change and development.

The current situation for Aboriginal mental health is that Aboriginal people are less likely to access mental health services than non-Aboriginal people and less likely to be identified as having a mental health problem by services in the community. In research that I conducted with David Vicary (Vicary & Westerman, 2004), we started going around and yarning with community about what happens if someone becomes unwell. What we found was that people were more likely to see it as part of someone's personality and part of their character rather than being pathological. There's a great deal of accommodation for mental illnesses within Aboriginal community. Some of that is due to the fact that the concept of mental unwellness is quite new for Aboriginal people. We're more likely to see something as being cultural. When someone becomes unwell, we tend to see that as a result of external factors. So if I go out to the community and someone's attempted suicide, they won't say he attempted suicide, they'll say he's been sung or been paid back or something like that. That's the externalisation of mental health problems that we tend to see. The community is struggling with the idea that individuals have actually internalised their unwellness rather than it being a result of external factors.

Aboriginal people come into services at the crisis level and at chronic stages. A client may come in in crisis, and after one or two sessions with them they don't come back and you may think you'll never see them again, and then you say, "I'm just going to close that file", and then they turn up again! It's quite normal for Aboriginal people to do that, because traditionally if we go to a healer, the reason we go to a healer is because they sort us and fix us, so it's quite normal that people will come to get fixed and when they feel they're fixed they won't come again. Another important issue is that they are less likely to be monitored, so we don't know much about the efficacy of any sort of psychotropic medication with Aboriginal clients.

There's a lot of stigma regarding mental health just generally, but with Aboriginal people it's greater, because of the external attributions and belief systems. If Aboriginal people become unwell, they often believe it's because they've done something wrong, so therefore the stigma is far greater.

What are the statistics on Aboriginal mental health? Suicidal behaviour is at least 2.3 times the national average and for some Aboriginal males aged 25-45 the rates are 3.4 times the national average. In 45% of Indigenous people, death by suicide occurs in people 26 and below, compared to the mainstream where there's an age average of about 41.3, and 80% of Aboriginal suicides in 1998 happened in men aged 25-35. There's a real vulnerability in that particular population in that particular age group. For depression, it's about double the rate in the general population, and for self-harm it's about three times the rate.

For PTSD, there is not a lot of data, but in my opinion, for every single Aboriginal person that comes in as a client, I would always explore the possibility of some form of PTSD as part of the normal assessment process. However, I've done a lot of work with Stolen Generations people and a real clear message that has come out from them is that they're sick of hearing that 'we're all traumatised'. There is a phenomenon called over-helping which is relevant here. We know that PTSD is an abnormal reaction to a critical event. In 90% of cases people experience PTSD after a critical event. Everyone experiences some maladjustment when they've gone through a critical event of some sort, but what we don't want to do is encourage people to feel that PTSD is a normal response rather than an abnormal response. We can tend to create the idea that people should be going through a particular process because they've been through trauma. In my experience people are saying, 'Look, all of us have been through this, but everyone makes sense of those experiences quite differently.'

Judith Herman actually talks about conflicted PTSD, which occurs when people are experiencing lots of different types of trauma. There may be primary trauma and secondary trauma, but people may just treat the tertiary trauma. When violence or even abuse has become normal within particular communities – and I'm not suggesting that every community is like that – and when people are isolated and there is no one to help the community, the behaviour becomes almost adaptive and normal because they don't have anything to compare it to. It becomes very easy then for a victim to become a perpetrator of abuse, so the community gets caught in cycles of violence.

I have also noticed that there is very limited validation of people's trauma if they are in communities where everyone's going through similar things. We know that for healing to occur, the first thing that needs to happen is that someone validates their trauma, so they can realise that what happened to them is wrong and should never have happened. But a lot of people haven't even had that basic validation. This is why it's so important to say "Sorry", because what that represents is that what happened during the Stolen Generations era was wrong and it should never happen again.

How Aboriginal people deal with trauma is very interesting as well. In a mainstream setting, how non-Aboriginal people feel as a result of trauma is a very individual reaction. When people go through an assault of some sort then what they have to do is to integrate that assault into their renewed sense of self concept. People who get stuck in the healing tend to define themselves purely on the basis of the assault or of the event itself. For Aboriginal people it's quite different. It's not an individual thing, it's actually a community sense of healing, so therefore if someone goes through a trauma of some sort, it then becomes a matter of reintegration of one's self into how the community views you. If anyone's going through the trauma, then their involvement with community makes it really difficult to heal.

If there has been a lot of trauma in the previous generation, there's fairly strong evidence that there's going to be trauma to some extent in the next generation down. There's a very good evidence base for the role of parental modelling of trauma. You only have to look at the Redfern riots[5] to see what happens when a critical event occurs. In that case a young man was killed. There were some young kids that actually witnessed that, and this death related to everyone in the community. There was no validation of hurt and trauma from government or any other services, so they had 12 hours of getting angrier and angrier. The young kids, because they couldn't make sense cognitively of the trauma, looked to how everyone around them responded to the trauma, and they all got angrier and angrier, and then there were 8 year old and 10 year old kids standing on the bonnets of cars throwing Molotov cocktails and other

---

[5] Redfern is a Sydney suburb with a high proportion of Aboriginal people. On February 17 2004 an Aboriginal youth 'TJ' Hickey was riding his bicycle when he spotted a police car that he thought was chasing him. While he was attempting to flee he accidentally impaled himself on a fence and died. Anger over the actions of the police led to rioting which continued into the night.

missiles at the police. That behaviour was actually quite normal in that situation. It's quite normal for young people to respond to trauma in that way if everyone is dealing with the trauma in that particular way. They look to see how people around them respond to the trauma.

There's a strong role for modelling bad behaviour but there's a strong role for modelling good behaviour too. In communities that I go to that have experienced a critical event, in some cases they have just that one trauma and don't seem to have another again. Those communities are different from the ones that tend to be stuck in traumas in that they have lots of people modelling adaptive ways of coping with critical events. As Aboriginal people have a learning style of modelling imitation, they're going to look to how people around them respond to events and take that on, and this is how we make sense of it. For instance, take mental illness. Statistics show that if you have a mother who is depressed you're up to three times as likely as the general population to be depressed yourself. So if you have a family or community history of trauma, you're likely to inherit trauma yourself.

What should be the priorities in Aboriginal mental health based on what we know? The first one is getting the assessment to be more reliable and valid. We've been doing a lot of work on developing a culturally validated tool for screening Aboriginal youth at risk. This is because there just aren't any culturally validated tools around, whether it be for mental unwellness or whether it be for cognitive testing, and as a result Aboriginal people either don't get tested at all, and therefore they're excluded from mainstream testing, or they're tested inaccurately. People who use all the mainstream tests, and do so appallingly badly, and use the most culturally unfair tests going around will say, 'A person's Aboriginality must be taken into account when interpreting these results.' But without culturally appropriate tools and proper training, how are they going to be able to do that?

We need to see whether an assessment is accurate: does the issue actually impair the person across different contexts? For instance, if someone's depressed in a mainstream context we would expect that they would be depressed in a cultural context as well, otherwise how could we say that the person is truly depressed? If the issue doesn't actually impair them within their culture - and the cultural judgement is always right, because that's where they're primarily from - are the assessments valid? Are the assessments constructed by Aboriginal people for Aboriginal people? What does intelligent behaviour looks like from our Aboriginal perspective? What does mental unwellness looks like from our perspective?   And have the tests been developed taking all that information into account in their construction?

Another consideration is whether the tests have face validity. There are lots of examples of tests where it's assumed that Aboriginal people are starting from a similar playing field to non-Aboriginal people, but many Aboriginal people can't even understand the concept of a test, and most of the tests rely on exposure to mainstream concepts and constructs and acquired knowledge. Some tests are much better than others, but there are too many examples of tests that Aboriginal people will fail just because of cultural difference rather than actually having a deficit, but often the results are interpreted as Aboriginal people having a deficit.

For example, recently I was using the Wechsler Intelligence scales with a young girl about 15 years of age who was interested in it and curious about it. Part of it was a picture completion test - which is no longer part of the latest version of the scale - where you have to point out which bits are missing from the picture. There was one picture where there was a chair with three legs, and she sat and looked at it for ages and ages and couldn't find what was missing, because all the chairs where she comes from have three legs. That's a classic example to illustrate that she would have failed that test.

How can we incorporate belief systems, spirituality, organisations, skin relationships, gender, sub-cultures etc into assessment protocols? How do people go about determining how much illness there is in the general population? Every now and then I do a little epidemiological study in which two standard deviations above the mean indicates the likelihood of clinical depression. But people administering these tests commonly don't look at clinical validation, whether those symptoms impair somebody within the community. I don't know anyone who actually does cultural validations.   There may be differential interpretations for every single item on a particular questionnaire. For example, there's a tendency for Aboriginal people to relate more to negatively worded items, which means that they're going to score more highly than non-Aboriginal people on depression scales. There's also fairly good evidence that the symptoms measured on the DSM-IV are actually different across cultures. Good work has been done in Canadian populations and African-American populations and Spanish- and Chinese-American populations, and we've done work here with Aboriginal-Australians, which look at the symptom variation across mainstream illnesses, and we've found variations around that, so are we really looking in the right directions, and do we know what we're looking for?

Take the MMPI, the Minnesota Multi-Phasic Personality Inventory, which is one of the main personality assessment instruments in use around the world. One of the subscales is the Psychopathic Deviance Scale. Research shows that there's a trend for minority populations, and that includes Aboriginal people, to score a peak on that particular subscale. What the Psychopathic Deviant subscale taps into is a different way of looking at the world, so highly intelligent people will also score a peak on the Psychopathic Deviance Scale because they look at the world in a different way. This is just one example of how cultural difference can result in a person being labelled as deficit or dysfunctional when they're really not.

At IPS we've done a lot of work on the two concepts differential and clinical diagnosis. The research that we did on homeland-dwelling[6] Aboriginal youth found that a third had high risk factors across three main illnesses - depression, anxiety, and alcohol and drug usage. That has massive implications for assessment, intervention, and particularly prognosis. The other thing that makes things more complicated is the fact that a lot of other things, if there's a lot of abuse around, can sometimes look like anxiety disorder. Drug and alcohol syndrome can also look like anxiety disorder. We need to consider differential cultural diagnosis, which means that cultural factors or cultural issues can sometimes be confused with clinical disorders. There's a lot of cultural-related illness. For instance, people who have been removed and dislocated from country can experience what we call a longing or crying or being sick for country[7], which looks exactly like mainstream depression. There's also a condition affecting the Stolen Generations people, people who were removed traumatically from land and country, called dissociative fugue, which means that they don't have any recollection of that removal from country or land. Their illnesses actually look like mainstream illnesses, but the causes of them are cultural and therefore the solution is a cultural one.

I've also done work on attachment disorders. A lot of Aboriginal kids have reactive attachment disorder, which means they seem to attach indiscriminately to anyone. However, in Aboriginal society the kids don't

---

[6] The term 'homeland' in this context refers to communities, usually remote from major urban centres, consisting almost entirely of Indigenous people. With some exceptions, non-Indigenous people are not allowed to enter a homeland without a permit from the community.
[7] The term 'country' in Indigenous contexts refers to where an Aboriginal person's traditional land is located. Aboriginal people have strong spiritual and other ties to their country.

just attach to Mum and Dad, they attach to a whole nucleus, the whole community, and they do so in a very hierarchically organised way. Hence, assessing attachment in Aboriginal kids is very different to assessing attachment in mainstream society.   For a non-Aboriginal person, attachments in Aboriginal young people may look chaotic, but there's predictability in the seeming chaos. For example, a kid may go home one day and if Mum and Dad aren't there they think, 'That's alright, I'll just go to Aunty's, because I know that she will feed me. At night time I know that I'll go to Granny's, because her house is safe[8].'   So there's a real distinction around the different types of attachment, which are organised depending upon what can be obtained, not necessarily emotionally but more in a practical sense, as a result of those attachments. So Aboriginal children have their own way of making sense of attachments.

Incorporating cultural differences into assessment is really important. Differential cultural diagnosis is a term that I invented when I was doing my doctoral studies. What it means is that, quite often, Aboriginal people may have a couple of clinical disorders but may also have a couple of cultural disorders. For example, if someone's been sung, they may actually also have a clinical disorder that needs to be treated. Quite often when I work with these communities, they say to me, 'You take care of the whitefella stuff, and we'll take care of the cultural stuff.'

With regards to the inequities in mental health statistics, we don't have a lot of good information. Various estimates of the prevalence of mental illnesses range from as low as 1.8% to as high as 51.2%. It does not instil much confidence, but unfortunately it marginalises us further because if we don't have accurate information we can't really advocate for appropriate services for our people.

Another important issue is the absence of the validation of cultural illnesses or cultural disorders. I recognised this about seven years ago. I gave a 20 minute presentation on getting assessments right by incorporating things like being sung, payback, and so on, and there were professors of child psychology in the audience, half of which had never even met an Aboriginal person in their life. At the end of the presentation one of the professors said to me, "This is all very interesting, but there's actually an absence of evidence that these things exist." To which I

---

[8] In Aboriginal societies, what westerners call aunts or uncles are commonly regarded as equivalent to mothers and fathers, with similar roles and responsibilities. In the same way, all of one's grandmother's sisters are commonly regarded as grandmothers. This stems from the traditional organisation of Indigenous society using the principle of the equivalence of same-sex siblings.

responded, "You're absolutely right, there is no evidence that these things exist - in the world in which *you* live!"

How can we validate cultural reliability in a way that protects the security and the safety of the culture and also gives people an understanding of what to look for? If someone's experiencing spiritual visits, how do we know when they're psychotic, how do we know whether that's appropriate within the culture, and how can we tell the difference between the two? We need to do a lot more work to answer these questions.

Indigenous Psychological Services is a private service without government funding. We are Indigenous-specific, with a strengths-based approach. For example, we don't focus on parenting *problems* but parenting *differences*. We look at strengths within a culture. We look at the skills that Indigenous people have and try to bring those into our therapy or our community interventions.

We use a brokerage model, which means that we don't have any full-time staff except secretarial support. If a community wants us to go out and do work with them, we link up with a couple of psychologists over there and out we go. We train those local people to deliver those services, and we only use people who are culturally competent and who are vouched for within their community. We are quite rigorous about how we use the cultural vouching system. It's something that's very important. I started this system of vouching many years ago, when I'd get people coming into my service and they'd say, 'Yes, I work with this community and I work with that community, I'm just really good at working with Aboriginal people.' So I'd say, 'No worries, so where did you work?' They'd say, 'I've worked at such and such, such and such,' so I'd ring up and see whether anyone would vouch for them. Cultural vouching is a really strong way of determining whether someone is as good as what they say they are. It's really important that the community itself determine whether someone is culturally appropriate and culturally effective.

We address relative disadvantage. Most regions wait up to three years for our services, because we have no government funding for anything that we do. So what we do now is provide 30% of our work at no cost. We charge people for the services who can afford it and that goes back into research as well as into community intervention services. I think the brokers dread when I ring them up because they know that it's either going to be a freebie or really cheap. We charge the people that can afford it so we can do the community based free-type work. I think as an educator of disadvantaged Aboriginal people it's our responsibility to do that.

With regards to the solution-based approach, we've been developing unique psychological tests. We've done a lot of work around the development of the Westerman Aboriginal Symptom Checklist for Youth. We've done a lot of screening of young people and we've now got data on about 223 kids across five different states, so we can now look at population differences across different issues. Because our focus is on suicide prevention, we've been able to develop programs based on those differences, but importantly we've been able to determine whether mainstream risk factors are the same or relevant for Indigenous people. So an example is, from our suicide research we've found that there's a different nature to it, and we're able to validate that across the population. For instance, for mainstream suicide there's usually a build-up of depression that you notice in cases when people become suicidal. For Indigenous people we've found that 60% of the variance is actually accounted for by impulsivity, which is quite different. So depression is a focus but it's actually not as big an issue as impulsivity is, so therefore we may have been focussing on the wrong factors. We're able to then identify what the key differences are and then mobilise communities around identifying those differences and then intervene in a more effective way.

Also we've developed a lot of protocols and proformas around the cultural formulation of assessment. We look at, for example, the differences between psychosis and spiritual reasons for self harm, depression or longing for country. We've developed a comprehensive set of guidelines around how to determine the difference between those cultural and clinical disorders.

We are also engaged in improving workforce and organisational cultural competencies, in which organisations engage us to do comprehensive cultural audits of their organisation. The first one we did about six years ago at an organisation that was state-wide. Probably 90% of their work was delivering services to Aboriginal communities, and they weren't being effective, so they wanted to figure out why that was the case. We have what we call an Aboriginal Mental Health Cultural Competency Questionnaire, which has involved six years worth of work in validation of the components that predict cultural competency and service delivery. Cultural knowledge is only a small component of how and why people are culturally competent in service delivery. In fact, we've had organisations where 80% of their staff have had training in cultural knowledge or cultural awareness but that has had no relationship whatsoever to cultural competence and service delivery.

The five key components of cultural competence that we assess are: local Indigenous specific knowledge; skills and abilities for being able to adapt or utilise mainstream training in a way which will be effective with Aboriginal clients; resources and linkages for the use of cultural consultants, cultural guides, and links with the local community; organisational structures - ensuring that those are consistent with culturally appropriate practice; and personal and organisational beliefs and attitudes, which is the most important component - if your behaviour is not consistent with your beliefs or if you have a negative attitude towards your Aboriginal client, then you can't be effective.

We have now undertaken cultural competence screening on well over 2,000 people, so we can compare how culturally competent one person is compared to the norm group. We can say, 'compared to other people working in the field you are at level 1.' The scale goes from level 1 all the way through to level 7, which is the culturally proficient level. For the first organisation that we did our cultural audit on, we got the individuals to fill them out and then we looked at how the group was functioning across those five different areas. We found that 80% of their organisation was at level 1, which is effectively the level of racism. We could see the blood draining from their faces, so I said, 'Well, the good news is the only way is up!'

People are really positive about cultural competency evaluation. It gives them a baseline, and then we give them very specific targeted strategies on how to improve it. We do a re-evaluation in 3-6 months time, and then people can see their shifts.

We have also developed the only known culture-specific client policies and procedures to protect workers, including things like the use of traditional healers, ethically, legally and culturally. We go into organisations and look at all their administration policies and procedures and make them more culturally specific. We have developed an Indigenous specific client information management system which comes in a CD-ROM. Say you have an Aboriginal client that comes in, and you need to do an assessment on them. The CD-ROM prompts you about the things to look for. For example, if you need a certain test it will tell you how to adapt that test, and it includes information about culturally bound syndromes and related issues. You just need to enter the information in and then it spits out an automated report at the end.

We've also developed unique training packages with an Indigenous mental health focus, including training around psychological testing, cultural and ethical dilemmas, suicide and depression, counselling skills and therapies, cultural learning styles, and mental health assessments, a whole range of things, from the starting point all the way through to high end therapeutic intervention. A total of 4,595 people have been trained in the IPS packages since the year 2000 in the absence of ongoing funding or support, since the organisations or communities themselves see value in it and invite us in.

When working with Aboriginal people, self disclosure is very important. In Western psychology training students are commonly told that they shouldn't disclose anything about themselves when working with clients, but Aboriginal people need to first decide if they like you. If they don't like you they're not going to come back. I know when I've engaged with an Aboriginal client when they ask me about myself personally. They'll say something like, 'Oh that fella, I saw you with, is that your brother?' That's when I know I've got them, because they're actually interested in me personally. But how do you actually protect yourself in that process where for Aboriginal people it's essential to self-disclose and yet you also need to then protect yourself in that process? I do a lot of work with the Stolen Generations counsellors who are all of the Stolen Generations themselves. We do a lot of work around vicarious trauma with them, because it's really tough to have to self disclose and yet protect yourself in that whole process as well. So I say you can only use self disclosure if it's to the benefit of your client.

The need to sit with people is a very interesting point. When you first go out to communities you just need to sit with the elders[9] and that's how you engage with the whole community. This is because they need to check out your spirit, to check out whether you come in with good spirit and a good intention. There's also a phenomenon that is not particularly enjoyable but it's normal. Part of the process is that people will growl you[10]. They'll growl you and they'll have a good go at you. When I first went out of Western Australia I went up to the Northern Territory and sat with the elders and they just raked me over the coals for about three hours. If you interfere with the growling, it's going to go on for much longer - that's the bad news! I used to take young psychologists out and I'd say, 'Just shut your mouth and don't say anything, and if you leave before an elder does, I don't want you coming back to the office.' So you

---

[9] In Indigenous societies the elders are the gate-keepers, the custodians of traditional knowledge and the main decision-makers. A person becomes an elder not just by reaching a certain age but through having earned that title through having lived according to traditional law.

[10] 'Growling' consists of testing a new arrival verbally, often provocatively.

just have to put up with being growled and growled and growled and growled. Growling is about people protecting the community from those who are not coming in with good intentions. Now, if I don't be growled, I think something's wrong.

We've also done a lot of work on treatment of culture-bound syndromes. If someone's longing for country, we can adapt mainstream counselling and therapies. For example, some people may have been removed from country and are unable to go back, because they're in locked wards of psychiatric units or they're in prisons, so they can't go home to fix the longing for country. We work on the longing for country adapting mainstream psychological interventions to do that.

We work on developing community capacity for whole of community interventions. For instance, we have developed Indigenous specific suicide intervention programs in which we train communities. We train service providers and we train youth in suicide prevention programs. We go into communities with high rates of suicide and we mobilise the whole community around providing interventions to those with suicidal issues. The reason why we do that is that a community with a lot of suicides can't afford to wait when someone wants to hurt themselves. It's usually not between 9 and 5, Monday to Friday. It's usually when the trained person's not around, like three in the morning on the weekends when there's no-one around, but they need to deal with it now. So we go out and train people up. The extraordinary strength in Aboriginal communities is that people will say, when there's someone that's unwell, 'Tell us what we need to do.' You wouldn't see that in mainstream culture, that's a massive strength that we have in our culture.

We have also done some work on whole of community trauma in New South Wales. For these interventions, the process is actually more important than content. One of my elders said three years ago that Aboriginal people are more concerned with process than we are with content. This means that if you have someone go out to a community - and I feel sorry for people that start off working in communities, because they have go through a baptism of fire, and I can see it all unfolding but it's not within my power to prevent it - and saying, 'I want to do this, I want to provide that, I've got this great program, I want to deal with this for you lot', and everyone's sitting there and taking it all in, then someone will pop up and say, 'Yeah, but who are you going to talk to and who are you going to engage with, who have you talked to, and where are you from anyway?' It's about process, process, process, process. If you get the process wrong and the protocols wrong, you're never going to even see the light of day. The process stuff is actually more important than the content. I've seen the best clinicians in the whole world get nowhere because they haven't got the process right.

With regards to our suicide prevention courses, we've trained over 1,095 people in four years, and 85% of those have been Indigenous. In one community we went to, the first time we delivered in this form we had 112 people come through in six days, whereas in mainstream training the facilitators would be lucky to get five or six Aboriginal people coming through. We average about 64 people every time we do an intervention program in the Aboriginal community.

We also evaluate them rigorously. We sit down with people and get them to look at their skills before the training and the skills after. We sit down for quite a while, then we feed back to people later on. We've been able to track what's happened in four communities 18 months after the training, and we've found that the biggest effect when you're going out to Aboriginal communities is at what we call the third phase, when there is a massive potentiating effect. When we go in the first time, people are struggling with the concepts. At the second time people are remembering some of the concepts, and the third time they're running the training themselves. That's building capacity within those communities, and when we evaluate it the whitefella way[11], they can't ignore the results and the outcomes that we've been getting.

One time I was in a place called Roebourne, in Western Australia. We had community elders who had English as a second or third language, yet their skill levels were assessed as equal to those of the service provider at the second phase. It was just brilliant to see the pride that they had in getting that feedback.

In our trauma intervention we focus on identifying people who are actually traumatised rather than making assumptions that everyone has been traumatised. This example is of a community who had three of their young people murdered about 17 years ago by a serial killer who came and worked in the town, and no-one cared, literally. After 17 years not one of those community people had had any counselling, any services, any intervention, nothing, until we came in. A lot of those people had never had anyone in to talk to them and say to them that what happened here was wrong, or anything like that. We've been going to that community now for three and a half years, and we've just been able to attract funding for two dedicated Indigenous mental health workers. We're also been able to develop a model whereby the families of the

---

[11] 'Whitefella way' is the mainstream (western) way, which often has to be followed, even in traditional Indigenous contexts, because the whitefellas rule the country and provide the funding for services

victims run and control the service itself. They founded a Steering Committee and decided that families need to be empowered, and they decided who was going to be employed and who wasn't. They did the interviews and the whole thing and I was just the facilitator of the whole process. If the workers don't do what they say they're going to do, then they're responsible to the family members of the Steering Committee. It's a really unique model and it's a strange model in that it's hard to imagine any mainstream services just saying, 'Yes we're going to let the families have more control over these conditions than we have.' It's fantastic that they've been able to get that sort of outcome and have some form of healing adjustment where there had been an absence of that through the legal system.

In conclusion, how do we move forward? We need to improve diagnosis, prognosis and interventions. We need models of best practice. What's stopping it? We need to work on empirical and cultural validation, replications of models for use with other issues, transferability across different groups, and longitudinal data about what is effective. We need to work on sustainability of results over time, genuine capacity building, and people being responsible for their own issues. Studies show that the success of programs depends upon community self management. We know that, we know the evidence is there.

Reference

Vicary, D., & Westerman, T. (2004). 'That's just the way he is': Some implications of Aboriginal mental health beliefs. *Australian e-Journal for the Advancement of Mental Health, 3*(3).

SEXUAL OFFENDER TREATMENT OF INDIGENOUS AUSTRALIAN MALES: HOW TO KEEP THE PROGRAM RESPONSIVE AND INTERESTING

KATHRYN STONE AND SARAH SUTTON

Abstract

Aboriginal studies and symposia have supported the concept that Aboriginal offenders should have access to assessment and treatment that are culturally and spiritually responsive. However, there has been a general absence of empirical evidence determining the effectiveness of therapeutic rehabilitation programs for Aboriginal people in Australia. This has led to uncertainty in knowing 'what works' for Indigenous people who have committed sexual offences. It is the view of the presenters that cultural factors have a primary role in improving engagement, assessment and sexual offender intervention strategies for Aboriginal people. In South Australia, the Department for Correctional Services provides a 6-9 months Sexual Behaviour Clinic (SBC) for those who have committed sexual offences against adults and children, based on the program provided by Correctional Services of Canada. The primary goal is to assist clients to develop the skills, attitudes and thinking abilities to meet their needs in prosocial ways so they can enjoy productive and enjoyable lives, and so they will no longer commit offences. The presenters also utilise a variety of experiential and flexible practices in order to assist and respond to all participants in the group. This paper provides examples of how such strategies are incorporated into the program in order to improve the responsivity of the program and increase participants' interest.

We work within the Department of Correctional Services (DCS) in South Australia, in a branch called the Rehabilitation Programs Branch, a new Branch that's been up for about two years now. One of us (Sarah) is a Senior Psychologist in the branch and the other (Kathryn) is a Senior Aboriginal Programs Officer. Kathryn's academic background is in the area of politics and gender studies. The Rehabilitations Programs Branch is a multidisciplinary team which includes social work, psychology, nursing and education.

I (Kathryn) am a Kaurna-Narungga woman. Kaurna land is the area across the Adelaide Plains, in which the conference was held, and Narungga is on Yorke Peninsula which is west of Adelaide.

Port Augusta[1] is where the northernmost prison in South Australia is situated, with a significant Aboriginal population. Traditional[2] Aboriginal men and women have to serve their time in that institution, and they come from many different cultural groups from right up north of South Australia. If an Aboriginal person commits a crime within South Australian borders, there is a high likelihood that they will go to that prison. The topic of this paper is a sexual offender treatment program that we facilitated there, called the Keystone program.

For me personally, as a young Aboriginal woman coming into this area and working with my own people and people from other cultural groups, I felt I needed to look back at the way things were done in the past, to understand where my own people have come from and how we are supposed to help people benefit from this western therapeutic model. Something I had to be careful about when I was doing it was not to stereotype Aboriginal people and think, 'Well this is the way it is for everyone'. There's no evidence for a single Aboriginal learning style, but there are some recurrent themes because of the way that traditional life was structured and organised.

Yami Lester is a man who was fortunate to receive traditional learning and lifestyle, and he provides this description of what education was like in traditional society:

> When you travelled along with your fathers or mothers they'd be teaching you. They will tell you stories, not only to do with the land, but also stories about how you should behave. The adults had the children with them all the time and they'd teach them how to talk and how to behave.

Prior to the European invasion young traditional Aboriginal people in Australia had a very intensive organised learning regime, a lot more intensive than what non-Indigenous people are learning within the western

---

[1] About three hours drive north of Adelaide, on the edge of what is often called the 'Outback', the low-rainfall lands in the centre of Australia
[2] In this context 'traditional' refers to peoples who have retained much of their pre-colonial culture. Traditional Indigenous people usually live in Indigenous communities away from cities and major towns

education system in school today. Learning in traditional life is directly related to behaviour, protocol, relationships, community lifestyle, learning from history and tradition. The responsibility for this learning was carried out by family members, specifically mothers and fathers – and the complex kinship system in Aboriginal society means that the sisters of the biological mother are also regarded as mothers, and the brothers of the father are also fathers. That teaching would start in childhood and it would go right through adolescence and into adulthood as well.

One of the main things that I have noticed about the Kaurna people is the level of role modelling that took place in Aboriginal traditional life. Learning was almost always in the presence of other people, because Aboriginal society was an oral culture. Information about the land, kinship, survival and religion was not written down but passed on orally through generations. It's a powerful way to learn, but also all it takes is for one generation for that not to happen and it's all gone. Learning occurred mostly through observing the way that things were done, listening and imitating, and it would be the aim in observing and watching another person to gain absolute mastery of a particular skill. Learning was about trying to achieve the models of perfection that were laid down in the past. Out of thousands and thousands of plant species people had to know which ones could be eaten, which ones were poisonous and which ones had medicinal uses. You had to know the land like the back of your hand so that you could locate water and other precious resources. Learning occurred over a long period of time. It would take many years for a person to build up their strength in a particular area. It wasn't expected that they would have a certain number of sessions and go away qualified.

In the area of learning there can be a conflict between structured learning and spontaneous learning.   The structure of learning was completely different in traditional life to what it is now. There were no eight hour school days, there were no work days, no set number of years spent at university, no set hours to undergo a therapeutic program, no tightly scheduled breaks, no two-hour programs, time slots, and no monitoring by bells and horns to indicate the end of one activity and the start of another. In traditional life learning was largely unstructured and occurred spontaneously within a concrete context. A concept would be taught when the opportunity arose, which made the acquisition of knowledge much more solid and easier to recall in the future.

Since Aboriginal culture is a collective culture, learning occurred in groups, through group processes to benefit the group. It was not an individual process, and in our therapy group we can see the collision of this with individualistic therapeutic models. We have noticed that they seem to make decisions around the best interest of the group rather than the best interest of themselves or even another individual member. Here is one example of this: because the program contains a cognitive behavioural therapy model, we were talking about challenging thoughts and challenging distortions. We found that the guys will avoid doing that, or when they do it, it's in a quite a gentle way because they don't want to create conflicts for the whole group. They're looking at the bigger picture, where the group's headed, and trying to protect that. In a collective culture one's whole identity is defined around relationship to other people: where they sit within that group, whether they are fulfilling their role and protocol within that group. Hence there is a different way of interacting.

Aboriginal people consider the relationships they have with another person, including a therapist, over and above how that other person will perform in an area. For instance, if you're working in a therapeutic relationship with an Aboriginal client, they will assess you and, based on your ability to relate to them personally, they will either respect you on that basis or they will ignore and avoid you. Even their perception of your ability to provide them with what they need is less important than their perception of your ability to relate personally to them. We often see Aboriginal people walking away from services that even they know they desperately need. This is because Aboriginal people belong and identify with person-oriented cultural practices and not information-orientated cultural practices.

Many people seem to have a misconception that Aboriginal people are incapable of abstract thinking, that concepts have to be concrete. I don't believe this is correct. A psychologist will assess abstract thinking by asking questions like, 'In what away are an apple and a banana similar?' If you were to answer that they are all similar because they're both fruit, then you demonstrate that you're capable of abstract thinking. The idea is to find out if a person can think outside the square, contemplate different theories, and be able to reflect on intangible ideas and different ways of doing things. Aboriginal people are good at this. An example of this is being able to travel long distances by the use of mental imagery and find a way to get back home through many different possible routes and tracks if there was flooding or burn-off time[3]. Even young children were able to do this. Also, Aboriginal spirituality is very abstract. The core of our spirituality is The Dreaming, a complex system of beliefs about how the world was created and reasons for being. It's very abstract. It's an

---

[3] It was, and still is in many parts of northern Australia, the custom to burn off tall perennial grass after each Wet Season in order to renew the plants to provide fresh food for animals such as kangaroos which were hunted for food.

intangible concept. You can't touch it or feel it. We find that Aboriginal guys in our group really benefit from abstract activities.

Another example of an abstract concept in Aboriginal culture is the framework for social and emotional health and well being, the holistic model. This is multi faceted and is about Aboriginal people recognising all aspects of a person. When they're coming to our groups, they are coming in with their model of knowledge, which incorporates the emotional, the spiritual, the physical, the cognitive and the social. The CBT (cognitive behavioural therapy) model, which is basically about thoughts and feelings leading to behaviours, really needs to be enhanced when working with Aboriginal people. For instance, someone will come in and we'll ask him questions such as, 'What were you feeling at that time?', and if he says, 'I just didn't feel right', or 'It wasn't me, I wasn't right inside', then it's tempting to think, 'Oh, that's about his inability to articulate'. But it's not. It's a reflection of the incompatibility of the two models.

We realised that the learning environment that we offered from our perspective was unfamiliar to both Aboriginal and non-Aboriginal cultures. I was reading recently the book *Why Do Warriors Lay Down and Die?* in which the concept of culture shock was explored. The book explained that culture shock is experienced by both groups when they're forced to move from their own familiar cultural set-up to another, and they describe it as being "the loss of emotional balance, disorientation and confusion that results from moving from the familiar to the unfamiliar". It sounds really negative, uncomfortable, and we noticed in our groups that when the guys come in they sometimes get anxious and frustrated because they are unsure of what we want from them. They don't know what we're actually asking. We're speaking another language without speaking another language. We've got to remind ourselves all the time that this is a culturally foreign environment for them, in which they don't have all the familiar cues that they're used to. As the result of this discomfort and tension, a couple of things can happen. People may start feeling really bad - get depressed, feel angry. A lot of them start to really question themselves and this can affect their self-esteem. In the case of non-Aboriginal professional workers, they may blame the other cultural group and leave the team or stop working in an Aboriginal community. We often see that non-Aboriginal people are only able to last a really short period of time working in Aboriginal communities. Non-Aboriginal people can grow really frustrated or angry with the process because they are used to accomplishing things at a certain pace and then they go into an environment that's completely different. All the cues are gone, the processes are different, it's completely foreign. Some people feel that they're not able to achieve what they want and just leave in a state of hopelessness.

Following on from the concept of culture shock and the unfamiliarity of a learning environment, it can appear that Aboriginal people don't participate as much as other people, and are then branded as 'Lazy' or 'Un-responsive'. Facilitators need to allow Aboriginal people the time to process information through a reflective learning style, because it's the reflection which is going to allow people time to mull over the concept for themselves, deconstruct what's been spoken about and re-create meanings for themselves personally. Another major thing to remember is that often Aboriginal people won't speak out until they know they've got it right. It's a balance about not putting too much pressure on someone, not making them feel you're backing them into a corner, but also wanting them to develop and grow.

Aboriginal people also face what we call the invisibility syndrome. This describes what happens when facilitators don't have enough time or resources and therefore avoid or ignore Aboriginal culture and diversity in the group. An Aboriginal person in this position will as a result not experience the same degree of social and emotional support that the other participants do, and this can be a consequence of the facilitator avoiding talking about issues or not wanting to explore culturally specific issues. I've heard people say, "I didn't want to offend them, but...". I don't know if I believe that statement. I don't think I could ever offend someone by asking a question, it's all about the way that the question is asked. Not asking questions is about fear, when you've got a group of other people that expect you to be the leader, and you're supposed to know all the answers, and not wanting to come off looking like you don't know things that you may think you are supposed to know.

Another thing that can happen is benevolent racism. This refers to professional staff having a lower set of expectations for Aboriginal clients and people. They think that they're being kind if they 'don't expect too much' from 'them', for instance, 'We know they probably can't keep up, the work won't be to the same standard.' This is incredibly damaging because it sends out the message to everyone that Aboriginal participants have 'a place that they belong to' and they're 'destined for failure'. Aboriginal people are capable of operating at the same level as other participants. Be careful of value judgements, since they lead to further alienation of Aboriginal people within the therapeutic environment.

It's about finding the balance between responding to culturally specific learning styles without setting unrealistic expectations. I personally take the approach that I think it's possible to work with two different cultural identities. Aboriginal people have their traditional identity - they have their identity within the community that's collective - and they have another identity, the western identity in the western world, and those two things, I think, grow and develop independently of each other. We've received feedback from the guys in the group saying, 'We want to feel like we want to come to this program and we don't want you to be taking away Aboriginal culture from us'.

As a non-Aboriginal Psychologist, I (Sarah) would like to conclude by presenting some examples of techniques that we have found useful, since I believe psychologists are not generally taught these principles through their post-graduate training. For example:

- **Slowing down and taking time to connect with the Aboriginal participants rather than doing what I had learnt in my psychology training** - which was following the modules of the particular program and educating group members in the principles of cognitive behavioural therapy;

- **Focusing on understanding the group member's experiences and views** – you know, working out what is really going on for this fella - rather than a simplistic perspective of their problems and their life from reading their file or some psychological report;

- **Building trust with the group members by trying to actively reduce the 'professional' barriers** – having cups of tea with the guys during breaks and having a yarn – Kathryn once said to me that she thought I had built trust with one particular group member as after months and months of one fella being in the program and not speaking much to me, he offered to make me a cup of coffee in a break!! Kathryn said "you're in";

- **In Psychology, I was taught about individuals rather than *interactions* between individuals, and without reference to the cultural and historical context of individuals and groups**. Obviously, this is only part of the story, therefore I need to remember that the behaviours of the Aboriginal participants in a group have been committed in a social, emotional, health, spiritual, historical and political context, and as Tracy Westerman and Yvonne Clark state, these contexts include factors such as oppression, loss of identity, racism, invasion, misunderstandings, stress, trauma, unresolved grief, ill health, displacement and cultural genocide;

- **Providing positive messages** – such as promoting positive states of well-being and encouraging and reminding participants that they are able to make changes in their lives – especially given that they had experienced negative messages throughout their lives, including mistrust of government agencies and negative experiences of institutions and organisations such as Correctional Services;

- **Ensuring transparency in the program** – being straight up when discussing issues and when giving feedback to participants, rather than "*meandering* around issues" as the fellas pick up the body language and see straight through this – feedback I have been given is "Yeah right, just tell me what you *really* mean". However, I've also found that feedback I do give must also be balanced as often the fellas are highly sensitive to challenges – which is not surprising given Aboriginal history in the last 200 years has been shaped largely by government policies;

- **Given that the Aboriginal participants are particularly sensitive to power imbalances, allowing them to make their own changes, rather than imposing my own thoughts on them** – particularly being careful that I am not imposing my westernised beliefs on them as this would obviously just continue the history of oppression that Aboriginal people face. This is similar to the work by Xavier Amador on people with mental illness when he stated that the "doctor knows best approach does not work, because collaboration is a goal not a given";

- **Awareness of my own biases** – I try to monitor and challenge my own values, biases and prejudices and attempt to ensure that these don't affect my interactions with people from other cultural groups;

- **Providing role-modelling of reconciliation by working collaboratively** with my Aboriginal colleague, Kathryn.

Overview of the Sexual Behaviour Clinic

The SBC is one of the programs within the Rehabilitation Programs Branch (RPB) – other programs include the Violence Prevention Program and Correctional Services Core Programs such as Anger Management and Ending Offending with Aboriginal Participants. The RPB is multi disciplinary and includes a manager, Aboriginal programs officers, psychologists, social workers, and evaluation officers.

The SBC has an "open" group format and each participant is involved for 6-9 months duration. It is based on the Correctional Services Canada program. It has a variety of modules such as Emotion Management, Empathy and Victim Awareness, Cognitive Distortions, Intimacy and Relationships, Self-Management, and Deviance.

There are mixed cultures within the groups, of both Aboriginal and non-Aboriginal participants. Our group began in November 2006 and out of ten guys, there were 8 Aboriginal guys. There is also a variety of abilities of the participants, for example literacy levels and concentration

Therapeutic Techniques that can assist in Building Cultural Responsivity

Before talking about some of these techniques, I want to first quickly mention something that Bobbie Sykes talks about and that is the caution that must be used when professionals learn a little about Aboriginal society and then use this knowledge to make decisions on behalf of Aboriginal people. I want to make it clear that although these are some tools that we have found effective, they are of course only just that and therefore may or may not be useful to other service providers.

Dinner table: with other group members, participants act out their life, with the family sitting around the dinner table. This is an easier, non-threatening way to demonstrate the factors which have influenced them rather than having to verbalise this to other group members.

Attachment continuum: placing cards on the floor reflecting a secure attachment style and three non-secure (such as preoccupied, fearful and dismissive) and asking participants to walk over to the one that reflects their different relationships with a variety of people such as their mother, father, the victim of their offence, etc.

What would you be if....: Asking each participant to say what all other group members would be if they were a .... Car, Flower, Era in time, Building, Foreign country, etc. For example, Kathryn might describe me as a cactus, or something like that. Basically, it is a useful way to build trust between group members and to practice giving feedback to others.

Role plays: for example we role-play different communication styles such as aggressiveness, assertiveness and being passive. We also video tape these role-plays and play them back and we watch as they give each other feedback. For example, we find that often the guys think that they're acting assertively, but it is actually aggressive. We do the same at the conclusion of the Empathy module. For example, the fella plays the role of their own victim in order to demonstrate whether they can imagine what their victim must have felt and experienced as a result of the offence.

Talking stick: sometimes in group we use this for the person who is speaking and only the person with the stick can speak. For example, we use this during 'check-in', where each person talks about how they're going and whether they have any issues. This sometimes help the group run smoother as it reduces people talking over other people, and I think this also assists in giving each group member power and control even if it is in only a small way. Also, when group members enter the program, we initially conduct the check-in, but over time we give the group members increased responsibility and they run the check-in.

30 best or worst seconds of their life: they stand in a position as though it is a still camera snapshot of that part of their lives, and everyone else has to try to guess what it reflects. We've found this can be less threatening than telling the story, and it also encourages additional discussion about feelings, body language, and many other concepts learnt in the program.

The good the bad and the ugly: basically, it is working out three ways to solve a problem, with ugly being the worst possible way that you could act.

Collages: as part of the program, we ask the guys to present an autobiography of their life, but in order to be flexible they can either write it down or use paints and canvases and magazines to create something which represents them and their life.

Obstacle course: this involves partnering up. One member of the pair is blindfolded, and their partner has to somehow get them across the room around or over various obstacles without touching them but using only words, such as 'turn left', 'two steps forward', and so on.

Masks: near the beginning of the program, we show the group members different face mask pictures. We explain to them that everyone has masks that they use with different people or in different settings: such as the joker who often clowns around and has trouble being serious, the tough guy who doesn't speak up much in group or directs the conversations, or the protector/helper who often colludes or inappropriately supports other group members. Once everyone has an understanding about the different masks, if we later notice people using these masks during a discussion or activity in the group program, we can openly challenge or question them about this, without being confrontational or threatening.

Pass Clap: this is a good activity to recognise and improve non-verbal behaviour, not to mention coordination. We all stand in a circle and one person starts the clap, and it is passed between the group members without using words and getting faster and faster. Can then add two claps going at once and it is hilarious.

Emotion Bingo: (although it is not really bingo − except that each person has a sheet of paper). On the paper there are printed a range of different emotions each with a corresponding cartoon face representing

that emotion.   We go around the circle and each person must pick a
different emotion and use it in a sentence. For example, 'I feel….. anxious
…. when I have to give presentations to other people'. The person that is
able to think of the most emotions is the winner. Obviously it is a good
way to build their emotional vocabulary, and to improve their recognition
of particular emotions.

Finally, what we do after each activity is ask the group why they think
we did it, and they are usually pretty good at identifying the reasons. So
they are not just one-dimensional activities that we do for fun, but rather
they are useful in many different ways to illustrate the concepts of the
program and build group trust and cohesion.

References

Amador, X. (2006). I am not sick, I don't need help! Research on poor
     insight and how we can help. Adelaide: Mental Illness Fellowship of
     Australia Presentation, September 2006.
Bergman, J., & Hewish, S. (2003). *Challenging Experience.* Oklahoma:
     Woods 'n Barnes.
Berndt, R.,   & Berndt, C. (1996). *The world of the first Australians,
     Aboriginal traditional life: Past and present.* Melbourne: McPherson's
     Printing Group.
Clark, Y. (2000). The Construction of Aboriginal Identity in People
     Separated from Their Families, Community, and Culture: Pieces of a
     Jigsaw. *Australian Psychologist, 35*(2), 150-157.
Courtin, R. (2007). Becoming your own therapist. *Presentation at the
     Happiness and its Causes Conference,* June 2007, Sydney.
Dudgeon, P., & Pickett, H. (2000). Psychology and Reconciliation:
     Australian Perspectives. *Australian Psychologist, 35 (2)*, 82-87.
Keyes, C. L. M. (2007).   Promoting and protecting mental health as
     flourishing: A complementary strategy for improving national mental
     health. *American Psychologist, 62,* 95-108.
Marshall, W., Anderson, D., & Fernandez, Y. (1999).   *Cognitive
     behavioural treatment of sexual offenders.* Chichester: Wiley.
Mattingley, C., & Hampton, K. (Eds.) (1988). *Survival in or own land.*
     NSW: Hodder & Stoughton.
Norton, A. (2007). Aboriginal Victim Awareness Program. *This Week in
     Corrections, Winter Edition 2007,* Department for Correctional
     Services, South Australia.

South Australian Education Department (1989). *The Kaurna people: Aboriginal people of the Adelaide Plains: An Aboriginal studies course for secondary students in years 8 – 10*. Adelaide: Publications Branch.

Sykes, B. (1978). White doctors and black women. *New Doctor, 8,* 33–35.

Trudgen, R. (2000). *Why warriors lay down and die*. NT: Aboriginal Resource and Development Services Incorporated.

Vicary, D., & Westerman, T. (2004). That's just the way he is: Some implications of Aboriginal mental health beliefs. *Australian e-Journal for the Advancement of Mental Health, 3(3)*, 1-10.

Wessels, M. G., & Bretherton, D. (2000). Psychological Reconciliation: National and International Perspectives. *Australian Psychologist, 35*(2), 100-108.

DEVELOPING A STRUCTURED AND APPROPRIATE PROGRAM TO SUPPORT PARENTS WHO HAVE HAD THEIR ABORIGINAL CHILDREN REMOVED BY THE STATE AND THE PROCESS THAT THEY NEED TO ENGAGE IN TO HAVE THEIR CHILDREN RETURNED

LISA WHITE, JOYLENE WARREN AND TRISH HICKEY

We would like to acknowledge the traditional owners of the land on which the conference was held, the Kaurna people. One of us (Joylene) is from the far west coast of South Australia. On my mother's side I am from the Mirning people and Narrunggar from my father's side[1].

AFSS (Aboriginal Family Support Services) was established in 1978 as an Aboriginal Child Care Agency, involved in matters relating to Aboriginal child welfare. There was a name change in 1998 to Aboriginal Family Support Services, which is an Indigenous community-based organisation. The programme that we work in is Family Care, which is about re-unification. We work alongside birth parents who have had children removed. We receive a referral from Families SA[2] and we support parents with the re-unification journey. This may also involve working with extended family members, foster parents, Families SA and other relevant agencies in the community.

This paper is about cultural considerations. When we've been engaging with Aboriginal families the issues are health, welfare, family, shame, grief and loss, and injustices. We need to develop a framework of

---

[1] Mirning country is in the southern part of the Nullarbor Plain which is located north of the coast spanning far eastern Western Australia and far western South Australia. Narrunggar country covers Yorke Pensinsula in South Australia

[2] The South Australian Government organisation that looks after the needs of families

understanding of the culture of Aboriginal people, families and the
communities. We also need to develop a culturally appropriate framework
for developing our services, particularly engaging Aboriginal families.
What could be considered appropriate and of value in the mainstream
professional setting may have a different or no meaning for Aboriginal
people.

Health and welfare is a collective experience in Aboriginal cultures
and not an individual concept. It includes the wellbeing of wider family
members. Health and welfare includes issues such as loss, grief and
socioeconomic factors, such as medical, housing, employment, social
work and so on. Most Aboriginal people do not see particular issues as
separate from all other things happening in their lives. However,
professionals and agencies often treat individual issues separately and
work against the holistic needs of the Aboriginal people. For example, in
South Australian Aboriginal communities, there are five different health
welfare programs dealing with the needs of the Indigenous children and
families, and at any one given time five different workers can and will
interface with a particular family for different issues. In this setting
opportunities to work effectively for family wellbeing are impeded as the
family is locked into separate issues with separate solutions.

The Aboriginal approach to the desertion of family and community
breakdown is about healing and rebuilding services to function in a
supportive, holistic capacity, that is, health and welfare cannot be
separated. Mainstream services generally slot issues into separate
compartments and pay attention only to the individual. Aboriginal people
are not divorced from their kinship system and any intervention needs to
reflect that.

The next issue is about families. Families are of central importance in
Aboriginal people's lives and its meaning differs from a non-Aboriginal
society's definition. Aboriginal children float around amongst the whole
family network - among aunties, grandparents, older cousins - and get
cared for much more on a collective basis. Aboriginal children get well
looked after and it is a good way of sharing in the care of children for
developing a strong sense of kin and extended family network, duty and
responsibilities. If we respect the Aboriginal community care philosophy
we accept that Aboriginal children are best cared for within their family
network.

An individual person's health is also linked with the wellbeing, unity
and wholeness of the family. If a family member is isolated from the
family network, then the Aboriginal person is emotionally and spiritually
deflated. It is important to keep this in mind when providing a healing

approach to an Aboriginal person. While one-to-one counselling is sometimes appropriate there is a strong feeling that Aboriginal people need to receive culturally appropriate healing practices. Professional practitioners need to recognise the prime importance of collective family health, and meetings have to have the involvement of elders, seniors, and other family members to form the basis of any intervention.

Non-Aboriginal people have some difficulty in understanding the concept of shame, but recognise that it does impact powerfully upon the lives of Aboriginal people. Shame can be described as embarrassment and humiliation. The current practices of mainstream services are, we feel, shaming, providing a barrier to especially needed services or to participation more fully in the wider society - for example, to sitting down and talking about personal issues. There is a real reluctance for Aboriginal people to talk about their problems to non-Aboriginal people, because it might add to already existing violence or racist views and could widen the gap between black and white Australians. Also, Aboriginal people need other Aboriginal people to share their stories with because Aboriginal people are unwilling to place themselves in the position of putting down their own people in the company of others. This could be perceived as disloyal to the Aboriginal cause.

Additionally, for Aboriginal people sharing deep and personal traumatic information with non-Aboriginal people is an uncomfortable experience. Aboriginal people need to have the support of other Aboriginal people to validate their experiences, otherwise it is seen as a shame job. We often hear other Aboriginal people saying, 'Hey, that's a real shame job.' That's how Aboriginal people communicate with each other about these shames.

Grief and loss are a constant presence in Aboriginal people's lives in a way that is usually incomprehensible to most non-Aboriginal people. This grief and loss is from a variety of factors, including a long history of different issues and genocide, the loss of a lot of children, deaths in custody, ill health, suicide, high infant mortality rates and very short life spans, generally 20 years less that the national average. Many Aboriginal people are dying young. Many Aboriginal people have mental issues normally associated with old age. This usually results from substance abuse. Poverty, alcoholism, poor health, etc are connected to past injustices. However, the naming of injustices is a key entry point and not always an exit point as a solution to our problems. The central aspect is to find out from Aboriginal people about the strength and knowledge that have evolved enabling Aboriginal people to survive in the face of overwhelming injustices.

One of the main effects of colonisation has been to step on Aboriginal people from a sense of belief in their inferiority. People draw upon a variety of strengths and knowledge and it forces us to hold our families together. For example: self pride, determination and hope, turning negatives into positives, family connections, having respect for others, returning to homelands, sharing stories, Aboriginal ways and knowledge, and so forth.

Don't assume.   Don't assume that non-Aboriginal professional practitioners don't have to take any responsibilities for Aboriginal people at all. For example, take the hospital situation: if Aboriginal patients are about to leave, see if you can organise transport home, or ask what they're here for and how you may be able to help.

Don't assume that Aboriginal people, Aboriginal culture and values are the same as the dominant white psyche. Recognise the diversity of Aboriginal people and communities.   For example, don't ask the Aboriginal person to be the expert on all Aboriginal issues. Don't assume that you know all Aboriginal people and you can make decisions on their behalf, even when you have known Aboriginal people for quite a while. Also, don't assume that because you are white and you have a qualification and they are a particular age or gender that you can appropriately engage with an Aboriginal man or a woman. There are particular customs and practices in Aboriginal culture which require strictly gender appropriate responses.

Recognise that Aboriginal people have an identity and a culture which is characteristic. Recognise each Aboriginal person as an individual, but also as a part of an existing extensive family system. Recognise their strong traditional concepts, which maintain a very strong influence on contemporary culture. Recognise that Aboriginal people from all over Australia have different cultures. That is diversity. Recognise that 200 plus years of oppression by the dominant white society has affected the attitudes and the actions of Aboriginal people today. Aboriginal people today need opportunities to publicly name these injustices that they have experienced. Recognise that some Aboriginal people, for example, metro/urban Aboriginals, have a contemporary culture and they need to get access to their traditional culture. However, the more remote the areas, the more prevalent the Aboriginal traditional law and customs are practised. Recognise that the Western economic system has resulted in hardship for most Aboriginal people in the areas of income, health, hygiene, employment and education.

We want now to tell the story of a fella called Brian. We told him that we were going to tell everybody the story of our service. Brian had been unified with his children and it was a really good story so we asked him if we could share it. We said that we would not use his name. He said, "Use my name. I want to share this story and tell our men to stand up as men." This is Brian's story.

He's a 42 year-old man living in metropolitan Adelaide. He had his two children removed, a boy who was three years old and a girl who was two years old, through issues around domestic violence. What we set about doing was engaging with Brian. We got to know that Brian had very strong links with his family, very strong links with his mother and father. He played a really major part in their life and we also got to know that Brian was very angry, very angry at the services that were supposed to help him, and he had a lack of clarity around what he had to do to get his children back. At AFSS, we worked with Families SA in meaningful ways so that we could all work together towards reunification of Brian with his children, and that is often a really hard thing. It sounds simple, but it's actually very hard, because they (Families SA) are the people that have removed their children.

A major part of our role is to sit at quarterly review meetings and make sure that the conditions of the Court Order which Families SA enact are stated really clearly and it's clear what the guys are asked to do. We work with them so that they understand clearly what they have to do. And also it's about fear and we try to get them to see that it can be done in a way that's possible and that can be achieved. The major thing with Brian was that he didn't have that clarity. He had been involved in services for quite a while prior. Brian came into our service eight months ago and he didn't have that clarity at all. One-on-one counselling is asked for, and reports in regard to that relationship are passed back to Families SA and back to the Court, and especially with Brian that was a hard thing to try and organise. He is a man who is completely connected to family. He's got a really strong head, a very strong cultural link.

He really loved his kids, absolutely. When he came in he was so angry, but he could just work through that because he's just driven to get his children back, absolutely driven. When the benchmarks were changing, time and time again, both he and his mother, although they were so angry, confirmed that they would keep persevering because they wanted the children back. They are their children and they're part of their family. In the end AFSS did engage a long-term counsellor because that was something that couldn't be re-negotiated. There was a counselling agency in Adelaide that worked two ways[3], with an Aboriginal man and a non-

---

[3] Working 'two ways' or 'both ways' are terms commonly used in Indigenous contexts to refer to using both Western and Indigenous ways of doing things

Aboriginal social worker working together. They were able to engage with Brian in a way that worked for him and they did have a meaningful relationship that could be followed through, and I think it showed in the time that we worked with Brian.

What we notice a lot with our clients that we engage with in re-unification is that there will be Court Orders that come back that specify that they want to see certain criteria met before children are re-united with their parents, and what we often see is the most incredibly difficult benchmark that people have to meet. It's just so difficult to be able to really put into practice and bring about the kind of changes that they want to see so that kids can go back, and that's where our role mainly lies. It's about trying to make these criteria that the Court Orders are setting down a little bit more realistic. It's incredibly hard because our clients have got the most difficult circumstances. For example, sometimes it might be basic needs that need to be met. Re-unification includes these huge hurdles that our clients need to overcome, and it makes it really, really difficult, because from a cultural perspective it's just so far away from where people are at with these benchmarks that are set, which are assessments made by non-Aboriginal social workers.

With Brian we did see some really significant changes. He went from a place of being very very angry in regard to engagement with services that were there to support and to work with him. He moved to a psychological space where he used his anger to engage, so he could get to look after his kids. And he did, he got his children back full-time a month ago and that was after seven months of working with us.

A very common thing that we see in assessments that come out of the welfare system is that assessments are often made using a non-strength perspective, but if you can look at the same person using a strength perspective to do an assessment you get a completely different picture. The use of the strength perspective really advocates a lot on the client's behalf when it comes to psychological reports. Psychological reports are very powerful, they have profound impact on people's lives. In Brian's case his strength perspective was that he had a really, really strong family connection. He had support to call on at any time.

What this is about is that you can look at a particular time-frame or time span in a person's life. When we receive the referral we may work with clients for a long term, maybe over twelve months, and you can look at various events that have happened in that person's life. If you view them from a negative perspective they can be very sensationalistic and very damning and very controversial. If you use a strength perspective, you can actually unpack some of those crises and actually see extraordinary acts of courage, acts of perseverance where people have just been taken to the end of their rope and gone beyond the end of their rope and they've still hung in there, and you see how you can get two completely opposite perspectives. It's like looking at a situation from a negative perspective and then looking at that same situation from a positive perspective.

In closing, preparedness to learn about Aboriginal cultural aspects - for example, values, knowledge, beliefs, customs, relationships and being open to different meanings for Aboriginal people about health, family, loss, grief, and caring - are essential in developing an effective rapport and intervention that will enable you to work with Aboriginal families in a culturally sensitive manner.

REFLECTING ON KOORI COMMUNITY-DIRECTED HEALTH PROMOTION IN THE GOULBURN VALLEY

RACHEL REILLY, JOYCE DOYLE, BRAD FIREBRACE, DENISE MORGAN-BULLED, MARGARET CARGO AND KEVIN ROWLEY

Abstract

This paper describes a health promotion program conducted within the Koori community of the Goulburn-Murray region of northern Victoria, Australia. The state-funded program was community-directed and involved university researchers in a supportive role. The program comprised a number of separate but related activities devised and carried out within a framework derived from community psychology and participatory action research, with the aim of promoting nutrition and physical exercise. Although the activities did not always meet all their intended aims and problems arose with the quantitative evaluation of some activities, results of qualitative and ecological evaluations indicated that they made a valuable and sometimes unexpected contribution to health promotion in the community. Principles of participation and collaboration were central to the program's success. Challenges and benefits of working in genuine partnership are discussed.

Introduction

The Goulburn Valley in northern central Victoria is known as the state's food bowl, in reference to the large number of agricultural industries the region supports (Feehan, 2007). The richness of the land meant that following European migration to the area, land was highly sought after for farming and from the mid-1800s, Aboriginal people were forced, indiscriminately and on a large-scale, to relocate from their traditional lands to large, centralised communities or missions (Anderson, 1988; Kettle, 1991a, 1991b). The disruption to social structures, cultural knowledge and health systems that stemmed from this era had a devastating effect on the wellbeing of communities, who were already vulnerable from the introduction of previously unknown diseases and the loss of community members through the violence and massacres that occurred during the aggressive invasion of the Europeans (Saggers & Gray, 1991).

Aboriginal resistance to the destruction of their communities has been relentless. The Aboriginal Community Controlled Organisations (ACCOs) now existing in the Goulburn-Murray region are the legacy of early resistance efforts. These organisations continue to advocate for the empowerment and promotion of health, defined in its broadest sense, for the Aboriginal population of the region, which constitutes the largest Aboriginal population in Victoria outside of Melbourne. The health promotion activities described here were devised as a partnership between three key ACCOs and university researchers. A brief description of each of the partner organisations is included in Table 1.

The health promotion program was devised within a framework that acknowledges social and emotional determinants of health, including those found to be of specific importance to this community, including history, relationship with mainstream, connectedness and a sense of community and individual control (Reilly, 2005). In designing the project, the researchers and community project workers committed to work in genuine partnership and adhere to the values outlined in the National Health and Medical Research Council's Guidelines for Ethical Conduct in Aboriginal and Torres Strait Islander Health Research (2003, Figure 1).

The program is part of a broader, ongoing program of collaborative work conducted under the banner of the Heart Health Project (The Heart Health Project Steering Committee, 2007). Early findings from cardiovascular risk-factor screening indicated that the health behaviour of community members relating to diet and physical exercise were generally not in line with the national guidelines (Australian Government Department of Health and Ageing, 1999; National Health and Medical Research Council, 2003a, 2006). A key recommendation from this work was to develop community-directed, culturally-aligned programs to promote improvements in nutrition and physical exercise (Reilly, Doyle, & Rowley, 2007; The Heart Health Project Steering Committee, 2007).

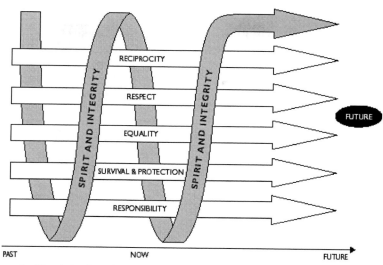

Figure 1: Aboriginal and Torres Strait Islander Peoples Values Relevant to Health Research Ethics (National Health and Medical Research Council, 2003b, p.9).

The program sought to address these recommendations by pursuing two aims. The first was to evaluate afore mentioned nutrition and physical activity guidelines from the perspective of Koori community members with a view to creating guidelines with relevance to the specific social and cultural context of the community. The second, more general aim was to devise relevant health promotion interventions to improve nutrition and fitness. An over-arching objective of the program was to develop the capacity of local Koori researchers to carry out and evaluate health promotion interventions (Reilly et al., 2007).

Table 1: The Partner Organisations

Rumbalara Aboriginal co-operative	The Rumbalara Aboriginal Cooperative is a Community-Controlled organisation responsible for programs relating to cultural heritage, health, housing, education and justice issues in the Greater Goulburn Valley, Hume and Binjurru Regions. Rumbalara co-op was established as a community centre in the early 1970s. The site had previously been a settlement for Aboriginal people leaving the Cummeragunja Mission Station in the 1940s (Rumbalara Aboriginal Cooperative, 2003)
Rumbalara Football Netball Club	The Rumbalara Football Netball Club (RFNC) was officially launched in March 1997. The club's vision focuses jointly on sport and wellbeing: "to be one of Australia's best regional sporting clubs and a leader in promoting community well being." It aims to "…be consistently successful at football and netball, provide a place for people to connect and use additional resources and partnerships to develop the health, education and personal development outcomes our members need" (Newton, 2004, p.1). Health promotion has been an important aspect of the club's activities since its inception, in particular through an ongoing "Health Lifestyles Program."
Viney Morgan Aboriginal Medical Service	The Viney Morgan Aboriginal Medical Service (AMS) is the primary community-controlled health organisation in the relatively geographically isolated Aboriginal township of Cummeragunja, located on the NSW side of the Murray River, approximately 60km north-west of Shepparton. The Viney Morgan Aboriginal Medical Service (AMS) itself was opened in 1988 as a result of lobbying by community members. The predominant objectives of the AMS are to provide an accessible source of health support and referral for medical services. However, it also provides services related to youth, education programs and housing as well as providing emergency relief to residents in need.

Onemda VicHealth Koori Health Unit	This multidisciplinary unit is situated within the School of Population Health at the University of Melbourne. The unit aims to foster an academic environment that values Aboriginal knowledges and methodologies, and supports ethical practice and Aboriginal self-determination through its work in research, community development and teaching.

Table 2: Components of the Koori Community Directed Health Promotion Program

Activity	Description	Outcomes
Researcher Training	Three Koori community members attending a training course on Aboriginal Health Promotion at Queensland University of Technology.	Participants reported: - Many problems are common to vastly different community settings - Greater awareness of their own expertise. - Ideas for health promotion activities using this expertise.
Hungry for Victory	A program targeting U/14 and U/17 footballers at RFNC. Participants attended nutrition education sessions, were provided with healthy breakfasts before games and were involved in mentoring.	- 40 participants overall, netballers did not participate until the end of the season for unrelated reasons. - 4 nutrition workshops were well attended. - Coaches reported greater confidence in players and observed greater connectedness between age-groups in the club and with other clubs due to provided visitors with breakfast.

Activity	Description	Outcomes
Focus Groups	To address the first aim of the program, a series of four focus groups were conducted with a cross-section of community members to evaluate the guidelines.	- Knowledge of the recommended nutrition and exercise was not seen as a major barrier to positive health behaviours. Instead, participants described a lack of food security as the primary concern. - Suggestions arising included developing a community garden, a Koori cook-book and an educational video.
Cummeragunja Women's Wellbeing Group	A group which was formed following advocacy by the women themselves, who did not wish to participate in a focus group, but instead suggested forming an essentially social group in which health issues could be discussed. A four-week pilot is now an ongoing program run by the women.	- An average of 25 participants each group. - In early groups facilitators observed a high level of motivation for exercise and friendly rivalry.
Canteen Fruit-share project	Food provided to the canteen was analysed using the 'store-turnover method' (Lee, O'Dea, & Matthews, 1994) over the 2005 and 2006 seasons.	- The variety of fruit and vegetables supplied by the canteen increased. - Pies, pasties and sausage rolls decreased by a third. - Vitamin content of foods sold increased significantly.

Activity	Description	Outcomes
10-Week Body Challenge	Employees from the Rumbalara Aboriginal Co-operative used pedometers to ensure they walked 10,000 steps per day for ten weeks as part of the 10-Week Body Challenge.	- 20 participants completed the program, no drop-out. - They reported a high degree of satisfaction with the program - The program is likely to be repeated.

Methods and Results

The program comprised a number of different activities devised within a participatory action research framework. Within this framework, program development proceeded in iterative cycles of reflection and action (Reilly et al., 2007; Stringer & Genat, 2004). Community members were encouraged and supported in developing skills enabling them to take control of the research process with the ultimate goal promoting change in the direction desired by the community (Kidd & Kral, 2005; Stringer & Genat, 2004). The project was overseen by a steering committee comprising senior community and university representatives, and was bound by an earlier memorandum of understanding between participating organisations that stipulated rules for community ownership and storage of data (Reilly et al., 2007; The Heart Health Project Steering Committee, 2007). University researchers played a supportive role in the development of activities, providing mentoring through regular meetings, and technical assistance when required. They also took part in evaluating and report writing. The activities implemented were described elsewhere (Reilly et al., 2007) and summarised briefly in Table 2.

Joyce Doyle: "The 'Hungry for Victory' programme was the first part of actually training people within the community and three of us went to Brisbane and we started nutrition training at university there. We worked on what might work back into the community and asked for the input of the Koori people[1], who had the ideas while we had the academic knowledge. The Committee of the Football Netball Club sat there with us

---

[1] The term Koori refers to the Indigenous peoples of Victoria and most of New South Wales apart from the north-east.

and then the three with the training worked on important programs that we needed to take back.   We developed the 'Hungry for Victory Programme' for the Rumbalara Football Netball Club and worked with the Under 17 young boys that play football[2]. We did want to work with the young netballers, but we didn't have the resources to do that.

"We called it the 'Hungry for Victory Programme' because for the young boys playing football it was important for them to win, and because they're in a sports club they're out there on show and get very competitive. We used it as a subtle way of saying, 'Well, let's look at nutrition, and let's look at exercise' and that way we hoped to make some changes in their awareness. We subtly did that without them realising what was actually happening, instead the whole focus was on messages like, 'We need to win a game guys, come on, you need to win this and this is how you've got to do it. You've got to bulk yourself up, you've got to look at carbs[3], and you've got to look at not smoking, not drinking.' There was a whole range of things that we brought in, and we used people throughout the club to reinforce that, and even their coaches and the managers that worked with them were on board with it.   There was a whole group of people that worked in together trying to work with the under 17s. They're a hard bunch of kids to work with, because they've already got set in their minds that when they've got a few dollars they'll go and spend it on something they want to buy or they'll eat at somebody else's house, and they don't think about what it is they're actually putting into their tummies or what they're doing the night before they play the game the next day. We brought that to the surface and worked with that.

We gave them their own t-shirts, so they were there parading around when they were training in their own t-shirts, and the rest of the groups – there are five teams who belong to the Footy Club - were saying, 'Well, what's happened here with this Under 17s programme? You know, what are these t-shirts for?" It created conversation, and then it created an awareness of, 'Oh, yeah, the Hungry for Victory Programme'. We looked at nutrition and exercise, and from that a breakfast programme was developed for the very senior players. Of the young ones who played at 9:15 in the morning in the fog, some never even had a breakfast. The 'Hungry for Victory Programme' aimed to try and get those young children to have some sort of breakfast; if not, when they had their break they were encouraged to eat something before they went back on. We did

---

[2] In Australia 'football' commonly refers to Australian Rules football, a game quite different to soccer.
[3] Carbohydrates

that throughout the season and they became, not a one-to-one mentor but a group of mentors for each other just by being in the under 17s group.

"We had water bottles and encouraged water to be carried around. We invited in a nutrition speaker. We also invited them to have a three course meal the night before, in which we were bulking them up for the game the next day. We talked about what we were eating and why we were eating it and how they would perform the next day, and when they came off the field after that game and said they felt much better, they had more energy. And although they wouldn't say it out loud, they were aware of what was actually happening here. The juniors in the programme were looking up to the seniors, who had the focus of the club on them, because they were the backbone to the whole Football and Netball Club. If they weren't winning and they weren't fit and they weren't well, then the whole Football Club wasn't well. The juniors were looking up to the seniors and saying, 'We're doing this, you know, what are you doing?', which was really a good outcome.

"Later we brought together some focus groups to look at nutrition and what it meant to our whole community in the area in which we work. We looked at a range of people from a young age to an older age. We talked about things like, 'What in the food chain do you understand? What does that mean to you?' There were a lot of things that came out of the discussions, and of course budget was always talked about because there was not enough money to work with.

"The community we're referring to is Cummeragunja. It's rather isolated, about 40 minutes drive from Shepparton[4], and it's right on the Murray River. There's always a border issue there because it's just in New South Wales, but also it is serviced by Victoria. We were asked to do some work with the women that were isolated and not able to get out, who had no transport and there was nothing to do there. We didn't want to do focus groups there, because they said, 'We don't want to talk about those, you know, health stuff or anything like that. We just want women to talk and whatever comes out is how we will take it from there.' It was just amazing how when the women actually sat down they said, 'We want to know about how to be healthy, we want to know how to stay fit, we want to know how to make a budget meal if we've only got a few things in the cupboard.' So they put those things on the table themselves and we never even stated that to them; they did it for themselves. So they did want to know about it, but they wanted to take control and do it themselves.

---

[4] Shepparton is in central Victoria

"We worked with them for four or five weeks. We got a small walking group going; we gave them a pedometer each and they started to test their walking, their steps, and we looked at the 10,000 Steps Programme and we worked with that. That was really successful. They came from everywhere to get one of those. They thought they were very special getting one of those, and we tried to monitor that. And we did health checks. They asked for health checks. They wanted their blood pressure, they wanted their BMIs, they wanted their height, their weight, and they wanted basic little diets given to them telling them how they can make changes for themselves. We worked with setting up a tray of food on display and talked about the choices they could make between eating some veggies or more hot chips. They were really interested and they learnt a lot from that.

"However, then it came Christmas time and it sort of died down then, but I believe that they've got some dollars to run it again next year. So hopefully it will grow from there and then onto the next stage."

Evaluation and Reflection

A lack of suitable resources for formal, systematic quantitative evaluation processes for this program limits our ability to demonstrate the effectiveness of the programs using conventional measures. Redressing this limitation through the development of culturally acceptable evaluation tools and processes is a priority for future research in this community. For some activities, such as the Hungry for Victory programme, planned evaluation processes using questionnaires measuring health behaviour and attitudes were not completed because the survey itself was unpopular (Reilly et al., 2007). However, project participants and facilitators provided qualitative feedback via surveys and interviews that has provided information about the barriers and facilitators of success of the activities. Surveys were adapted from an 'ecological analysis' methodology which assumes that the degree to which a health promotion program accesses multiple levels of social systems within a community determines its effectiveness (Richard, Potvin, Kishchuk, Prlic, & Green, 1995).

The activities outlined above were designed by local community members for their local context and as such it may not be possible to generalise findings to other communities. On the other hand, given the commonality of underlying health problems that led to the need for the program, there may be principles or activities that are useful in other communities. The survey data collected indicated that most activities were perceived by facilitators as meeting many of their planned objectives. The majority of activities were considered to be organised within a cultural framework with some western influence. None were seen as driven purely by a western model. Factors that were identified as barriers or facilitators to implementation by participants and facilitators are displayed in Figures 2 and 3 (the numbers on the y axis refer to the number of responses – some factors were mentioned more than once by some people).

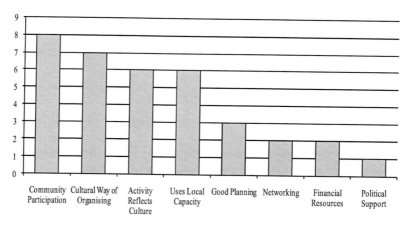

Figure 2: Facilitators of Implementation of Activities as Rated by Project Workers

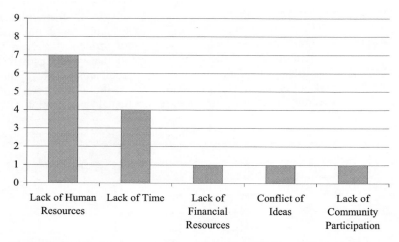

Figure 3: Barriers to success of activities as rated by project workers

Results indicate that a lack of time and lack of human resources were the main barriers to implementation. This may reflect the fact that skilled workers in the community are coping with a large number of different and sometimes competing responsibilities. It's also been previously documented that skilled workers are carrying a greater burden of stress, reflected in higher rates of depression, relative to the broader Koori community (McKendrick & Charles, 2001). Success was perceived as relying most strongly on a cultural way of organising activities, the utilisation of local capacity, and community participation.

Overall, the outcomes from the projects were positive and sometimes unexpected in that even where activities did not meet all their planned objectives, they resulted in information that will be used by community members in the next phase of activity development. For example, the focus groups did not result in a new set of Koori guidelines, but they did allow other arguably more relevant barriers to healthy eating to be identified, and generated some potential solutions that are now being considered by community leaders, such as a community vegetable garden.

In general, the more aligned with community values the activities were, the more successful they were. Furthermore, it has been argued that within this series of activities, those that were most aligned with participatory action research principles in their design have resulted in the most sustainable outcomes, which provides support for participatory approaches to health promotion (Reilly et al., 2007). The Cummeragunja

Women's Wellbeing Group, for example, aligns strongly with participatory principles - it began as a result of negotiation and advocacy by the participants on their own behalf, and involves the women discussing health-related issues, devising interventions and reflecting on them in a cultural and social context that is acceptable to them. Following their experience of the four-week pilot program, the participants advocated for and have received further funding to continue the program.

Conclusion

Despite the lack of systematic data allowing a formal evaluation, the health promotion interventions described here offer support for collaborative, participatory approaches to research and health promotion with Aboriginal communities. Where activities were devised by community members and conducted in a way that reflected community values and respected social processes, the outcome was perceived to be of greater benefit than in those situations where either the problem or solution were defined or imposed by those outside the community (Reilly et al., 2007). The intention at the outset was that control should be wholly in the hands of community members. In practice, there was ongoing communication and negotiation between community participants, university researchers and the funding body. Thus it should be acknowledged that the transfer of power was not absolute, which is unsurprising given the nature of two well-established institutions and a relatively small community group. Nonetheless, participatory action research and other approaches with a focus on participation and capacity exchange provide a framework within which communities can be empowered to advocate on their own behalf to understand and improve their health, and universities and funding bodies can respond to community needs as partners, rather than leaders in the process.

Acknowledgements

We thank The Heart Health Project Steering Committee: Paul Briggs (Rumbalara Football Netball Club), Sharon Charles (Rumbalara Aboriginal Co-operative), Julie Calleja, Rochelle Patten (Viney Morgan Aboriginal Medical Service), Sharon Lawrence, Roland Watson, Jane Winter (Department of Human Services Victoria). This work was funded by the Department of Human Services Victoria Public Health Research scheme. RR is supported by an NHMRC Program Grant (#320860). KR was a VicHealth Public Health Research Fellow. Thanks to Rob Ranzijn for editorial assistance.

References

Anderson, I. (1988). *Koorie Health in Koorie Hands: An Orientation Manual in Aboriginal Health for Health Care Providers.* Melbourne: Koorie Health Unit, Health Department Victoria.

Australian Government Department of Health and Ageing. (1999). *An Active Way to Better Health: Physical Activity Guidelines for Australian Adults.* Canberra: Australian Government Department of Health and Ageing.

Feehan, P. (2007). *Goulburn-Broken River.* Retrieved 27th June, 2007, from http://mail.toolkit.net.au/focus_catchments/goulburnriver.html

Kettle, E. S. (1991a). *Health Services in the Northern Territory: A History 1824-1970 Vol 2* (Vol. 2). Darwin: Australian National University.

—. (1991b). *Health Services in the Northern Territory: A history 1824-1970 Vol. 1* (Vol. 1). Darwin: Australian National University.

Kidd, S., & Kral, M. J. (2005). Practising Participatory Action Research. *Journal of Counseling Psychology, 52*(2), 187-195.

Lee, A. J., O'Dea, K., & Matthews, J. D. (1994). Apparent dietary intake in remote Aboriginal Communities. *Australian Journal of Public Health, 18*, 190-107.

McKendrick, J., & Charles, S. (2001). *Report of the Rumbalara Aboriginal Mental Health Research Project.* Mooroopna: Rumbalara Aboriginal Cooperative.

National Health and Medical Research Council. (2003a). *Dietary Guidelines for Australian Adults.* Canberra: Commonwealth of Australia.

National Health and Medical Research Council. (2003b). *Values and Ethics: Guidelines for Ethical Conduct in Aboriginal and Torres Strait Islander Health Research.* Canberra: National Health and Medical Research Council.

—. (2006). *Food for Health: Dietary Guidelines for Australians, A Guide for Healthy Eating*: Australian Government: Department of Health and Ageing.

Newton, K. (2004). *Rumbalara Football Netball Club: More than just a sporting club.* Shepparton: Rumbalara Football Netball Club.

Reilly, R. (2005). *Identifying Psychosocial Determinants of Indigenous Health (doctoral thesis)*. Unpublished Doctoral Thesis, University of Melbourne, Melbourne.

Reilly, R., Doyle, J., & Rowley, K. (2007). Koori community-directed health promotion in the Goulburn Valley. *Australian Community Psychologist, 19*(1), 39-46.

Richard, L., Potvin, L., Kishchuk, N., Prlic, H., & Green, L. (1995). Assessment of the Integration of the Ecological Approach in Health Promotion Programs. *American Journal of Health Promotion, 10*(4), 318-328.

Rumbalara Aboriginal Cooperative. (2003). *Rumbalara Aboriginal Cooperative Services Information* (Information provided by Rumba Co-op). Mooroopna: Rumbalara Aboriginal Cooperative.

Saggers, S., & Gray, D. (1991). *Aboriginal Health and Society: The Traditional and Contemporary Struggle for Better Health*. St Leonards, NSW: Allen & Unwin Pty Ltd.

Stringer, E., & Genat, W. (2004). *Action Research in Health*. New Jersey: Pearson Merril Prentice Hall.

The Heart Health Project Steering Committee. (2007). A collaborative cardiovascular health program for Aboriginal and Torres Strait Islander People in the Goulburn-Murray region: development and risk factor screening at Indigenous Community Organisations. *Australian Journal of Primary Health, 13*, 9-17.

Respecting Culture: Telling Stories of Suicide Prevention in Rural Communities

Jennene Greenhill, Harold Stewart and Kerry Dix

Abstract

This paper discusses a process of developing and evaluating suicide prevention strategies which was able to bridge cultural boundaries. It tells a story about overcoming adversity in rural communities as they marshaled their local resources to develop locally owned suicide prevention strategies in a whole of government approach. The evaluation assessed the impacts and efficacy of the processes used to implement the initiative and identified future actions and directions.

Flinders University Rural Clinical School was engaged by the South Australian Department of Health to conduct the external evaluation on the Suicide Prevention Initiative for Country South Australia. There were seven country regions involved in the project. Each region was responsible for establishing local action plans with their main target group, young men, in particular young Indigenous men.

The people and systems operating at the local level in rural communities presented powerful messages relating to service delivery with particular reference to Aboriginality. The importance of inclusivity, relationships, connections, credibility, building trust, networking and holistic approaches that are intrinsic to Aboriginal culture were identified as essential to project success.

The evaluation provided valuable knowledge that can inform policy on the challenges and successes. It has the potential to provide direction for future initiatives to maximise success and sustainability. The lessons also provide insights into primary health care practice with Aboriginal communities.

In this paper, Harold Stewart introduces the project, Kerry Dix and Jennene Greenhill describe the process of evaluating the suicide prevention initiative, and Harold Stewart makes some concluding remarks.

Harold Stewart

I wish to pay my respects to the Kaurna people, the traditional custodians of the land where the conference was held, both past and present.

I worked a few years in the Department of Health and Ageing. I come from a career of 23 years in the Australian government, which has taught me a lot about getting things done, and now I work in government policy. The thing that keeps me going is knowing people in the Aboriginal community and knowing what's happening out there, and what isn't happening, and what needs to happen, how people are suffering and how we need to change things for the future. That's what keeps me in my work specifically as a policy adviser in the Mental Health Unit, about strategic policy and how to influence the policy along cultural lines.

The project came about through money being made available to deal with a very serious issue in the Aboriginal community. South Australia has one of the highest rates of Indigenous suicide in Australia, but we are making some headway.

I come from a community called La Perouse, which is a French name. La Perouse Aboriginal community is on Botany Bay in Sydney. The French landed on that side of Botany Bay first and that's why it's called La Perouse, so one of the first languages I learned to speak was French, which was quite unusual, but I also learned a smattering of words in our own language. When I was very young I was given my Aboriginal name. My Aboriginal name is Bundamurra. Bundamurra is the word in our language for lizard. The name was given to me by my Uncle Bob Sims and I didn't know it at the time but that name that he gave me means that I'll be a survivor wherever I go because the lizard doesn't drink. The lizard gets the moisture and the sustenance from what they eat so if they can't find water, they don't need to. So wherever a lizard is found, they'll survive and by giving me that name, he meant that wherever I go I was going to be a survivor. I think that says a lot about this project. It's about how we build resilience within the community, and Kerry and Jennene have been able to examine what were the essential elements of the project and what they gave to the community.

My role was as a member of the cultural reference group, which included other cultural experts that came together to give different perspectives on how we could work with the community, and the community was across seven regional communities at that time. The project had its own unique way of operating with each local community. The valuable thing about the project was that the local Aboriginal community was engaged and were enthusiastic participants. There was no prescribed model in how the project should be formulated. I think that's so important today because if we're going to do any work in the community, any lasting work, anything meaningful, the local community has to be engaged, not only in the project but in the design and the planning of the project so as to leave some lasting result from the running of these projects.

I also work in Suicide Prevention Australia (SPA). We don't like to talk about that word so much, but it's important to say that it is a very serious symptom of the sickness of a society when suicide rates are moving upwards, across every age group and across every social stratum. There are many in the Aboriginal community that believe that suicide was not a part of our history. Thirty years ago there was no indication of any knowledge of suicide in the Indigenous community, so that's why we believe that suicide is an indication of how sick a society is becoming. What we are trying to do though is build psychological wellbeing in the community and try to find out why some communities have resilience and what we can capture from that to build wellbeing in the community.

One of the things that I've been successful in influencing in mental health policy has been in looking at the broader context of social emotional wellbeing[1]. I've been able to influence thinking around the use of Ngangkaries, Aboriginal traditional healers, in the mental health setting and that's coming about slowly. It takes time but I think that we can learn from the projects that are happening around Australia, some of Tracy Westerman's work, and other work that's happening in other jurisdictions, and slowly we can influence change in South Australia.

Cultural dyslexia is a failure to read other cultures. It's not something that is unique to relations with the Indigenous cultures of Australia, but we've felt for a long time that the Eurocentric cultures had a lot of trouble reading our culture.

I'm a Koori. My culture is different from Nungas in South Australia and Murris from Queensland. We have to understand and work within that context. There's a diversity of cultures and when you have that sort of

---

[1]Many Indigenous people do not like the terms 'mental health' or 'mental illness', preferring instead the term 'social emotional well-being', which better captures Indigenous holistic conceptions of well-being and avoids the individualistic assumptions of the western terms mental health and mental illness

approach or understanding it can open up your mind to reading other cultures and understanding. At one time there were 56 Aboriginal languages spoken in South Australia. There are five Torres Strait Islander languages. Some of those languages were dialects but they said something about the number of nations in Australia. When you realise that, it gives you some understanding of the broad scope of cultural diversity. The suicide prevention projects that went through all the country regions of South Australia were across some of those cultural groups, and they totally adopted an approach to listen to the local people to come up with something useful, a project that was going to not only help them and meet their needs, but one in which they had a part, some ownership in the formulation and the modelling of those projects.

Let me say though that in anything good, there's no guarantee that government is going to support it. Sadly, this is why we need evaluation reports, especially the Australian Government. If something good happens, there's not always continuation. They'll wait for the evaluation report if there's going to be one and if it's a positive report, they may decide to fund it in the future. Sadly, for the project described in this paper, the funding has not continued. What's been said is the funding has to be found from within the present operating budgets. I'm in government, I understand what that means. I'm not always happy with that but I'm going to lobby the Minister and the Premier, because my role is a little bit different to other policy advisers. A normal policy adviser has to deliver: the Minister is your master. You're the servant. As a cultural consultant, I'm a little bit removed from that and I can say some things within particular license, but my role is to advocate for change and I will. I told them that when they asked me to come and work with them. I said "I'm not going to say what you want me to say. I'll say what needs to be said and I'll back it up with evidence and knowledge." What we have found is evidence and knowledge, and that's the best place to argue from.

Kerry Dix and Jennene Greenhill

We too would like to pay our respects to the traditional owners, the Kaurna people. We want to describe something about the journey that we have been on. In the next section we present an overview of the project, the challenges that we encountered, the results that we found, the indication of those results and a focus on the workforce issues that we found to be of major significance in the projects.

The 'Suicide Prevention Australia for Country SA' project was funded by the Social Inclusion Board of the South Australian Government, and it involves the (former) seven (administrative) country regions of South Australia. The target group was classed as young males and, in particular, young Aboriginal males. Aus$800,000 was provided over two years, but funding only came through near the end of the first year, so basically it was a one-year project. The aim was that each of the seven regions develop their local action plans to be community driven and flexible which incorporated the capacities of their local community.

The Department of Health's consultant as well as an external evaluation found that there was some confusion in the beginning, for all of the project officers, concerning where everybody fitted and how they were going to work together. The implementation consultant helped the project officers with their planning and also provided them with networking opportunities to find out what was happening in other regions. The initial challenges that we faced as external evaluators included the time frames, as it was a one year project, and since there were seven regions we were faced with a dilemma of how to connect with seven regions to evaluate this project with any sort of validity.

The foundations were rather unclear and there was some ambiguity from the project officers about exactly what they were being asked to provide. Deciding on the methodology, how we were going to go about this evaluation, was a difficult process for us. Basically, we called it a series of case studies, and because they were all unique we didn't make a comparative analysis of those.

Because we were not Aboriginal women, and very aware that that came with its own biases, we engaged two cultural advisers as well as a cultural reference group, and we were completely and utterly indebted to them in terms of their wisdom, experience and knowledge in helping us to work out how we would go about data collection and the actual design of the evaluation. We also had no credibility or history of working with the communities, so it was really difficult for us to actually undertake the project to begin with, which felt quite uncomfortable.

The results that we found related to: the people that were involved, the systems that were operating, service delivery options, and Aboriginality. What we noticed about the people that was most important was the personal qualities they had. If they had years of experience working within the communities that they then tapped into, that turned out to be really important. Identifying local leaders and working with them was important.

Workforce issues, such as the turnover of the workforce in rural communities, was a real problem for the communities in getting the projects off the ground. What happened was that the money was provided to the Mental Health program managers in each region, and they dispersed the money into the communities, but it was decided that administering it at the regional level would work best. Because of that, it was funded centrally and hence for the funding to get to the Aboriginal communities there had to be a connection with the communities. Those communities that had local leaders and people who had worked within the Indigenous communities successfully and for many years were able to really build on what existed. An example of feedback is, "Because I've actually worked in this area for the last three years, I've gained some credibility. Inspiring people within the organisation to pick up and make it happen was considerably challenging" (participant).

However, those communities that were unable to connect because they didn't have any relationships or any connections ended up with no Indigenous content, which was really unfortunate.

When there were discussions about local leaders and young Indigenous males who had the potential to be involved in these projects, there were comments like: "They are not keen to stand up because they will be inundated with pressure" (participant).

Institutional racism was identified as an issue: "I'm absolutely shocked at the level of racism coming through the service organisations" (participant).

Also, government policy, both local, state and Commonwealth policies, had changed within that year period, which really impacted on how the projects were able to roll out.

Each region was able to implement their own projects in the way that they felt would work best for them. Some focused on education programmes and implemented the Applied Suicide Intervention Skills Training (ASIST), others created their own education programme. Some had community development focuses which encompassed activities for kids to be involved in. There was a whole range of different approaches.

What we found worked best for a lot of the regions was, if they engaged an advisory group, often there would be existing groups within their region that they could tap into. The connections and the linkages with community and local leaders were really important and that's what gave their local action the greatest effectiveness. The projects that engaged their youth workers to be project officers were probably the most successful because they had the connections, they had a link with the young people. Partnerships were crucial, and working across whole of government with a primary health care approach to make sure they engaged as many organisations in initiatives as possible really did help.

Some of the quotes illustrated the enthusiasm with which the projects were taken up:

It really got the kids excited and enthusiastic. They have the opportunity to learn something new which I think they were really looking for". "It really did give them a sense of hope that they can do good things". "I can't believe that I did this to get out of school. This has really changed my life". "There was lots of dance and drumming workshops and things like that that they really gained a lot from."

What we noticed as well about the range of projects was that the culture of Aboriginality - the time, identity, trust, and a strong understanding of Aboriginal history - was really important, and those projects that were able to engage with local Indigenous workers and communities really managed to get something off the ground. On the other hand, those that didn't have an understanding of Aboriginality didn't even make a connection, so there was no way they could actually move forward. Some of the quotes to illustrate the importance of Aboriginality were: "The pain and hurt of parents past is put onto the next generation. People are coming in for counselling who grew up on a mission, grew up with twisted thinking".

Without that acknowledgement and understanding and awareness of Aboriginal history and colonisation, those mainstream services were unable to make any inroads at all. This illustrates the effect of cultural dyslexia.

Cultural dyslexia is among the most important learnings from the suicide prevention initiative. The initiative has been delivered in a way that emphasises how we view the differences in each other from pre-conceived paradigms. An example of this has been in the difference between community and bureaucracy and the terminology used. This way of thinking often restricts our ability to really listen in order to understand and learn about each other. In understanding the concept of cultural dyslexia and exploring its foundations, we can try and create some new approaches to working in cross cultural environments. By suspending judgement and surrendering ourselves to new experiences, we can see things through different lenses. This increased insight will help us to embrace the remarkable differences that make up our society to truly work alongside each other collaboratively with respect and care.

Overcoming cultural dyslexia is not just about white mainstream and Aboriginal communities. There's a range of different groups within our society that we fail to read properly, based on gender and socio-economic status as well as culture.

The implications from the evaluation were centred around time, taking the time to really get to know people and making sure that this happens for people who have had experience over a length of time in working in those communities involved.

The aim of the project was for it to be sustainable, which was very difficult given the short time frame, and the project officers were really concerned about the pressure on them to achieve that in that time frame. They came to realise that they weren't going to come up with a "gold standard in suicide prevention, but maybe establish a few building blocks on which they could build in the future" (participant).

The whole of government approach was really beneficial because the networking and learning from each other provided them with a real solid base on which they could move forward, including laying the groundwork, planning, consultation and transparency. Some regions were really good at holding consultations with community to find out how it would be best to go about implementing their project.

Focusing more specifically on workforce issues, what we found really important in rural communities was the future need to address the concerns that were raised regarding workforce. The main issues were high turnover of staff and the lack of people on the ground to pick up and move with projects. We thought the best things people were saying could work were: mentoring programs, identifying home grown products and supporting them to build local capacity, collaboration, and working across organisations. Training and education was a big issue for the local workers, and another one was intergenerational learning. There were some fantastic examples of groups that were set up to talk about issues within the community and actually learn from each other. There needed to be some ownership and they needed to be locally driven. Without that, the community just wasn't interested in the projects. Adequate support and debriefing for the workers was important as well.

Harold Stewart

The essential element to all of these projects was that they were linked with a local health service, so it wasn't just a stand-alone suicide prevention project. It was linked in with the health promotion program that was run in a region, and there was ownership with the local health service. That integration is so important as far as looking at the total health needs, and introducing people to the range of health programs that run in their region. So it's about Aboriginal people being part of our total community out there because we used to be thought of as 'over there' or 'out there' or 'under there', not considered as part of that total community. This project was about getting the message across to the

Indigenous population in South Australia about the innovative ways we can find to work together collaboratively to have some impact on health.

Suicide prevention is not just about suicide prevention. It involves the ordinary social health of a community that has an impact on oneself, so if you don't address the whole wide range of community health, having a suicide prevention project that provides counselling for people is never going to work. That's what we're trying to show. The range of programs showed some innovative ways but further than just depression or those sorts of things, other major health problems and health needs also that need to be improved.

If we don't protect children, we don't have any future. We have to build a better world for tomorrow by looking after our children now and making them safer because every child comes into the world innocent.

Issues in Cultural Competence

Keith McConnochie, David Egege and Dennis McDermott

Abstract

This chapter summarises the panel discussion that closed the conference. While the term cultural competence is a contested one, as illustrated by the presenters, it is currently a useful term to help develop theory and practice. Each panellist gave a short presentation with their individual views on the topic. The ideas presented here are helping to refine a more sophisticated conception of cultural competence.

Keith McConnochie

Almost everybody who spoke at the conference talked about cultural competence, cultural awareness, or cultural safety at some stage in their presentation. In this brief discussion paper I would like to raise some questions and issues about the nature and application of the cultural competence model being developed by myself, Wendy Nolan and Rob Ranzijn. I will begin by briefly describing the model which we are using as a framework for planning the content, sequencing and structuring of the material that we cover in the University of South Australia undergraduate psychology courses in order to improve the levels of cultural competence in graduates. Then I will address three issues relating to the generalisability of the model:

1.   Cultural competence is a developmental process, not a one-off skill. The idea that you can develop cultural competence in a one or two-day workshop is simply not tenable;

2.   To be effective, cultural competence needs to be systemic; and

3.   Do cultural competence programs actually work? How much do we know about the effects of the hundreds of cultural competence

workshops that are run across Australia every year? What kind of effects are they having?

The model of cultural competence we have been using begins with the definition of cultural competence derived from Cross, Bazron, Dennis, and Isaacs (1989) and provided by the American Association of Medical Colleges (2005 - p. 1)

> Cultural and linguistic competence is a set of congruent behaviors, knowledge, attitudes, and policies that come together in a system, organization, or among professionals that enables effective work in cross-cultural situations. "Culture" refers to integrated patterns of human behavior that include the language, thoughts, actions, customs, beliefs, and institutions of racial, ethnic, social, or religious groups. "Competence" implies having the capacity to function effectively as an individual or an organization within the context of the cultural beliefs, practices, and needs presented by patients and their communities.

This definition emphasises three aspects of cultural competence:

- Cultural competence includes knowledge, attitudes and behaviour
- Cultural competence emphasises the capacity to function effectively
- Cultural competence extends beyond individual professional behaviours and includes organisations and systems

In developing our teaching program we have elaborated on the three components (knowledge, attitudes and skills) by placing them within an Australian Indigenous context, generating the following broad description.

1.   Knowledge.
This component includes two linked elements:
(i)   A broad or generic understanding of the nature of culture, and the implications of culture for understanding human behaviour, and,
(ii)   An understanding of the specific cultural and historical patterns which have structured Indigenous lives in the past and the ways in which these patterns continue to be expressed in contemporary Australia

2.   Values.
This component again includes two linked elements:

(i)   An awareness by the professional of their personal values and beliefs, and a capacity to move away from using their own cultural values as a benchmark for measuring and judging the behaviour of people from other cultural backgrounds, and

(ii)   Awareness of the values, biases and beliefs built into psychology as a profession, and an understanding of how these characteristics impact on people from different cultures.

3.   Skills.

This third (behavioural) component builds on the first two components to enable the practitioner to develop a repertoire of skills needed to work more effectively as a professional in Indigenous contexts – that is, to integrate values and cultural knowledge with professional knowledge and skills to develop more effective, culturally appropriate professional practice.

There is widespread agreement within the literature that the development of cultural competence is a continuous process, not a single event. Campinha-Bacote (2005 - p. 1) for example, notes that "competence is a process, not an event; a journey, not a destination; dynamic, not static; and involves the paradox of knowing". Wells (2000 - p. 192) provides a model which enables us to link the components of cultural competence (knowledge, attitudes and skills) to a framework for identifying stages in the development of cultural competence. Wells identifies six stages, along a continuum, as summarised in the following table:

Table 1: *Stages and Characteristics of Cultural Competence*

Stages	Characteristics
Cultural incompetence	Lack of knowledge of the cultural implications of behaviour.
Cultural knowledge	Learning the elements of culture and their role in shaping and defining behaviour.
Cultural awareness	Recognizing and understanding the cultural implications of behaviour.
Cultural sensitivity	The integration of cultural knowledge and awareness into individual and institutional behaviour.
Cultural competence	The routine application of culturally appropriate care interventions and practices.
Cultural proficiency	The integration of cultural competence into one's repertoire for scholarship (e.g., practice, teaching, and research)

By combining the components of cultural competence (knowledge, attitudes and skills) with this developmental sequence, we can generate a matrix which enables us to map the relationships between the two aspects (see Table 2). In structuring this matrix we have placed the developmental sequence along the horizontal axis, with the components on the vertical axis. The development of cultural competence then becomes a process of moving from the bottom left hand corner, through to the top right hand corner, as indicated by the arrow.

This framework has provided a useful guide for sequencing the content of undergraduate psychology courses within the University of South Australia. The program begins with a compulsory first-year course concentrating on the bottom left corner (the nature of culture, Indigenous Australian cultures, histories and contemporary cultures, some exploration of individual and institutional values and attitudes and a preliminary examination of the role of psychology in Indigenous Australia). This is followed by a combination of integrated content in other compulsory courses and a third year elective course focussing much more on the development of critical reflexivity, professional understandings and generic skills and strategies. Of course, this is not a simple linear progression - the journey frequently involves looping back to revisit earlier content in an iterative, reflective process.

Within this broad framework of cultural competence I would like to raise three issues for consideration.

Table 2: *Development of Cultural Competence*

	Cultural incompetence	Cultural knowledge	Cultural awareness	Cultural sensitivity	Cultural competence	Cultural proficiency
Professionally specific skills & strategies						
Generic skills & strategies						
Critically reflecting on profession or occupation						
Exploring Individual attitudes & values						
Culturally specific awareness (Indigenous)						
The nature and significance of culture						

1. Sequencing Cultural Competence Workshops

Clearly, the sequence described above is not something that can be covered in a brief one-off workshop. And yet, in many professional and organisational contexts, this is how the issue of cultural competence is handled – provide a one-day workshop on cultural awareness and the 'cultural competence' box can be ticked off. This is simply not going to work.

However, the model summarised above may provide a framework for mapping these kinds of workshops and locating different kinds of workshops within the sequence. Workshops which focus on exploring aspects of Indigenous cultures and histories are clearly located at the beginning of this sequence. Others (for example those dealing with very specific professional issues, such as Indigenous depression) may be right up in the top right-hand corner. There is currently no framework being used to map these disparate kinds of workshops, placing them within any kind of developmental pattern or sequence. Given the proliferation of these workshops, it may be valuable to explore the desirability and benefits of establishing some such scheme on a national basis.

2. Culturally Competence Needs To Be Systemic

The second point I want to make is that cultural competence needs to be systemic; it needs to be system-wide rather than dealing with particular groups of professionals. We need to locate the sequence of skills and understanding described in the model within a 'whole of the organisation' framework, involving all levels of the organisation, from the front end reception staff through administrative staff and processes, management staff and processes, professional staff and CEOs.

A significant amount of cultural competence training can be common for all levels. So, for example, the earlier stages (the nature of culture, Indigenous Australian cultures, histories and contemporary cultures, individual and institutional values and attitudes) are equally relevant to all staff in an organisation, and need not be run as separate programs. Indeed, there may be some real benefits in CEOs, professional staff and administrative staff joining together for these workshops. However, as we move further along the sequence we move towards increasing occupational or professional specificity. The kind of professional understandings and skills that are relevant for psychologists working with Indigenous clients may be very different to the kinds of understandings and skills needed by people who are working at front end reception.

3. Do These Programs Have Any Effect?

Finally - do cultural competence programs actually work? Do we have any evidence about whether participants actually change their behaviour as a result of these programs? There is virtually no Australian evidence (and very little from overseas) about the effects of these programs on individual behaviour. Given the extent of the 'cultural awareness/cultural competence' industry in Australia, within which hundreds (if not thousands) of these workshops are run every year, this would seem to be an important question to ask. I understand that some developmental work is beginning to be undertaken within the VET sector[1]. The VET sector is competence based, and they are doing interesting work on cultural competence - how to link and sequence the specific competencies and measure them. I also note with interest Tracy Westerman's instrument that she has developed for measuring cultural competence across agencies and organisations.

These are issues which need to be addressed urgently if the concept of cultural competence is to have any long term credibility.

David Egege

Firstly, I'd like to acknowledge Uncle Lewis O'Brien. Uncle Lewis is a Kaurna elder and has advised me on many occasions throughout the time I've been in Adelaide. I'd also like to acknowledge that we are on the land of the Kaurna people - the traditional owners of this part of South Australian country.

I often ask people, as I'm a guy of mixed heritage, where do they think I come from? As a black guy (I use that term for myself) I love telling people that I'm actually Welsh. I say it at times just to confuse people, because, as we all know Wales is a 'White country'. The reality of course is that there are many people born and bred in Wales who quite rightly can refer to themselves as Welsh, whilst acknowledging their ethnic roots. My mother was Welsh, my father was Nigerian, I am now Australian (I've been here 28 years). I was born in Liverpool, England; my wife is Scottish/Irish, two of my kids were born in Hamburg, Germany and my son was born in Australia. We are probably the personification of the multicultural family in Australia.

Having worked in most organisations within the health service in South Australia and within the health service in the Northern Territory it is

---

[1] Vocational and Educational Training sector of post-secondary education – mostly occupational training rather than academic in orientation

quite clear that the concept of cultural competence remains for most organisations purely a concept, and quite often a badly understood concept. I'm employed at present with Domiciliary Care SA (DomCare SA) to help implement their Aboriginal Services Strategy (I was previously the Aboriginal and Multicultural Consultant with Mental Health Services in Adelaide). My role has been to implement and update the Aboriginal and Torres Strait Islander Services strategy.

DomCare SA, with a staff of 800, had done some prior work addressing the needs of the Aboriginal community but lacked real direction. The first thing that I needed to concentrate on was the formulation of both a reconciliation statement and plan put together with support from Reconciliation SA[2] . They were launched a few weeks ago. It was a start to addressing the cultural needs of the Aboriginal community whilst seeking to educate an organisation on the reality of cultural competence in action.

I have worked in many agencies and departments in Australia, and just as often I have been the only black guy in the organisation. It did not take me long to understand that there were some inherent problems in the way that organisations were addressing Aboriginal affairs. The concentration on purely cultural awareness training is problematic, and at worse may be ineffectual in achieving long term change. This train of thought has resulted in a belief that a more skills based paradigm over one of mere sensitivity is now an imperative. Cultural competence at the organisational level is not solely a program or initiative, but rather a commitment that is shared by not only members of the board and staff, but is reinforced in all aspects of policy development, recruitment and retention, program management and service delivery.

From the perspective of DomCare SA it was essential that our Chief Executive and senior staff were on board, understood what was required to achieve our goals, and more importantly were seen to attend our cultural competence training. We have a young executive team and in many ways they were very open to ways which can truly help the executives of DomCare with new ideas and as a consequence they were supportive.

As a service that is HACC[3] funded, DomCare SA mainly provides services to older people who may be frail or are experiencing the long term effects of illness and wish to stay living in their own homes. We

---

[2] Reconciliation SA is a not-for-profit organisation working towards reconciliation between Indigenous and non-Indigenous Australians
[3] Home and Community Care system – a Commonwealth Government-funded scheme to provide support to enable people with disabilities to remain in their own homes as long as possible before requiring residential institutional care

received funding from HACC to begin the process of incorporating the concept of cultural competence within DomCare SA. I have been working with the concept of cultural competence for the last five years and it is quite obvious that although the term and concept has become quite popular in the last few years the familiar gap between theory and practice abounds.

Research also revealed that there were very few organisations in Australia who had taken on board the four dimensions of cultural competence: organisational, systemic, professional and individual. The question has to be asked, why this was so? It has become abundantly clear in many countries outside of Australia that purely sending staff off to cultural awareness training is problematic, and at worse may be ineffectual in achieving long term change. Cultural sensitivity does have its place, but more and more I find staff want the skills to put it into practice. Cultural competence has the capacity to operate from a more skills-based paradigm, and this is precisely what was required at DomCare SA.

Once funding had been allocated, we at DomCare along with my colleague Sophie Diamandi from the University of South Australia devised a program together. Sophie had been very involved in diversity training and it did not take long to put our program together. This process was absolutely essential as it was my belief that very few staff had even heard of cultural competence and therefore had no idea what it was. It was decided to run a one day training program introducing the concept to staff and a more intense one and a half day program for Team Leaders, HR and policy staff. The interesting thing for me is that most people that went through didn't even know what cultural *awareness* was, and that's an interesting indictment. It was essential that all staff attend the training, inclusive of senior executives and our Chief Executive. I was firmly of the opinion that all staff, including equipment services staff, administrators, and executives should attend training.

The introductory training of our cultural competence program is of course only the first step, but a vitally important one, as it has a strong self-reflective component. It is this component, that is so powerfully utilised in an environment that is as guilt-free as possible, that can be so effective. As a Black European living in Australia, 'white guilt' is a phenomenon that appears to be endemic amongst many health professionals and is articulated to me when discussing services, problems with services etc. It has the impact of rendering some professionals impotent as they relate to Aboriginal people from a perspective that is guilt ridden, and, alas, culturally incompetent. The workshops themselves were of great value as people were able to (perhaps for the first time in a group) speak their mind.

One time I was working with a group of social workers. I had asked them about their relationships and thoughts on Aboriginal people and communities. It became quite clear to me that they were of the opinion that they couldn't say what was on their mind, they in fact were completely quiet, it had to be teased out. Finally a young social worker put her hand up and stated that Aboriginal people scared her. At this point a male social worker turned to her and almost started to chastise her because of her view. At this point I had to state that in fact out of the 25 social workers there she was the only one that had the courage to say, 'Aboriginal people scare me.' The moment that this thought was articulated we had something to work with, because I know that a lot of health professionals feel the same. Finding out what it is in fact that 'scares' them is part of the self-reflective process that can be so richly enlightening.

At present we have had 320 staff go through our cultural competence introduction training, with 400 more staff to go. The training consists of:

- developing a knowledge of cultural competence
- the Cultural Respect Framework[4]
- the differences between cultural awareness and sensitivity
- developing a cultural competence understanding from state to community program level
- domains of cultural competence (organizational, systemic, professional and individual) and
- the future directions of our organisation in relation to an overall Cultural Competence Strategy.

Part of this process includes a self reflective process that speaks to all staff, be they a paramedical aide, a chief executive, a team leader, policy maker or administrator. The objective is to ensure that no longer will services utilise cultural awareness as just an add-on to their organisations (try adding wings to a caterpillar and see what happens) but will have their own role to play in the incremental transformation of the culture of their organisation. Ultimately this has an impact on all of us. All of us have a responsibility and a role to play. This is not only best practice, it is social

---

[4] The Cultural Respect Framework was developed by the Australian Health Ministers Advisory Council after significant consultation with Indigenous stakeholders. It includes strategies for incorporating the principles of cultural respect within government organisations (Australian Health Ministers' Advisory Council, 2004)

justice, and we have no longer the luxury of time in getting it right, we simply have no choice.

Be inspired. This is a glimpse of how some things are working here in South Australia. This will happen and we are beginning to make those changes. So on those days when you're a bit low, and this feels so hard - and it is hard, it is hard - be inspired. We're making those changes.

Dennis McDermott

I think Keith and David between them have covered a lot of the territory here. I think the three things that stand out for me are:

- Firstly, what do we imply by the term 'cultural competence'? I'd particularly like to put a question mark on *'competence'*.
- The second thing that comes up is exactly what David was saying just then. How do you successfully change workplace or organisational culture, in itself? What about the dynamics of that, and successfully picking up on that?
- The third question is allied to what Keith was saying about the difficulty of measurable change, and we're all struggling with this. It's how you get genuine and lasting change.

I think Wendy Nolan was saying, 'It's one thing for me to go out there and do a cultural competence workshop and think I've got it all together with the people going through the workshop or the course, and then the buggers go out and they do something to put their foot right in it, or they do something patronising. How do I get around that?' Of course, we don't yet know the answer to that.

The first question is around the term 'competence'. I was working for about four or five years in the Faculty of Medicine at the University of New South Wales. I'm a psychologist, not a medico. In such a faculty, working around doctors, you realise they love competence. Competence is what it's all about. It's about looking for proficiency - and quite rightly, because we have a duty to work with people properly. In my keynote speech I mentioned Mason Durie's work in New Zealand about cultural competence. In New Zealand there are Mental Health Competency Standards that mandate cultural competence, and you must go through extensive training. In professions such as nursing cultural safety training is mandatory. If the public see you as a professional, that's what's expected of you. But the thing I got from Mason Durie is an approach that, roughly stated, comes across as: 'Whatever you're doing, sure it's about skill – it involves a range of skills - but it's more about you as a whole person. It's what you bring to the encounter, what you bring to that cross-cultural situation that's important,' and I think that's spot on. I see it as a meta-skill.

I would suggest it's something we need to get down and think about, and just keep thinking through that notion of competence, too. One of the best critiques I've heard about it comes from a paediatrician in the United States called Dr Melanie Tervalon.   She's an African-American paediatrician, based I think at Oakland, and she says that cultural competence is the wrong term for her. The term that she thinks is far more relevant is cultural *humility*. She's developed her ideas through questioning around competence, working to change workplace and organisational culture, real, lasting and genuine change. Her ideas about cultural humility arose out of her experiences in a particular hospital environment in the San Francisco Bay area, where things were going pear-shaped or, as they say across the Tasman, when it all turned to custard[5]. Things were going really bad in the hospital in terms of what the Americans call 'race relations', and she was asked, 'Well, how do we do it differently? How do we do it better?' She discovered the process as she went, including extensive conferring with all her colleagues and developing an organic program that turned the hospital inside out. They built on the idea that you had to not only get top-down agreement, but somehow get the whole organisation behind you and then work your way through it.

She's still struggling with finding any specific way to put all these various dimensions together. We now have to undergo this sort of process ourselves here in Australia. Twenty or thirty years ago there was only a cultural awareness model to base training on. As I said before, I'm not here to disagree about cultural awareness training. I think it's integral: cultural knowledge and cultural awareness are integral parts of any particular program. It's specific, though, to local needs, local situations and local cultures - and local people need to teach it.

Looking again at this notion of cultural competence, we've gone too far in a sense. We've produced a check-list mentality. We've produced people who are rigid in the way they apply what they're doing, and I think that's really worth taking on board. So, what's important? Agility, flexibility, finding ways to get past that tick-the-box, check-list approach. What's also important is an awareness of fitting cultural competence with

---

[5] 'Pear-shaped' is a term used in Australia to indicate that things are starting to go wrong. 'Turn to custard' is the equivalent term in Aoteoroa (New Zealand – across the Tasman Sea from Australia)

the notion of cultural safety. There is an organisation that is applying these concepts to medical education and medical curricula around Indigenous health, the Leaders in Medical Education (LIME) who held a conference at the University of New South Wales in September 2007. One of the items on the agenda was to work towards an Australian definition of cultural safety. So far no-one's got it right, everyone's struggling with it. Is it the right term for Australia? Is it portable, does it apply here? I will say I believe there must be some place for the notion of a culturally-safe encounter.

Along with a culturally-safe person-to-person encounter, there is the need for a culturally-safe organisational set-up. If that's not happening, then you might as well pack up and go home. The system is supposed to be client- or person-driven, isn't it? It's about us really listening to someone, to where they want to guide us and how they want to be treated. It's not about me being a great anthropologist that knows everything about the person in front of me. I can't presume to know that, but I do need to know *myself*, know who *I* am.

This is an important question: who the hell am I? That's sometimes a vexed question that raises all kinds of issues. We need to build in that idea for any program that we do, that we start with our self, and then going from the knowledge of our self we are then able to work with someone else. But that's also where it gets difficult, I think. It often involves discomfort. But the opposite of discomfort is safety. I just don't mean cultural factors; I'm thinking of how to create safety in a learning environment. You have to build that right in. We need to find some way for participants to say what they really want to say, and they need to be safe to move through their issues. We have to find a way to factor this in.

The second question is how to change organisation and workplace culture. When I used to work at the University of New South Wales, in the Faculty of Medicine, there was no reconciliation statement, but to their credit, over about a 12 month period, they sat down, consulted, and worked out a statement, which then was applied. It helped legitimate and naturalise blackfella[6] perspectives and ways of treating each other, and I think it actually changed the cultural safety of the organisation, of the workplace. Before, we were finding that when Indigenous students coming into medicine would go into a class, if there was one racist student in the class, which there often was, everyone else would shut up because no-one knew how to tackle the situation. After the plan was rolled out

---

[6] Blackfella. This is a term which is sometimes used by Indigenous Australians to refer to themselves. It is a term which should be used very cautiously by non-Indigenous speakers as it does have some derogatory historical connotations.

they started saying, 'Not only can you not do this here, but there's actually support in this institution for doing things differently.' It also meant that we started bringing in Indigenous protocol and ritual into the faculty, with the idea that each time a new course was instituted, there would be an appropriate welcome to country, and from then on we would acknowledge country as part of each semester's start–up. This was a small gain, but the difficulty then was in moving things on from tokenism. It's about change in *actual* culture - that is a very difficult thing to do, but I think a necessary thing to do.

The third question is, how do you get genuine and lasting change? I like the idea that I picked up from the anthropologist, Ghassan Hage - at a conference in Christchurch about bi-culturalism and multiculturalism - that it's about building in genuine interaction and opportunity for interaction, where people can meet on a number of levels over time. To my mind that's setting up a chance for genuine and lasting change in attitudes. And without that knowledge of each other, it's so hard. Ghassan's take was that it's a bit like being like a family. With family, you can have your disputes, you can even fight. It doesn't matter, you know, as long as you've got that underlying small-'r' respect for each other built up and the knowledge of each other and a trust in each other that only comes from rough-and-tumble type interaction. It comes from honest thinking and honest dealing.

Environments that encourage that sense of being real, that provide opportunities for cultural interaction, could be based around food. For most cultures, doing it around a feed is a really great way of de-formalising it and getting it happening, with some genuine over-the-barbie[7] kind of conversations.

There are just two more things I want to say. In relation to workplace and organisational change and getting genuine lasting change in people working in health and mental health, the two came together for me when I was asked to go along to a Sorry Day[8] event at St Vincent's Hospital, a big Catholic hospital in inner-Sydney, right in Darlinghurst just near King's Cross, where you see everyone from people having their drug and alcohol problems at King's Cross to Kerry Packer - when he was alive - in the

---

[7] Barbeque.

[8] One year after the release of the Bringing Them Home report in 1997, a National 'Sorry Day' was established to acknowledge the wrongs that had been done to Indigenous families and to contribute to the healing process. Sorry Day is held on the 26th of May every year, and while it is not a public holiday it is marked by a range of activities across Australia. Information about 'Sorry Day' can be found at the National Sorry Day Committee web-site; http://www.nsdc.org.au/.

private wing of the hospital. And not only do they get local Kooris[9] in there, but, as a major hospital with particular national referrals, blackfellas from all over. We talked about doing some work with specific people there around some of these cultural competence and cultural safety issues, but the man I was talking with said, 'Well, no. We can't just train this or that unit, because in fact you should hear the comments coming from those in charge, in charge *up there*, you know. We have to work with the whole hospital to get somewhere, have to work as a whole organisation.' I think that's true. If we're looking at getting lasting change, we better make sure the environment itself changes.

The final thing I want to say, again referring to cultural safety, is something I picked up from the Cultural Safety Research Group at Victoria University of Wellington (New Zealand). When I talk about reflection and building a reflective practice, this is something that's been done with students, especially with students' use of reflective journals. What about people who go through cultural safety or cultural competence programmes? We could ask them to keep a reflective journal to diarise at the time what's happening with their encounters and how they encounter a particular situation that's culturally fraught, how they then deal with it, what they consider they learnt, and which of their insights they would then share. It might be another useful tool.

References

American Association of Medical Colleges. (2005). *Cultural Competence Education for Medical Students.* [Electronic Version] from http://www.aamc.org/meded/tacct/culturalcomped.pdf.

Australian Health Ministers' Advisory Council. (2004). *Cultural respect framework for Aboriginal and Torres Strait Islander Health.* Adelaide, SA, Australia: Department of Health South Australia.

Campinha-Bacote, J. (2005). A culturally conscious approach to holistic nursing. Paper presented at the Holistic Nurses Association Conference. Retrieved June 11 2008 from http://www.medscape.com/viewarticle/513607.

Cross, T. L., Bazron, B. J., Dennis, K. W., & Isaacs, M. R. (1989). *Towards a culturally competent system of care: A monograph on effective services for minority children who are severely emotionally*

---

[9] Koori (or Koorie) is a term which is often used by Indigenous Australians from New South Wales or Victoria to refer to themselves. It is derived from a similar word in a number of East Coast languages which translates as person or people

disturbed. Washington, DC: CASSP Technical Assistance Center, Georgetown University Development Center.

Wells, M. I. (2000). Beyond cultural competence: A model for individual and institutional cultural development. *Journal of Community Health Nursing, 17*(4), 189-199.

CONTRIBUTORS

Professor **Judy Atkinson** introduces herself as coming from the three I's: Indigenous, Invader and Immigrant. She identifies as a Jiman (from Central west Queensland) / Bundjalung (Northern New South Wales) woman who also has Anglo-Celtic and German heritage. Judy has a BA from the University of Canberra and a Ph.D. from Queensland University of Technology. She is presently the Head of the College of Indigenous Australian Peoples at Southern Cross University, and Director of the Healing Circle, (Collaborative Indigenous Research Centre for Learning and Educare). Her major academic focus, and the extensive work she has conducted within Indigenous communities across Australia, has been in the area of violence and relational trauma, and healing for Indigenous, and indeed all peoples. She developed the We Al-li / Indigenous Therapies Program designed to address the critical needs of Indigenous communities around violence, trauma and healing. She co-authored the Aboriginal and Torres Strait Islander Women's Task Force on Violence Report for the Queensland government. Her book: Trauma Trails – Recreating Songlines: The transgenerational effects of Trauma in Indigenous Australia, provides context to the life stories of people who have moved/been moved from their country in a process that has created trauma trails, and the healing that can occur as people make connections with each other and share their stories from within a deep educaring process. She developed the undergraduate degree Indigenous Studies - Trauma and Healing; the Masters in Indigenous Studies (wellbeing) degree; and a Professional Doctorate – Indigenous Philosophies. 2009 will launch a Diploma in Community Recovery in response to her work in Timor Leste and across Australia in Aboriginal communities, designed to be delivered on the ground in communities, interactively with process evaluation research: action to practice – practice to evidence – evidence to policy.

Martha Augoustinos is Professor and Co-Director of the Discourse and Social Psychology Unit (DASP) in the School of Psychology, University of Adelaide. Martha has published widely on 'race' and prejudice in Australia and in the field of discursive psychology. She is co-editor with Kate Reynolds of *Understanding Prejudice, Racism and Social Conflict* (Sage, 2001) and co-author of *Social Cognition: An Integrated Introduction* (2nd ed, Sage, 2006) with Iain Walker and Ngaire Donaghue.

Margaret Cargo is Senior Lecturer in Health Promotion at the University of South Australia. Her research interests include the evaluation of community-based health interventions with a focus on accounting for context and implementation to interpret intervention outcomes. She has worked in partnership with Aboriginal communities in Canada and Australia for the last 10 years. Her recent work expands the social/environmental justice and knowledge translation roots of participatory research to include Aboriginal self-determination.

Michelle Dickson is the director of the Social Health program at Macquarie University, with special responsibility for teaching Indigenous students, and an associate lecturer in the Department of Psychology.

Kerry Dix is the research assistant at Flinders University Rural Clinical School (FURCS). Kerry has Diploma of Applied Science - Nursing and completed her Graduate Certificate in PHC – Research and Evaluation in 2006. She has worked extensively as a Registered Nurse in rural Community Care and Outreach services prior to joining the Clinical School. Kerry has a broad range of skills in both service provision and program management of rural primary health care services and initiatives. Kerry has been instrumental in the progressive expansion of rural community services in the Riverland. Since joining FURCS she has been engaged in the evaluation of a range of Public Health and Primary Health Care initiatives.

Joyce Doyle is a senior Aboriginal community member who has worked in the health sector for the Goulburn Valley Aboriginal community for over 20 years. She was one of the first graduates of the Institute of Koorie Education at Deakin University, completing her teaching degree in 1989. Her work has included four years in the teaching system, primary health care service delivery and management, and health promotion delivery, research and evaluation.

David Egege was born in the United Kingdom and lived for a number of years in various countries in Europe (including four years in Germany) finally settling in South Australia in 1981. David graduated from Flinders University (South Australia) with a Bachelor of Social Administration and a Bachelor of Arts majoring in Sociology and Politics. He worked for many years as a clinician in both the Northern Territory and South Australia. His postings included work with a variety of health agencies and organisations as a Senior Social Worker and Team leader. David has had broad experience in mental health, disability, aged care, multicultural and Aboriginal services, hospitals and Correctional Services. In the last few years he has occupied senior policy positions with a number of Government Departments as a Multicultural and Aboriginal Services Consultant concentrating on the implementation of Cultural Competence. David has his own consultancy 'First Street Consultants'

Danielle Every is a researcher at the Hawke Research Institute for Sustainable Societies, University of South Australia. Her work on antiracism, refugee advocacy, humanitarianism and nationalism has been published internationally in journals such as Discourse and Society and Journal of Refugee Studies. She is currently working on an ethnography of Ethiopian restaurants in South Australia as places of community building, intercultural exchange and everyday multiculturalism.

Brad Firebrace was born and lives in Shepparton and has worked at Rumbalara Football Netball Club for a number of years. He has played senior football for the team for nine years. As part of the Heart Health Project team he has assisted with implementing and evaluating programs such as heart disease risk factor screening, communicating research results to community, and led the design of the 'Hungry for Victory' nutrition project. Bradley is a graduate of the Academy of Sport Health and Education.

Diane Gabb is a psychologist and educator who worked in cross-cultural counseling with international, immigrant and indigenous students in secondary schools and universities, and also with newly-arrived immigrant and refugee adults in Australia and New Zealand from 1974 to 1994. She then moved into the field of transcultural mental health where she developed and delivered professional development programs for clinicians, teachers and welfare personnel within the Victorian Transcultural Psychiatry Unit in Melbourne, Australia. Since 2003, Diane has collaborated with Dennis McDermott on programs focused on Australian Indigenous mental health and well-being, facilitated from within the transcultural paradigm, where understanding the culture and values of both client and practitioner are considered critical for successful clinical and professional intervention.

Jennene Greenhill is currently Director of Flinders University Rural Clinical School and Coordinator of the Masters in Clinical Education program. Her PhD from the University of Queensland Business School was a longitudinal study of organizational change and inertia in health services using complexity theory. She also holds BA in Sociology and a Master of Social Planning and Development with a dissertation on institutional reform in mental health services. She has had an interesting and diverse career in health services spanning 20+ years with experience at senior levels in clinical, management, education and research in acute and community-based health services. She leads a research team and manages a research program including several funded projects aimed to improve health systems, investigating health service change and integration, aged care mental health and health education.

Trish Hickey was born in New Zealand and has worked in Community Health settings in New Zealand, England and Australia. Trish has broad experience in mental health, disability, aged care and Aboriginal health, working in urban, rural and remote settings within Health and Correctional Services in the Northern Territory and South Australia. She currently is working for a Mental Health Peak Body in Adelaide.

Keith McConnochie has worked in Aboriginal education and Aboriginal studies for over thirty years. He has published extensively in this field, including books on race relations, Aboriginal education and Indigenous archaeology. Keith has been a member of the Psychology and Indigenous Australians project team since the group began in 2004.

Dennis McDermott is a Koori psychologist, academic and poet. His mother's people made their home on Gadigal land in inner Sydney, though their country is more likely Gamilaroi, which is where Dennis grew up, in Tamworth, NSW. His father's mob is from Donegal. He has trained Aboriginal foster carers, supervised counsellors to the "stolen generations" and worked with families dealing with a death in custody. In 2005, he was made an Honorary Fellow – He Pūkenga Taiea of Te Mata o te Tau – the Academy for Maori Research and Scholarship. Recently, Dennis was awarded the 2006 Dr. Ross Ingram Memorial Essay Prize by the Medical Journal of Australia. He chairs the judging panel for the David Unaipon Award for the best unpublished Indigenous manuscript, part of the Queensland Premier's Literary Awards. His poetry collection, Dorothy's Skin, was short-listed for the 2004 Brencorp Prize for Poetry and the Prize for Indigenous Writing at the 2004 Victorian Premier's Literary Awards.

Denise Morgan-Bulled has a background in education and was one of the first Koori Kindergarten Assistants and Koori Educators in Victoria in the 1970s. She is currently the Public Health Worker at Viney Morgan Aboriginal Medical Service, Cummeragunja. Denise is a graduate of the Institute of Koorie Education where she studied environmental and heritage interpretation.

Wendy Nolan is Deputy Director of the Centre for Indigenous Studies, Charles Sturt University and a founding major member of the Psychology and Indigenous Australians team. She has completed a Bachelor of Arts and a Master of Arts in Aboriginal Studies, and was the leader of an Australian Research Council-funded project 'Patterns of Engagement: The Contexts, Frequency and Characteristics of Psychological Practice with Indigenous Clients'.

Tracey Powis is completing her PhD through the Department of Psychology, Macquarie University (Sydney, Australia). She is currently working in Te Kura Hinengaro Tangata/ The School of Psychology, Massey University (Aotearoa/New Zealand). Contact T.Powis@massey.ac.nz

Rob Ranzijn is a Senior Lecturer in Psychology and the leader of the Psychology and Indigenous Australians project team at the University of South Australia which has been working since 2004 to improve the skills of psychology students and psychologists in the area of effective practice with Indigenous Australians. He was instrumental in instigating the Indigenous sub-committee of the Australian Association of Gerontology. He is the leader of the Australian Government-funded Learning and Teaching Council project 'Disseminating Strategies for Incorporating Australian Indigenous Content into Psychology Undergraduate Programs throughout Australia'.

Rachel Reilly is a descendant of Irish and Scottish immigrants to country South Australia. She completed a Doctorate in Health Psychology in 2005. Rachel has worked with Aboriginal community organisations in the Goulburn Murray region on a variety of health promotion and research projects in her role as Research Officer at the Onemda VicHealth Koori Health Unit, University of Melbourne. Her current interests include defining models of Indigenous health promotion, psychosocial determinants of Indigenous health, investigating the link between diet and mood and devising interventions to reduce workplace stress. In addition to her research activities, Rachel practices as a Clinical Health Psychologist in the private sector.

Damien W. Riggs is an ARC postdoctoral fellow in the School of Psychology, University of Adelaide, Australia. He is the president of the Australian Critical Race and Whiteness Studies Association and editor of the APS journal Gay and Lesbian Issues and Psychology Review. He has published widely in the areas of lesbian and gay psychology and critical race and whiteness studies in peer-reviewed journals and is the editor of two books: Out in the antipodes: Australian and New Zealand perspectives on gay and lesbian issues in psychology (with Gordon Walker, 2004, Brightfire Press), and Taking up the Challenge: Critical race and whiteness studies in a postcolonising nation (2007, Crawford Publishers). He is the author of two books: Priscilla, (White) Queen of the Desert: Queer rights/race privilege (Peter Lang, 2006) and Becoming Parent: Lesbians, gay men, and family (2007, Post Pressed).

Kevin Rowley was born in Melbourne and is an Australian of Celtic background. His research has been in the areas of diabetes and cardiovascular disease, and the evaluation of Indigenous community-based health interventions. Currently a Senior Research Fellow at Onemda Vichealth Koori Health Unit, he has collaborated with Aboriginal community-controlled organisations in northern Victoria over a number of years to develop the Heart Health Project, from which the work reported here evolved.

Harold Stewart was the Principal Aboriginal Mental Health Consultant working in the Mental Health Unit in the Department of Health, South Australia, until his retirement in 2008. His role was to provide strategic policy advice in the development, implementation and evaluation of mental health strategies, programs and initiatives to ensure they are inclusive of and responsive to the mental health care needs of Aboriginal people.

As a "tjilpi" (Pitjantjatjara meaning elder) he was deeply committed to reducing the soaring levels of suicide in the Indigenous population in South Australia. Harold believes the way forward for Aboriginal people is to return to traditional Aboriginal cultural values and cultural respect.

He has a background as a policy advisor in the Aboriginal Health Division of the Department of Health. During that time he had direct input into the development of the Aboriginal and Torres Strait Islander Social Emotional Wellbeing Strategic Framework for the SA Aboriginal Health Partnership.

Whilst working with the Australian Government Department of Health and Ageing in the Office for Torres Strait Islander Health he had a role in

the national consultation group on the development of the "The National Strategic Framework for Aboriginal and Torres Strait Islander Peoples' Mental Health and Social and Emotional Well being."

He has lived and worked in South Australia for over 30 years where he has mainly worked with the Australian Government. Harold also was the Manager of Yaitya ("yaitcha") Warra Wodli Language Centre where he advocated for Aboriginal language research, retention and revitalisation. During this time he gained some knowledge of the Kaurna, Wirangu and Pitjantjatjara languages. He is a member of the Federation of Aboriginal and Torres Strait Islander Languages, the national peak body for Indigenous languages.

Kathryn Stone is a Kaurna-Narungga woman, (from the region which reaches from the Yorke Peninsula to the Adelaide Plains) and has family connections with the Ngarrindgerri people (of the Coorong of South Australia). As an Aboriginal person who belongs to a local Aboriginal family group, Kathryn has maintained connections with the Aboriginal community around South Australia all of her life. Kathryn completed a Bachelor of Arts Degree at the University of Adelaide with a double major in Politics and Gender Studies and has been employed by the Department for Correctional Services in South Australia for 5 years and her primary role has been to assist and support Psychologists and Social Workers to engage Aboriginal offenders in therapeutic treatment. During this time Kathryn has continued studies at the University of Adelaide within the area of Education and Psychology and remains passionate about addressing Social Justice issues for Aboriginal people throughout Australia.

Sarah Sutton is the Principal Clinician of the Rehabilitation Programs Branch, Department for Correctional Services. Sarah completed a Masters Degree in Forensic Psychology (1999-2002) at the University of South Australia following an Honours Degree in Psychology (1998) and a Bachelor of Science Degree (1995-1997). Sarah has worked for the Department for Correctional Services since 2003, and over this time has sought to improve her competency in working with Aboriginal clients. Her co-facilitation of the Sexual Behaviour Clinic with a group of Aboriginal men has been a valuable learning experience for her professional development in this regard.

Joylene Warren works for the Aboriginal Family Support Services, Adelaide. She is from the far west coast of South Australia. On her mother's side she is from the Mirning people and Narrunggar from her father's side.

Dr **Tracy Westerman** is of the Nyamal people in the far North West of Western Australia. She is the founding Managing Director of Indigenous Psychological Services. She developed IPS for the purpose of addressing the inequities that exist between the rates of mental illness in Indigenous populations and the levels of access to appropriate services. Dr Westerman holds a Post Graduate Diploma in Science Psychology, a Master's Degree in Clinical Psychology and Doctor of Philosophy in Clinical Psychology. She is the only Aboriginal person in Australia to have earned a PhD in Clinical Psychology. Her PhD thesis received a commendation from the Chancellor an honour bestowed on the PhDs considered to be in the top 10% of those submitted. Her extensive list of presentations includes numerous keynotes throughout Australia and internationally. She has developed, evaluated and implemented a range of indigenous specific training packages and intervention programs throughout Australia focusing on suicide prevention, depression and trauma management. She has also conducted numerous national tenders and research projects into mental health service delivery specific to Indigenous people.

In 2006 Dr Westerman was awarded the Suicide Prevention Australia LiFE award for contributions to suicide prevention in Indigenous Health. In 2002 Dr Westerman was awarded the NAIDOC award for "National Scholar of the Year" and currently holds an NHMRC Post Doctoral Research Fellowship (2003-2006) to investigate Attention Deficit Hyperactivity Disorder (ADHD) in Aboriginal populations. She is the first Aboriginal person to receive such a Fellowship. Other awards include Scholarships with the Australian International Development Assistance Bureau, Graduate Scholarship, and 1990–1992, the Department for Community Development (DCD) Scholarship 1995 – 1997, Curtin University Mark Liveris Seminar, School of Health Sciences, PhD presentations, Winner of Certificate of Excellence for Best oral presentation for PhD research.

Lisa White has focussed on program design and implementation of Aboriginal Services in the metropolitan regional and remote areas of South Australia in the Government, non-Government and Aboriginal Community Controlled sectors. Her background includes child protection, antipoverty and gambling rehabilitation. She holds a Degree in Social Work and

Diploma in Narrative Approaches for Aboriginal People in Community Development and Counselling.